To Angelina Peet Kostas,
who inspired my love and appreciation for good food and nutrition
through her example, education, and emphasis on wholesome, deli-
cious meals prepared with artistry and love,

and

George James Kostas,
who emphasized healthy, delicious meals as a basis for optimal
health, preventive medicine, and enjoying life to the fullest.

Thank you, Mom and Dad.

CONTENTS

The Guilt-Free "Comfort Food" Cookbook

The Guilt-Free "Comfort Food" Cookbook

Soups   111

Salads   121

The Guilt-Free "Comfort Food" Cookbook

Beef, Pork, Veal, and Lamb   *139*

Chicken and Turkey   *161*

The Guilt-Free "Comfort Food" Cookbook

The Guilt-Free "Comfort Food" Cookbook

Desserts *259*

The Guilt-Free "Comfort Food" Cookbook

OREWORD

A sensible and well-informed approach to eating is essential to good health.

In 1968, when my first book *Aerobics* (Bantam) was published, and in 1970, when I founded The Cooper Aerobics Center in Dallas, preventive medicine was still a new concept. I wanted to help move medicine away from a strict emphasis on disease treatment toward disease *prevention* through exercise, diet, and stress control.

Although aerobic exercise is the component of wellness that I have spent much of my life promoting, I use every opportunity to talk about the other ingredients of a healthful lifestyle. I encourage everyone I meet to find tools for managing stress, to have regular preventive medicine examinations, to avoid smoking, to use alcohol only in moderation, to walk or participate in other aerobics activities, to do strength training, and to maintain proper weight through good nutrition.

The Cooper Clinic, which has helped more than 60,000 patients adopt healthier lifestyles, opened a Nutrition Department in 1979. Georgia Kostas, M.P.H., R.D., L.D., coauthor of *The Guilt-Free "Comfort Food" Cookbook*, started the Clinic's nutritional services and is the Clinic's Director of Nutrition.

From the beginning, we emphasized aerobics and nutrition. The two go hand in hand. Not that it's always easy to eat right or to change ingrained habits—our busy lives put our nutrition at risk. We grab food on the run without thinking about what we are putting into our bodies. When we do try to eat better, we are often confused about what we should eat.

The Guilt-Free "Comfort Food" Cookbook

At The Cooper Clinic, Georgia and her colleagues educate patients about food and its role in well-being. A registered and licensed dietician, Ms. Kostas is extremely successful at motivating people to make needed dietary changes. She makes it simple. She helps people get past their fear of failure and deprivation and learn to enjoy food in a balanced way.

Now her simple, clear, and fun approach to eating better is available to a much wider audience—including you! She and her colleague, Robert A. Barnett, a well-known nutrition journalist, have created a wonderful cookbook that will help you rediscover the fun of eating foods that taste good and are good for you.

The Guilt-Free "Comfort Food" Cookbook is full of delicious, "down-home" food that fits into the preventive nutritional guidelines of The Cooper Clinic. Nutritional information is explained clearly and simply. It even includes an easy to use system, based on the United States Food Guide Pyramid, that makes it easy to create a balanced eating pattern without having to memorize a lot of numbers or formulas.

Readers are guided gently toward healthier eating habits. Careful attention has been given to creating delicious, tempting, and enjoyable recipes—all based on the same sensible-yet-effective nutrition guidelines we use at The Cooper Aerobics Center and The Cooper Clinic.

It's great news for all of us that we can enjoy new dishes and old favorites without worry or guilt. *Bon appetit!*

Kenneth H. Cooper, M.D.

APERSONAL NOTE FROM GEORGIA KOSTAS

In my sixteen years of nutritional counseling at The Cooper Clinic, I have met thousands of health-conscious consumers seeking greater vitality and health through food and fitness. It is one of the greatest satisfactions of my work to participate in each enthusiast's quest for a healthier lifestyle—to help reorient pathways and to share in the glow of good feelings that come from success. Healthful eating really does make a difference in their lives, my patients tell me, providing not only improved health and fitness, but a renewed sense of well-being.

You can feel it too!

Lifestyle changes are never easy, to be sure. But with strong motives, delicious meals, a sensible, clear game plan, and persistence, we can all learn ways to enjoy food and stay healthy. Knowledge of nutrition is not enough. "I know what to eat," I hear daily, "but I can't seem to do it." "I don't want to feel deprived." "I don't want to fail," they admit. "I want to like what I eat."

Confusion about nutrition often blocks healthful changes. Which is better: margarine or butter? Olive oil or corn oil? Popcorn or pretzels? Fear of boredom and deprivation ("Will I have to give up chocolate?") may also stand in the way of good intentions.

So what *does* work? Real food! Healthful, fun recipes; planned-for-you menus; favorite foods; tasty, attractive meals—these are at the heart of transforming nutrition principles into happy, health-changing meals and habits.

The Guilt-Free "Comfort Food" Cookbook

Life experiences centered around food often give us our fondest, richest memories. Shared meals strengthen the bonds of family and friends. Who doesn't savor the rich, enticing flavors of favorite foods? Who doesn't find comfort in the foods of childhood? A good meal with the people we love makes us feel better. It nourishes the body—and the soul.

To work, any eating plan must take into account the many ways that food nourishes. Often the most effective changes are modest, gradual, and easy rather than dramatic and overwhelming. Over the years, my patients have proven to me that several factors enable one to make desirable changes in one's eating style:

- small, simple changes
- a balanced system of blending higher-fat and lower-fat foods to provide satisfying meals that average lowfat over the day or week
- enjoyment of one's favorite "indulgence foods" in smaller portions, less frequently, or in lower-fat, lower-sugar versions
- cooking strategies for lightening homespun favorite recipes— our "comfort foods"

Healthful eating can be simple, exciting, and bountiful. To show you how, we created *The Guilt-Free "Comfort Food" Cookbook.* Let it become your guide to a healthier lifestyle. Each recipe incorporates healthful eating principles. Each menu provides you with *balance, variety,* and *moderation,* the formula for optimal nutrition. All the recipes are rich in nutrients and low in fat, saturated fat, cholesterol, and calories.

By simply trying the recipes in the book, you will find yourself eating better and very likely lowering your cholesterol, blood pressure, and weight—while enjoying every biteful.

Best of all, you'll have more energy, maybe even more zest for life, and you will look and feel your best!

$\mathscr{A}$CKNOWLEDGMENTS

$\mathbf{F}$irst thanks go to Deborah Maugans of Birmingham, Alabama, for her creativity, professionalism, and good cheer in the development and testing of the recipes. Debby's fondness for American, and particularly southern American, cooking, combined with her practiced culinary skills, her experience in lowfat cooking, and her sense of fun, made her an ideal partner in this project.

We'd also like to thank Dana Schwartz, M.S., for her careful work in analyzing (and often reanalyzing) the recipes for nutritional content and for providing helpful suggestions. (Thanks also to Marion Nestle, Ph.D., chair of the Nutrition Department at NYU, for helping us find Dana.)

For helping illustrate these nutritional principles, we thank Tomaso Milian for early sketches of the Eating Right Pyramid and the "icons" that follow each recipe, Robert Graf for his design suggestions, and Linda Eger for her art research.

We thank Leslie Peterson, our editor, for deftly shepherding the manuscript through the production process. We are grateful to literary agents Herb and Nancy Katz, who saw the potential in this project from beginning to end, and to Alice Martell, who helped clarify our mutual responsibilities.

To the staff of The Cooper Clinic, who supported Georgia's time for this project, and particularly to Linda Nash, who facilitated countless calls, faxes, and overnight mail deliveries between us, we extend our heartfelt thanks. We'd also like to thank the thousands of patients at the Clinic whose individual stories of dietary change inspired us to make this book.

Finally, grateful acknowledgment goes to Dr. Kenneth Cooper, founder and executive director of The Cooper Clinic. Dr. Cooper's leadership and vision in promoting prevention through eating and exercise, his encouragement of a healthful diet as part of total well-being, and his support of the Nutrition Department at the Clinic is the ground in which this book took root and grew.

Georgia G. Kostas and Robert A. Barnett

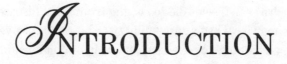

$\mathscr{I}$NTRODUCTION

Welcome to *The Guilt-Free "Comfort Food" Cookbook.*
Here is a book for people who love to eat. It is for anyone who
wants to learn how to enjoy favorite "comfort" foods without guilt.
Join us in discovering a positive approach to eating right, motivated
by pleasure rather than anxiety, joy rather than fear, plenitude rather
than deprivation.

The bounty of foods we bring back to the healthful table may sur-
prise you: barbecues and bacon, pizza and nachos, cream sauces, biscuits, pies, and layer cakes. And each recipe is carefully crafted to fit
into the most modern nutritional concepts. All you have to do is follow
our directions, and enjoy the food. Along the way, you'll learn valuable
lessons about healthful cooking and menu planning so you can bring
your family's entire eating plan into a joyful balance.

Here are the American foods you love, transformed into lighter versions that will keep you hale and hearty enough to enjoy them for a
good many years. Fond of Banana Cream Pie? Look on page 271. Like
your grits cheesy? Try Creamy Cheese Grits (p. 78). Do you believe
that a healthful diet means you have to say good-bye to your favorite
beef and pork dishes? Then you haven't met our Beef Stroganoff (p.
148), our Pot Roast with Plum-Peach Ketchup (p. 144), or our Salis-
bury Steak with Mushroom Sauce (p. 142). Like fried chicken? There's
Country Oven-Fried Chicken (p. 163). Did you grow up on tuna casserole? Our "The Works" Tuna Casserole (p. 203) will bring back memories, but leave the fat behind.

Learning how to cook favorite foods healthfully and how to balance
your diet has many benefits, both now and in the future. Everyone to-

day knows that what we eat can help lengthen life . . . or shorten it. Perhaps you've seen friends die too young from heart disease—friends who may have had a susceptibility to heart disease yet weren't able to change their diet or exercise regularly or quit smoking. Today we all know that too much saturated fat, the kind found in fatty meats and full-fat dairy foods, can clog arteries.

A good diet—low in fat, high in fiber, rich in grains and fruits and vegetables and beans, with modest portions of lean animal foods (beef, poultry, seafood) and low fat dairy foods—can also help protect us from stroke, diabetes, many common cancers, osteoporosis, and gall bladder disease. Every day scientists add to the list. In 1994 a study found that people who eat greens such as spinach or kale a few times a week had a significantly lower risk of developing macular degeneration, the most common cause of blindness over age sixty-five.

Delicious food that's low in fat and high in fiber also makes it easier to control weight, and weight loss is often the first step to controlling high blood pressure, high cholesterol, and diabetes; often, losing a few pounds can have dramatic results.

The biggest benefit to eating better, however, isn't preventing future diseases but looking and feeling your best—energetic with a sense of well-being—now.

One benefit to eating more high-fiber fruits, vegetables, beans, and whole grains is to improve digestion and elimination, helping prevent constipation and diverticulosis. In the long run, your risk of developing colon cancer is also reduced. But you'll also feel better, right now.

Food and fitness go together. Learn to eat better, and your body will get the nutrients it needs when it needs it, and you may find you have more energy during the day and sleep better at night. If you are physically active—and each of us should be—you'll find that our lowfat meals, rich in complex carbohydrates, help fuel a program of walking, running, swimming, bicycling, or gardening. You may even have more energy on the golf links and the tennis court.

But change isn't easy. We grew up with favorite American foods, and it's not easy to skip the burgers and munch on "rabbit food" and tofu. Fortunately, you don't have to. One way to enjoy your favorite comfort foods without guilt is to learn to substitute lower-fat ingredients for higher-fat ones. You'll find examples of smart, lighter-cooking techniques and ingredients throughout this book. Often we explain at the beginning of a recipe exactly how we achieve these rich, satisfying tastes with a fraction of the fat the old, heavier recipes used.

But that's just the beginning.

The best way to enjoy your foods, yet eat in a healthier way, is to learn the proper *proportion* of foods. This is what nutritionists mean when they talk about balance. And this may be the source of the greatest confusion about nutrition today. Some people think about food as either good or bad. But eating too many servings of cheeseburgers and too few of spinach doesn't make one food good and another bad. It's not the single food that's good or bad, it's the *balance* of foods we choose.

Many of us eat too many high-fat meats, cheeses, snacks, and desserts and too few high-fiber breads, grains, beans, vegetables, and fruits. What we need is balance. We need to learn the proper proportion of breads and grains, vegetables, fruits, dairy foods, and protein foods, including beef, pork, lamb, chicken, turkey, fish, shellfish, and beans.

Learn the right proportions, and you can eat everything you like. Our recipes will give you hundreds of tips on how to cook favorite foods with less fat. They are also designed to help you—easily, simply, almost intuitively—provide for yourself and your family the kind of dietary balance that keeps people healthful and appetites satisfied.

Once you learn the secrets of balance, eating your favorite American foods without guilt becomes second nature.

Balancing Health and Fun: The 80/20 Principle

The key tenets of sound nutrition are variety, balance, and moderation. Let's start with *variety*.

For optimal health and energy, consume a wide variety of different foods daily and throughout the week. Often we forget this simple principle. The greater variety of foods we consume, the greater the likeli-

The Guilt-Free "Comfort Food" Cookbook

hood that we'll consume enough of the nutrients we need and not too much of any substance that's not good for us.

Consider these two foods: beef and sweet potatoes. Beef is rich in protein, iron, and B vitamins; sweet potatoes are low in protein, but they are rich in fiber, vitamin C, and vitamin A in the form of beta-carotene. Eat only beef, and you'll be missing fiber, and you may also get too much artery-clogging saturated fat. Eat only sweet potatoes, and you won't get enough protein. But eat a small amount of beef, two or three ounces in a stir-fry, and a baked sweet potato, and you'll get plenty of protein, iron, B vitamins, fiber, vitamins C and A, and little saturated fat.

Next is *balance*. Balance refers to the proper mix, ratio, or proportion of foods. The greatest emphasis is on fresh produce, grains, and starches, with smaller amounts of lean meat, fish, poultry, beans, and lowfat dairy products. Whenever possible, choose lowfat versions of these foods.

The third principle is *moderation*. Moderation applies both to our selection of high-fat foods and to the portions we eat. Do you like chocolate? That's okay. You can eat chocolate and still have a wonderfully nutritious diet. One way to indulge a sweet tooth is to learn how to make or buy lower-fat versions of your favorites. For example, if you like chocolate, you might try our Chocolate Sorbet with Cinnamon and Vanilla (p. 286); lucky for you, it has only 160 calories and five grams of fat per serving. You can also have high-fat chocolates, in small amounts, once in a while.

Moderation also means portion control. Even our chocolate sorbet will put pounds on if you eat two or three or four servings at a time. In this book we label foods we want to eat only in moderation as Extras. Extra foods include fats (oils, margarine, butter, dressings, mayonnaise), snacks (such as chips and dips), and sweets (candy, cakes, cookies, soft drinks). If you drink alcohol, that's an Extra too.

It's perfectly fine to have a few Extras in your daily diet. But if all you eat is dessert, even if that dessert is fat-free, you won't be giving your body what it needs. The same goes for portion control. Even a varied, balanced diet will make you fat if you eat too much!

All foods contribute nutrition in varying degrees and are part of life's enjoyment, so enjoy them all—moderately! You don't have to

The Guilt-Free "Comfort Food" Cookbook

skip fun foods, "comfort" foods, or richer foods. Simply balance your overall food selection with more nutrient-dense foods and smaller, or less frequent, portions of richer foods. This way you can enjoy the best of all worlds—taste, variety, balance, and moderation.

We call this the "80/20 principle." By selecting healthier foods 80 percent of the time, you may select less nutrient-rich fun foods 20 percent of the time and still consume a health-promoting diet overall.

This is an innovative principle of balance that makes sense. It works in the lives of the health-seeking consumers we counsel at The Cooper Clinic. Instead of eating low fat all the time, it's more enjoyable and liveable to mix fat-free and lowfat foods with higher-fat foods so your *average* fat intake is reasonable. This is a balancing act that is satisfying, nutritious, and restores the fun in meals. Take, for example, these two meals from recipes in our cookbook:

- Poached Sea Bass with Pesto Verde (p. 191), Tex-Mex Corn Saute (p. 239), Asparagus with Warm Citrus Vinaigrette (p. 255), and Short-and-Sweet Strawberry Shortcakes (p. 265)
- Skillet Beef Puff (p. 150), Curried Squash Soup (p. 117), Green Beans with Caramelized Onion and Tomato Relish (p. 257), and fresh fruit salad for dessert

Both meals combine higher-fat and lower-fat foods so the average fat and calories meet the criteria for healthful eating. In the first meal, the entree has only seven grams of fat in a serving, so there's room for the eleven grams of fat in the shortcake. But the Beef Puff has twelve grams of fat per serving, so a nonfat fruit salad keeps the meal modest in fat and calories.

We've analyzed all the recipes in this cookbook to help you put your own "balancing act" into practice. All our recipes are fairly low in fat, saturated fat, and calories. You can use *our* recipes to balance out any high-fat foods you may eat elsewhere, in restaurants, or when using other recipes. Before long you'll be putting your own higher-fat/lower-fat menus together without having to count calories or fat. You can trust the recipes in this book to be:

The Guilt-Free "Comfort Food" Cookbook

- very low in added fat and especially low in saturated fat (the kind that comes from animal fats such as beef fat, butter, cream, whole milk, and cheese)
- high in complex carbohydrates
- high in fiber
- moderately low in added (refined) sugar, including syrup and honey
- low in salt, or with salt as an optional ingredient (After about six weeks of consuming a lower-sodium diet, you'll find that you need less salt in your food for it to taste "right.")
- drawn together from a wide variety of everyday foods
- blended from lowfat and high-fat foods to create moderate, balanced dishes
- designed to help you plan menus based primarily on grains, vegetables, and fruits, with smaller portions of lowfat animal protein, including lowfat and nonfat dairy products
- created to emphasize the enjoyment of food

Once you learn this new way of cooking and putting meals together, you'll have the best of all possible worlds—delicious *and* healthy food.

Putting Nutritional Information to Work for You

For each recipe in this book, we've included a complete set of nutritional information. That way, you can tell at a glance how many calories a dish has and how much fat, saturated fat, cholesterol, sodium, protein, carbohydrates, fiber, vitamins, and minerals.

For example, here's the analysis that comes after our Picnic Potato, Corn, and Butter Bean Salad (p. 130):

Per Serving: 280 Calories, 4 g Fat (2 g Saturated), 8 mg Cholesterol, 340 mg Sodium, 10 g Protein, 56 g Carbohydrates
A Great Source of: Fiber (7 g), Vitamin B6 (32%), Vitamin C (48%), Potassium (1,040 mg)
A Good Source of: Vitamin B1 (24%), Vitamin B2 (10%), Vitamin B3 (16%), Folic Acid (20%), Pantothenic Acid (16%), Copper (22%), Iron (12%), Magnesium (20%), Zinc (10%)
Pyramid Equivalent(s): 2 Vegetables

The first thing you'd probably notice is the drawing of a pea pod on the side of the page. That's our symbol for the Vegetables category in the Food Guide Pyramid. Look above the pea pod, and you'll find that this recipe provides 2 Vegetables; that is, two servings from the Vegetables group. This is actually the most important information we give you about this (or any other) recipe. We'll spend the rest of this section explaining how to use the Food Guide Pyramid to balance your family's meals easily, without much thought, or a bunch of numbers.

We also provide a full set of nutritional information for anyone who wants to learn more. As you can see, we tell you that each serving of this dish provides 280 calories and four grams of fat (two of them saturated). It's a pretty lowfat dish. With only eight milligrams of cholesterol, it's also very low in cholesterol. It's low in sodium too: only 280 milligrams. It's got a fair amount of protein, lots of carbohydrates, and a wonderful amount of fiber: seven grams. And it is a *Great Source* for certain nutrients and a *Good Source* for others.

Here's what all these numbers mean:

Calories

There's no set amount of calories that's right for everyone. Each of us has a caloric amount that's just enough to keep us satisfied without gaining weight. How much you need depends primarily on how large you are and how active you are. For example, a small woman who is fairly sedentary may need only 1,600 calories a day. If she were to walk two miles a day at a moderately brisk pace, she might need 1,800. Men are usually larger than women, so a sedentary man might need 2,200 calories. A large active man might require 2,800 or more. Because our recipes are generally low in fat, they tend to be fairly low in calories. If you need more calories, have a second helping!

Fat

Fat is a very compact source of calories, so too much fat makes it hard to control weight and increases the risk of many chronic diseases. Most Americans get about 34 percent of calories from fat; a healthier amount would be 20 percent to 30 percent of calories from fat. That translates as thirty to eighty grams of fat a day—about thirty to sixty for women and fifty to eighty for men.

A gram of fat has nine calories. So if your daily needs are 1,800 calories, 30 percent of that would be 540 calories. That's sixty grams of fat. That's your daily fat "budget." Most of our entrees have ten grams or less fat per serving. We'll give you more information about fats below in the section on Extras.

Saturated Fat

Saturated fat, found primarily in fatty meat and full-fat dairy foods, raises blood cholesterol and increases the risk of heart disease as well as some cancers. We should strive to keep saturated fat to less than 10 percent of our total calories—or one-third of our total fat. Thus, if your fat budget is sixty grams, you'd want to keep your saturated fat intake to one-third of that—twenty grams. Our recipes have between zero and five grams of saturated fat per serving; most are under three grams.

Cholesterol

We should have no more than three hundred milligrams of cholesterol a day. Too much dietary cholesterol may raise blood cholesterol. Our recipes are low in cholesterol.

Sodium

Too much sodium can raise blood pressure in susceptible individuals. We should strive to keep sodium intake at 2,400 to three thousand milligrams a day. A good rule of thumb is to keep sodium to five hundred milligrams per dish and one thousand milligrams per meal. Most of our dishes are low in sodium; a few that are at the higher end are actually nearly complete one-dish meals. Most of the sodium in our diets comes from processed foods, so as you cook fresher foods, you'll automatically lower your sodium intake.

Protein

This should make up 10 to 20 percent of calories. Protein has four calories per gram. So if you consume 1,800 calories a day, 10 percent would be 180 calories, or forty-five grams. A good rule of thumb is that if a dish has fifteen to twenty grams of protein, it's a good source of protein—a main dish. Most of us get plenty of protein—more than we need, actually. It's the *source* of our protein that's the biggest problem: fatty meats and full-fat dairy foods high in saturated fat. That's why this book emphasizes smaller portions of lean-protein sources with only two or three ounces per recipe serving.

Carbohydrates

These should make up the majority of our calories—50 to 70 percent. As with protein, a gram of carbohydrate has four calories, so 50 percent of an 1,800-calorie diet would be nine hundred calories, or 225 grams of carbohydrate. Most of these should be complex carbohydrates, the kind found in the Breads section; wherever possible, we should get our complex carbohydrates from whole grains, but refined grains, such as white rice and white bread, are also sources of complex carbohydrates.

Simple sugars are also carbohydrates—simple carbohydrates. These should make up only a small part of our daily carbohydrate intake.

Under each recipe, you'll also find a section that lists nutrients that are a *Great Source* and another that lists those nutrients that are a *Good Source* of nutrients, from fiber to iron. This tells you which nutrients a particular recipe is rich in. Our criteria is the United States Recommended Dietary Allowances (USRDAs). These are set high enough to ensure that the vast majority of Americans would meet their individual nutrient needs (known as RDAs) if they got 100 percent of the USRDA. Here are the criteria we used:

A Great Source of:

These are the nutrients that are present as 25 percent or more of the USRDA. For fiber we choose the lower end of the daily range recommended by the National Cancer Institute (twenty to thirty-five grams), which means that five grams is a *Great Source.* For potassium, it's 625 milligrams. If you can get a quarter of your day's needs for a specific nutrient with one serving of a single dish, you're doing pretty well!

A Good Source of:

These are the nutrients that are present as 10 percent to 25 percent of the USRDA. For fiber, that turns out to be two grams. For potassium, that's 250 milligrams.

Following are the nutrients we list:

Fiber

The benefits of fiber are discussed in our "Go with the Grains" section later in this introduction. Most Americans get only about ten grams of dietary fiber a day. We should strive for twenty to thirty-five grams a day. Our recipes make it easy!

Vitamin A

Vitamin A is important for vision, the health of the skin and all the inner linings of the body, growth and development, and reproduction. Vitamin A comes in two forms: preformed vitamin A found in animal foods such as milk and dairy products, and beta-carotene, a plant form that the body converts into vitamin A. In addition to its role as a building block for vitamin A, beta-carotene, as well as the related carotenoids found in yellow and green vegetables, is an antioxidant, which may help protect us from heart disease and many cancers. Many of our recipes that are good or great sources of vitamin A are also good or great sources of beta-carotene.

Vitamin B1

This B vitamin, also known as thiamin, helps our bodies convert carbohydrates into energy, helps maintain the tone of muscles, and is needed for nerve transmission.

Vitamin B2

This B vitamin, also known as riboflavin, helps the body metabolize proteins, fats, and carbohydrates.

Vitamin B3

This B vitamin, also known as niacin, helps the body metabolize fats and proteins and convert carbohydrate to energy.

Vitamin B6

Like B1, B2, and B3, vitamin B6 helps release energy from carbohydrates, fats, and proteins. It also helps convert certain amino acids, the building blocks of proteins, into serotonin, a brain chemical involved in pain, appetite, and sleep. This vitamin may also help protect the heart; low levels of vitamin B6 may lead to elevated levels of homocysteine, an amino acid. Elevated homocysteine levels have been demonstrated to increase the risk of heart disease. Vitamin B6 is abundant in whole grains, beans, seeds, nuts, bananas, seafood, and chicken. Many of our recipes are rich in B6.

Vitamin B12

This nutrient, found only in animal foods, is necessary for the formation of red blood cells and for energy metabolism. If you don't get enough, you can become anemic. However, unless you abstain from all animal foods for years, you'll get plenty of B12.

Folic Acid

Another B vitamin that many of us need to get more of, folic acid helps protect DNA, the genetic code, from damage and may help protect against certain cancers. It also helps protect fetuses from "neural tube" birth defects such as spina bifida. Folic acid also works with vitamin B6 to regulate homocysteine levels. Fresh fruits (including orange juice) and vegetables, especially greens, are the best sources of folic acid, along with beans and nuts. You'll find many of the recipes in this book are very good sources of folic acid.

Pantothenic Acid

Pantothenic Acid is also a B vitamin involved in the metabolism of carbohydrates, fats, and proteins as well as the regulation of nerves. It is abundant in the food supply.

Vitamin C

An important antioxidant, vitamin C works with vitamin E to protect us against potential carcinogens and heart disease. It also helps wounds heal, helps to build collagen, may help fight infections, and aids in the absorption of iron.

Vitamin E

Another important antioxidant, vitamin E keeps cell walls strong and less permeable to injurious substances. It protects against many cancers. It prevents LDL ("bad") cholesterol from turning into a damaged oxidized form that adheres to artery walls, and thus helps protect against coronary heart disease.

Calcium

This mineral is not only essential for building bone and protecting us against osteoporosis, but may also help keep blood pressure under control and plays an important role in nerve transmission.

Copper

A trace element, copper helps the body build bone and connective tissue, convert fat and carbohydrate to energy, and make use of iron.

Iron

An essential part of the red blood cells, iron helps carry oxygen to every cell in the body. It is important for growth and development. Low levels, over time, can lead to anemia.

Magnesium

Magnesium is important for bone growth, nerve and muscle function, and the maintenance of a regular heartbeat.

Zinc

Needed for normal skin, bones, and hair, this antioxidant also helps maintain immunity and promotes healing and growth.

Potassium

Potassium helps regulate blood pressure, the functioning of nerve and muscle, the body's water and electrolyte balance, and the balance of acid and base in the body. Found primarily in fresh fruits and vegetables, it may help prevent strokes.

These, then, are the nutrients we tell you about. You can use this information if you have specific health concerns. For example, let's say you need more calcium or iron in your diet. Flip through the pages until you find a recipe that's a *Great Source* or even a *Good Source* of these nutrients.

Most of the time, though, you don't need to memorize a bunch of numbers to eat a delicious, wholesome, balanced diet. Yes, you *do* need to learn how to balance your individual meals and your day's

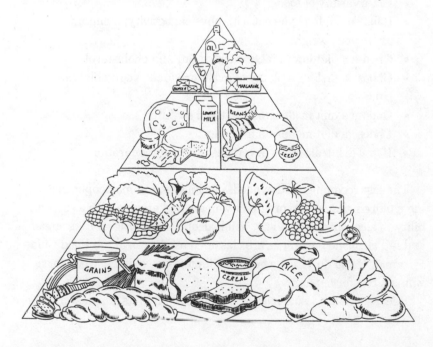

The Guilt-Free "Comfort Food" Cookbook

worth of meals and your week's meals. But we've made it easy for you. The best place to start is with the symbols on the side of each recipe.

These are the elements we want you to use every day. They correspond with the *Pyramid Equivalents* at the bottom of each recipe. They are based on the Food Guide Pyramid, sometimes called the Eating Right Pyramid, which illustrates in visual form the basic tenets of nutrition. To get the most value from this book, we want you to learn to tap the power of the Pyramid.

The Power of the Pyramid

The United States Food Guide Pyramid, established by the U.S. Department of Agriculture in 1990, is a pictorial guide of the Dietary Guidelines for Americans. The Dietary Guidelines, for healthful people two years old and over, provide up-to-date nutrition advice. These guidelines help people choose foods that promote health and may help reduce the chance of developing some diseases. They are:

- Eat a variety of foods.
- Balance the food you eat with physical activity; maintain or improve your weight.
- Choose a diet low in fat, saturated fat, and cholesterol.
- Choose a diet with plenty of grain products, vegetables, and fruits.
- Choose a diet moderate in salt and sodium.
- Choose a diet moderate in sugars.
- If you drink alcoholic beverages, do so in moderation.

The last recommendation needs clarification. Some people, including children, teenagers, pregnant women, and anyone with a susceptibility to alcoholism, should not drink alcoholic beverages. Like sugar and fat, alcoholic beverages are classified as Extras in the Food Guide Pyramid. If you do drink, a healthful limit is one drink per day for a woman, two for a man.

Because we are visual learners, the Pyramid in its simplest form reminds us to consume the majority of our food calories from the bottom half—the complex carbohydrates or "plant foods" (whole grains, fruits, vegetables). I like to follow the "¾ Plate Rule": Divide your plate into fourths, covering three-fourths of the plate with complex carbohydrates (grains, vegetables, fruits) and one-fourth of the plate with a three-ounce, protein-rich entree—about the size of a woman's palm or a deck of cards.

How is the Pyramid constructed to guide our food choices? It is divided into six Food Categories:

- *Breads (or grains):* six to eleven daily servings
- *Vegetables:* three to five (or more) daily servings
- *Fruits:* two to four (or more) daily servings
- *Dairy:* two to three daily servings
- *Meats (including poultry, seafood, beans):* two to three daily servings
- *Extras (fats, oils, snacks, sweets, desserts):* There is no set recommended daily serving for this group. Rather, the recommendation is to "eat sparingly."

As we'll see, the definition of a *serving* is smaller than many of us may expect. For example, a serving is half a bagel, three-fourths a cup of juice, half a cup of cooked vegetables, a cup (not a glass) of milk, or two or three ounces of lean beef, poultry, or fish. Often we'll eat two or three servings of a food in a single helping. That's why you'll often find that a single serving of one of our recipes may translate to 1 Bread, 1 Meat, *and* 1 Vegetable.

Right now, why don't you take another look at our artistic rendering of the Food Guide Pyramid on p. 13. It provides a graphic illustration of the proper balance of foods in the diet. Throughout the book, we've used smaller symbols with each recipe to provide visual clues to how each recipe fits into meal planning. Let's look at these symbols.

The first symbol is Breads. It's the base of the Pyramid.

The Guilt-Free "Comfort Food" Cookbook

The second symbol (you saw it earlier) is for Vegetables on the second tier of the Pyramid.

The third symbol is for Fruits.

Up one tier of the Pyramid is the Dairy group.

Then there's the Meats group.

Finally, there's the top of the Pyramid, the Extras group.

Let's explore the power of the Pyramid to help you balance your family's meals!

Go with the Grains

At the base of the Pyramid, whole grains are in the Bread, Cereal, Rice, and Pasta Group. Included in this group are whole-grained bread, breakfast cereals, oatmeal, brown and white rice, pasta, couscous, barley, quinoa, popcorn, bran muffins, corn or wheat tortillas, bagels, English muffins, crackers, pancakes, and pita bread.

These foods form the *foundation* on which good nutrition is based. Grains are the "staff of life," providing us with complex carbohydrates, the body's favorite fuel, plus a host of vitamins and minerals, including iron, zinc, and fiber.

Fiber is the missing element in many of today's diets. Most Americans consume ten grams of fiber a day; we need twenty to thirty-five grams daily, according to research and recommendations by the National Cancer Institute. Fiber improves digestion and the health of the colon, helps regulate both blood sugar and blood cholesterol, and helps protect against certain cancers (including colon) and heart disease. The fiber in the coating of the whole wheat bran kernel is *insoluble;* this roughage brushes through the colon, pushing food wastes along for easier elimination, faster transit, and a healthier colon. Health experts believe the less time that food wastes come into contact with the colon, the fewer potentially cancer-causing substances are produced from the normal interaction of intestinal bacteria with the food. Hence the risk of colon cancer is reduced. Perhaps 80 percent of colon cancer in men (it's the second leading cause of cancer in men) could be prevented if we ate more fiber.

A second type of fiber, *soluble* fiber, helps reduce blood cholesterol and regulates blood sugar and appetite. This kind is found in oatmeal, beans, apples, and pears.

For optimal health, we need six to eleven servings of grains daily. The number of servings we need is based on our daily caloric needs. That is, if you need fewer calories, you'll need fewer servings of grain. A grain serving is one slice of bread (a sandwich made with two slices of bread is two servings); a dinner roll; a tortilla; a pancake; half a bagel or English muffin or pita pocket; a half cup of rice, pasta, cereal, or other grain; or an ounce of ready-to-eat breakfast cereal.

When shopping, look for 100-percent whole-grain and enriched or fortified breads. Experiment with grains you may not be familiar with, such as barley, quinoa, and aromatic rices. But steer clear of commercial breads loaded with extra fat (sweet rolls, croissants, crescent rolls, biscuits, cornbread). They are often loaded with ten, twenty, or even thirty grams of fat per serving, most of it saturated. Use our recipes for biscuits and cornbread instead!

Select at least two grain servings at each meal to consume the minimal six servings a day.

Veg Out

Moving up the Pyramid, we come to the second tier: Vegetables and Fruits. Living by the "Five-a-Day" rule—consuming a minimum of three or more Vegetables, two or more Fruits—reduces our risk of heart disease and cancer. For example, in over one hundred population studies, people who eat the most fruits and vegetables generally have about half the cancer risk as people who eat the least amount of fruits and vegetables.

Vegetables provide us with complex carbohydrates; fiber (both insoluble and soluble); B vitamins; antioxidants such as beta-carotene, the protective plant form of vitamin A, vitamin C, and folic acid; and

The Guilt-Free "Comfort Food" Cookbook

minerals such as iron, magnesium, manganese, copper, zinc, calcium, and potassium. Fruits and vegetables also provide us with hundreds of other unidentified phytochemicals (*phyto* means "plant") that may protect us against heart disease and many cancers. For example, phytohormones (yes, hormones in plants!) may possibly play a role in protecting post-menopausal women from heart disease and breast cancer and men from prostate cancer; soybeans, and probably many other kinds of beans, are rich in these phyto-hormones. Much more research will be needed before we understand the true contribution these plant compounds may make toward health, but in the meantime, this book is chock-full of healthful vegetables, fruits, and beans!

Antioxidants are a key to preventing premature aging, cancer, and heart disease. These compounds, particularly the vitamins beta-carotene, vitamin C, and vitamin E, protect against the oxidation of LDL ("bad") cholesterol that causes atherosclerosis (hardening of the arteries) that leads to heart disease. They also protect many other kinds of cells from the kind of damage that can lead to premature aging.

And don't forget the indoles found in cruciferous vegetables (broccoli, Brussels sprouts, cauliflower, cabbage, bok choy, turnips, turnip greens), which help prevent cancer. Try to eat a cruciferous vegetable every day!

Consume three to five vegetable servings a day (a half cup cooked, one cup raw, or a dinner-sized salad). Here are some easy ways to do this:

- Eat a salad or coleslaw and two other vegetables daily.
- Go for color. It's easier and often tastier to eat one cup of mixed, colorful vegetables such as Oriental stir-fries or vegetables in a pasta salad than a cup of a single vegetable such as carrots or broccoli. Make sure one meal a day, lunch or supper, emphasizes vegetables, because often one or two meals contain none.
- When it comes to greens, the darker the more nutritious. For example, add a cup of spinach to a lettuce salad, and you'll increase its beta-carotene content tenfold!
- Add vegetables everywhere you can—as pizza, potato, and taco

The Guilt-Free "Comfort Food" Cookbook

toppings, in potato salads, bean soups, muffins, chili, rice and pasta dishes, and omelets. We've done it throughout this book. You'll find vegetables not only in the vegetables chapter, but throughout recipes in the breakfast, beef, poultry, and seafood chapters.

- Buy (in our order of preference) fresh, frozen, or canned. With canned vegetables, nutrients are lost in the water, and sodium is often added.
- Eat some vegetables raw; lightly cook others. Microwave, steam, or grill. Cook quickly and with little water to preserve the most nutrients.
- Potatoes, greens, cabbage, tomatoes, and bell peppers are all excellent sources of vitamin C. Eat at least one serving daily.
- Don't forget onions, green onions, and garlic!

I often tell my patients to double up on whatever vegetable portions they normally eat. Doubling usually allows the more appropriate amounts to be consumed. I also recommend at least three or four all-vegetable meals a week to balance out days without vegetables and to boost fiber and antioxidants. A few all-vegetable meals also help balance one's weekly calories for easier weight control. This includes all vegetable types: green beans, carrots, bell peppers, broccoli, tomatoes, salads, and starchy vegetables such as green peas, corn, and potatoes.

Be Fruitful

Fruits, like vegetables, are terrific sources of fiber, vitamins, minerals, and especially beta-carotene/vitamin A and vitamin C—critical antioxidants for health. Beta-carotene is found in the yellow, orange, and red fruits: apricots, cantaloupes, peaches, strawberries, and mangoes. (Beta-carotene is also rich in yellow, orange, red, and dark green vegetables: tomatoes, carrots, pumpkin, butternut squash, yellow squash, broccoli, bell peppers, sweet potatoes, spinach, kale, turnip greens, mustard greens, and cabbage.)

Consume ample fruit daily, and you may find your sweet tooth disappearing. Sweet, ripe fruit is nature's dessert. In our cookbook, turn any of our fruit salads, or even beverage recipes, into dessert.

Select two to five (or more) servings of fruits a day. A serving is one medium fruit (the size of a tennis ball): an apple, a banana, an orange, or half a cup of sliced fruit (berries, pineapple, melon). So is three quarters of a cup of juice (six ounces), or a quarter cup of dried fruit (raisins, prunes, dried apricots). To eat more fruit, try these practices:

- Have two fruits at breakfast; for example, juice and a banana.
- Have one fruit at each meal.
- Grab a fruit as you leave home each morning, and eat it later with lunch or as a snack.

The Milk Way

Moving up the Pyramid, the third-tier food categories primarily provide *protein*. Those are the Dairy products (skim or one-percent milk, lowfat or nonfat yogurt, reduced-fat cheeses), and the Meats (and substitutes), which include lean beef and pork and lamb, poultry, seafood, dried beans and peas (legumes), and eggs.

Let's start with milk and dairy products. These nutrient-dense foods can play a role in every part of the life cycle, infancy through adulthood. In infancy and adolescence, milk's calcium is crucial to growing bones and developing bodies. Throughout adulthood, dairy foods provide the calcium needed for maintaining bone strength, keeping muscles from cramping, nerve transmission, and many other things.

Because women reach peak bone mass by age thirty-five, and at menopause begin to lose bone mass, women especially need calcium to maintain strong bones and prevent or retard osteoporosis ("brittle bone disease"), which occurs in one out of three older women. Besides calcium, milk provides many other nutrients: protein, carbohydrates, the B vitamins (particularly B2, or riboflavin), B12, vitamins A and D, and minerals such as phosphorus, zinc, copper, and manganese.

How much milk or dairy products are needed daily? Two to three servings. A serving is a cup (eight ounces) of milk or yogurt, one and a half ounces of cheeses, or two ounces of processed cheese. Choose non-fat, skim, or lowfat dairy products. All our recipes include these products, so you can sample and taste for yourself how delicious lowfat eating can be. We have used nonfat milk, fat-free or reduced-fat cream cheese, reduced-fat cheeses (including naturally reduced-fat Parmesan, feta, and mozzarella), and lowfat cottage cheese and ricotta. We give you the option to go as lowfat as you choose in these recipes.

Don't forget: Growing children need two glasses or cups of milk a day, and growing teens need three to four glasses. Women ages twenty to forty need two or three servings a day, and during pregnancy or lactation, four. A postmenopausal woman needs three servings a day if she is taking estrogen, four if she is not. Men, although not as vulnerable as women to osteoporosis, still lose bone with age.

Since we are living longer, bone up on calcium now. Besides, calcium may help reduce high blood pressure and even reduce cancer risk. Milk isn't the only source of calcium. Dark green leafy vegetables and beans are also good sources; you'll notice that many of our non-dairy recipes are also rich in calcium. But in the American diet, milk and dairy products provide the majority of calcium.

Meaty Matters

Red meat, poultry, fish, shellfish, dried beans and peas, and eggs fall into the *meat* category and are rich sources of protein, the B vitamins, magnesium, zinc, copper, iron, manganese, phosphorus, and various trace minerals.

Choose primarily lean meat cuts (top sirloin, tenderloin, sirloin tips, top round, flank, eye of round), which contain less than ten grams of fat per three-ounce cooked portion. Lean cuts mean you won't get too much cholesterol, saturated fat, total fat, and calories. Excessive amounts of meat or high-fat cuts of meat may contribute to cholesterol elevations, weight problems, and colon cancer.

What is a reasonable serving size? As the Pyramid suggests, strive for two or three two-to-three-ounce meat portions daily. This translates into four to six ounces of lean meat per day.

At home and in restaurants one typically consumes six to eight ounces per meal, or twelve to sixteen ounces a day. It's okay to eat a larger portion from time to time, but the best way to help balance your diet is to start "leaning" toward smaller, leaner meat cuts. Here's a tip for eating out: Cut protein-rich entrees in half!

Most of our recipes that use animal protein provide two or three, or at most four, ounces per person. We fill up the plate with grains, beans, greens, vegetables, even fruits. Beef, pork, lamb, veal, chicken, turkey, fish, and shellfish give the dishes wonderful taste, but a well-balanced plate needs more than a big hunk of steak.

By leaning toward smaller, leaner portions—four to six ounces daily—you'll get only two hundred to 350 calories, ten to twenty grams of fat (two to seven grams of saturated fat), and one hundred to 150 milligrams cholesterol a day. That fits well within the American Heart Association and U.S. Dietary Guidelines. Their recommendations: No more than one hundred to three hundred milligrams of cholesterol and fifty to seventy-five grams of total fat, so that only 20 to 30 percent of our calories are from fat and only 10 to 20 percent of calories are from protein. In simple food language, four to six ounces of meat daily meets national criteria for optimal and cardiovascular health.

(As a side benefit, when we eat smaller protein-rich foods, we can balance our plates with more complex carbohydrates, so that we meet another U.S. Dietary Guideline: 50 to 70 percent complex carbohydrate calories daily.)

Look for variety in your protein sources. If you like red meat, that's fine, but every week try to eat some poultry, some seafood, and some meatless meals based on beans. A one-ounce meat/fish/poultry serving is the equivalent of eating one egg or a half cup of cooked beans or peas, a quarter cup of tuna or salmon, or five shrimp.

Always trim the fat off meat before cooking to cut back on fat, saturated fat, cholesterol, and calories. Buy water-packed tuna and salmon instead of oil-based products. As our recipes demonstrate, you can use lowfat cooking methods to prepare meats, fish, and poultry—stir-fry, grill, bake, broil, or roast, pour off the excess fat that drains off the meat, and remove poultry skin before serving cooked chicken.

Limit whole eggs to four weekly to prevent eating too much cholesterol. Use egg substitutes or egg whites. In fact, many great cooks pre-
fer to cook with egg whites or egg substitutes once they try it because
baking products turn out lighter, and omelettes are fluffier.

Beans are a particularly excellent protein source. They supply
quality protein, fiber, complex carbohydrates, and almost every nutrient known to man—iron, zinc, magnesium, copper, manganese,
potassium, calcium, chromium, all the B vitamins, and "phytochemicals" that may play an important role in protecting against certain
cancers. Our chapter on vegetable main dishes includes many entrees that combine a grain and a bean for a hearty, balanced, protein-rich main dish. Fish and shellfish are both excellent sources of
protein, low in fat and saturated fat. They are also rich in omega-3
fatty acids which have been shown to reduce elevated triglycerides
and high blood pressure and reduce the tendency of blood to clot,
which helps prevent heart attacks.

Extras: Fats and Sweets

At the tiny tip of the Pyramid are Extras. These include all the
foods we eat that provide fat, sugar, and calories but few nutrients.
They belong in the diet. But we need to be careful not to consume
them too liberally. These Extras include margarine, butter, cooking
oils, salad dressings, gravies, sauces, dips, fried foods, chips, and other
fat-rich snack foods. They also include sweet foods such as jam, jelly,
syrup, soft drinks, candy, ice cream, and desserts.

Fats may occur naturally as part of foods (in meat and cheese, for
example) or be added to foods (in cooking as spreads). The sugar re-
ferred to in the Pyramid is refined added sugar, not the naturally oc-
curring sugar in fruit and milk.

Use these extra calories sparingly. They are nutrient-poor, and
they often add pounds. They *also* add flavor and enjoyment to meals,
to be sure. Our recipes show you how to make these Extras more
healthful; for example, Carrot Cake (p. 264) is not only lower in fat
than most carrot cakes, but includes enough carrots to count as 1
Vegetable!

The Guilt-Free "Comfort Food" Cookbook

Fat is often a source of great confusion. In general, we should consume as little fat as we are comfortable with and specifically limit saturated fat as much as possible. Saturated fat is found primarily in meat and dairy products, primarily beef, ham, hot dogs, burgers, whole milk, cheese, sour cream, cream cheese, ice cream, coffee cream, and butter; it's also found in the coconut and palm oil added to some bakery products, snack foods, and popcorn. Another fat we should minimize are "trans fats"—the fat molecule has been changed from a natural "cis" form to a rare "trans" configuration—which are formed when vegetable oils are partially hydrogenated, making them act similarly to saturated fat. For example, trans fats raise blood cholesterol levels. On average, we consume less trans fat than saturated fat, so it's less of a health threat. But it's a good idea to minimize our consumption. Trans fats are used in hard stick margarines and in many commercially processed baked goods, including cookies, pies, crackers, and filled candies. Any food that lists partially hydrogenated oils in its ingredient list contains trans fatty acids. When purchasing margarine, choose those that contain liquid oil as the first ingredient, and avoid those that contain partially hydrogenated oils, especially as the first ingredient.

In this book, we use stick margarine only when it's absolutely necessary (in pie crusts, for example), and even then in small amounts. Fortunately, soft tub margarines, and especially reduced-fat soft margarines, contain very little saturated or trans fatty acids, so we use them more frequently in this book.

The other major types of fat are polyunsaturated (in corn oil, mayonnaise, most vegetable oils) and monounsaturated (in olives, olive oil, avocados, nuts, canola oil). When used in place of saturated fat, each of these kinds of fat can lower blood cholesterol. Each can play a role in a healthful diet. However, very high amounts of polyunsaturated fats may act as oxidants—the opposite of antioxidants—and so monounsaturate-rich oils are preferable for the bulk of fat calories. A good rule of thumb is to limit saturated and polyunsaturated fats to one-third each of your fats and let monounsaturates be a third or more.

The Guilt-Free "Comfort Food" Cookbook

We recommend olive oil and other monounsaturated fats such as canola oil be used first, as a primary oil or fat. Minimize both margarine and butter, and especially butter, because it is more saturated. Avoid or limit all saturated fats.

There are marvelous spreads for bread besides butter and margarine—marinara sauce, tomato paste, lowfat cream cheese, a little olive oil, jelly, apple butter (which contains no fat at all), and lowfat cheeses. A baked potato can be topped with lowfat shredded cheddar or mozzarella cheese, lowfat Ranch dressing, nonfat cottage cheese or sour cream, salsa, marinara sauce, barbecue sauce, soy sauce, or even mustard!

Remember: Although oils, dressings, mayonnaise, and the like are 100 percent fat, they pose no health problem when consumed moderately and as part of an overall balanced (20 to 30 percent fat) diet. The guideline of 20 to 30 percent fat does not apply to individual foods, but to the amount of fat in the total day's food.

The main point to remember is that fats and sugars, while an integral part of many healthful diets, are Extras and to be consumed in moderation. Don't fall into the trap of swapping sugar for fat either. Just because a food is fat-free doesn't mean you can eat all you want of it and not gain weight. It may be primarily sugar!

Putting It All Together

That's it. It's pretty simple when you get the hang of it. And this book makes it easier, especially when planning meals. Flip through the chapters. You'll see that at the bottom of each recipe there are Pyramid Equivalents. The little pictures beside each recipe are your first signal; use the nutritional information next to them to discover exactly how many servings from each Pyramid group the recipe provides. For example, here's Creole Bean Soup (p. 118).

Next to the nutritional information, you'll see these now-familiar symbols:

This tells you at a glance that this lovely soup provides you with three parts of the Pyramid. It's a good beginning to a balanced meal! Looking more closely at the nutritional information, you'll find it says:

Pyramid Equivalent(s): 1 Bread, 2 Vegetables, 1 Meat

That shows you that this soup, a nutritious starter, could even be the basis for a main dish. Served with bread and a side vegetable, you'll have a dinner meal that has 2 Breads, 2 Vegetables, and 1 Meat. Have cookies and fruit for dessert, with a glass of lowfat milk, and you'll get every part of the Pyramid that matters.

We hope you'll start thinking in terms of the Pyramid as you flip through the book, looking for recipes. Planning dinner? Look for 1 Meat, 2 Breads, 2 Vegetables, perhaps 1 Dairy and 1 Fruit. Making breakfast? Try for 2 Breads, 1 Dairy and 1 Fruit. Here's a rule of thumb for planning daily meals:

- *Breakfast:* 2 Breads, 1 Dairy, 1 Fruit, Extras
- *Lunch:* 2 Breads, 1 Meat, 1 Fruit, Extras
- *Supper:* 2 Breads, 1 Meat, 3 Vegetables, Extras
- *Snacks:* 1 Fruit, 1 Dairy, Extras

Another way to practice Pyramid nutrition is to follow the "Rule of Threes." Every day, eat:

- *Three Whole Grains:* These include whole wheat breads, brown rice and whole oats, whole yellow cornmeal, popcorn, corn tortillas, bran cereals, barley, quinoa, and rye and pumpernickel breads.
- *Three Starches:* These can be white rice, white bread, bagels, crackers, pretzels, pasta, most ready-to-eat cereals.
- *Three Vegetables*
- *Three Fruits*
- *Two to Three Meats:* Remember, a serving is only two to three ounces, and includes lean red meats, poultry, seafood, and beans.

The Guilt-Free "Comfort Food" Cookbook

- *Two to Three Cups Milk/Yogurt:* Choose lowfat!
- *Three Teaspoons to Three Tablespoons Oils/Fats*
- *Three Teaspoons to Three Tablespoons Sugar*

Remember, a *serving* is not a *helping!* If you have a cup and a half of rice, you're actually consuming three servings. Similarly, a five- or six-ounce piece of beef, chicken, or fish is two servings. You'll notice this difference when you peruse the Pyramid Equivalents at the bottom of each of our recipes; often, one recipe serving provides a Pyramid Equivalent of 1 Bread, 1 Vegetable, and 1 Meat. Looking through these recipes should help you get a gut sense of how easy it is to get at least six servings a day from the Breads group, two from Fruits, three from Vegetables, two to three from Dairy, and no more than two to three from Meats.

The Pyramid Equivalents don't tell you everything, to be sure; that's why there is a full set of nutritional information for each recipe. For example, one thing the Pyramid Equivalents won't tell you is how many calories you'll be consuming. According to the Pyramid, a cup of milk and a cup of skim milk are the same thing: 1 Dairy. But one has lots of fat and the other none. So you'll have to choose lowfat versions of the Pyramid (that's easy in this book), and figure out your calorie needs. That's easy too. Most of the recipes in this book are quite modest in calories. But how many servings of each recipe you need will depend on whether you need 1,600, or 2,200, or 2,800 calories a day. As you move toward lower fat foods rich in fiber, however, such choices will become easier. You may find yourself reaching for second portions of main dishes and side dishes and still losing weight! Be aware, however, that even our lower-fat and lower-calorie desserts are still Extras.

If you choose lower-fat, lower-sugar versions of foods in the Pyramid categories, you're bound to be fine. Whether you choose from the lower number of servings or the higher one depends on your individual calorie needs—and whether you need to gain, maintain, or lose weight. Here's a rough guide to Pyramid Equivalents based on caloric needs:

The Guilt-Free "Comfort Food" Cookbook

	Many women, older adults	Children, teenage girls, active women, most men	Teenage boys, active men
Calorie Levels[*]	1,600[†]	2,200[†]	2,800
Breads Group Servings	6	9	11
Vegetables Group Servings	3	4	5
Fruits Group Servings	2	3	4
Dairy Group Servings	2-3[‡]	2-3[‡]	2-3‡
Meats Group (total ounces)[§]	5	6	7

[*]Reach these calorie levels by eating lower-fat foods from the five food groups and by choosing fats, oils, and sweets sparingly.

[†]Women who are pregnant or breast feeding may require more calories.

[‡]Teenagers, young adults to age twenty-four, and women who are pregnant or breast feeding need three servings.

[§]Notice that the meat group is based on total ounces, not servings. Thus, an older adult or woman who is not physically active needs only five ounces from the meat group a day, including eggs, beans, fish, poultry, and red meat.

The above servings create an eating pattern that is 50 to 70 percent carbohydrate, 20 to 30 percent fat, 10 to 20 percent protein—and there are no calories or fat to count!

Remember: If you follow the Pyramid as a picture of health, you'll surely become a picture of health yourself!

The Guilt-Free "Comfort Food" Cookbook

$\mathcal{E}$ATING WELL ON A BUDGET

$\mathbf{E}$ating well on a budget can be a challenge. That's especially true when you are learning how to eat a little differently. For example, many of the recipes in this book call for fresh fruits and vegetables, and these can be expensive. But the approach to cooking and eating we are introducing can also save money even as it protects your health and delights your taste buds.

The same balance that improves health can also save money. Many of the recipes in this book use smaller amounts of meat prepared to enhance their flavor, combined with larger amounts of carbohydrates such as rice. That's a good way to lower fat and saturated fat, preserve taste, *and* save money. As an example, consider Gourmet Burritos (p. 146). It combines a pound of ground beef with a can of black beans to make a meal that serves six. Beans are cheaper than beef. Combining the two makes sense in three ways: taste, health, and saving money.

But you won't necessarily save money just by using these recipes. If you make a summer recipe that calls for fresh strawberries in the middle of winter when strawberries are both more expensive and less flavorful, you'll be wasting your money. Wherever possible, and when it doesn't compromise taste, we've included cheaper alternatives (for example, frozen strawberries). But you'll want to use common sense to get the best value from this book. Here are some suggestions:

- Use the recipes in this book to cut back on your purchases of expensive, unhealthful snack foods (potato chips, corn chips) and

The Guilt-Free "Comfort Food" Cookbook

desserts (candies, cookies, cakes, pies). Many of our recipes are cheaper and more healthful.

- Buy in bulk—but only if you are going to use it. A large box or bag of rice makes sense, but enough marshmallow cream for five years is no way to save money. Check prices; the unit prices for bulk items bought at discount food supermarkets are often as high or even higher than regular-sized items in regular super-markets. That's especially true when you add in supermarket store sales and coupons.

- Shop with a list. Go through this book, and plan out three or four dinners plus a few breakfasts, lunches, and snacks. Then you can buy a week's worth of groceries that you will actually use. Nothing is more expensive than wasted food.

- Buy seasonally. Are eggplants on sale? Make Neapolitan Eggplant Pizzas (p. 253) and use the rest for Roasted Eggplant Dip (p. 52). In the winter, when acorn squash is cheap, make Streusel Acorn Squash and Apples (p. 242). In summer, when tomatoes are cheap and good, Tomatoes Stuffed with Tuna Tabbouleh (p. 58) is a good choice.

- Invest in a freezer, and buy meats and poultry in bulk and on sale. Shop in the evening when these meats and breads are often marked down. One approach is to cut fresh meats up into one-pound or half-pound amounts, cover tightly in freezer-tight bags or containers, and freeze. Then you have enough for a meal for two or four when you need it.

- Eat vegetarian meals a few times a week. Beans are the secret here. They are nutritious, lowfat sources of protein—and very cheap. Try Posole Bean Chile (p. 216) or Greens and Beans over Grilled Polenta (p. 220) and you'll be helping to lower your cholesterol even as you save money.

As you learn to eat in a more healthful manner, you'll find your own ways of saving money. You may be spending a little more money on fresh fruits and vegetables, but you'll save money as you consume less meat and more breads, grains, and legumes. That way you'll not only be saving money—you'll be saving your health.

The Guilt-Free "Comfort Food" Cookbook

A BUYER'S GUIDE TO LOWFAT RED MEAT, POULTRY, AND SEAFOOD

The cuts called for in the recipes are, in general, lean. These are the leanest cuts:

- *Beef:* loin, top round, top sirloin, sirloin tips, eye of round, and bottom round. (Make sure they are well-trimmed.)
- *Veal:* rib and loin chops, steaks, and roasts
- *Pork:* tenderloin, loin, and center cut ham (both fresh and cured)
- *Lamb:* Leg, arm, and loin
- *Poultry:* The main fat comes from the skin (and abdominal fat), so our recipes discard the skin either before or after cooking. White meat is leaner than dark meat.
- *Fish:* White fish such as flounder tends to be lower in fat, but all fish is low in fat and especially saturated fat, so every kind of fish is a good choice. As with chicken, the skin is mostly fat, so it's best to avoid it.
- *Shellfish:* Again, all kinds are healthful. Some, like lobster and shrimp, have a little more cholesterol than bivalves such as clams, but all shellfish tend to be low in fat and saturated fat. So all kinds fit in a healthful diet. It's the cooking method that makes the difference: Boiled shrimp is healthier than fried clams!

HEALTHFUL INGREDIENT SUBSTITUTIONS FOR YOUR FAVORITE RECIPES

As you read the recipes in this book, you'll discover many ways to bring taste and texture to lowfat recipes. Here are a few general substitutions:

- *Whole milk:* skim or one-percent lowfat milk (in some recipes thickened with cornstarch)
- *Cream:* Evaporated skim milk can be added to soups and sauces instead of cream. It's also a good substitute in coffee!
- *Sour cream:* lowfat or nonfat yogurt or nonfat buttermilk. Letting yogurt drain in a cheesecloth-lined strainer in the refrigerator for several hours or overnight creates a "yogurt cheese" with a consistency similar to sour cream. Also nonfat or lowfat sour cream.
- *Full-fat cream cheese:* lowfat cottage cheese plus reduced-fat cream cheese or lowfat cream cheese
- *Whole milk ricotta:* part-skim or nonfat ricotta
- *Whole eggs:* egg substitutes or egg whites. In some cases, a whole egg plus egg whites provides rich yolk taste with only a small amount of cholesterol.

The Guilt-Free "Comfort Food" Cookbook

MENU PLANNING

Now that we know the principles, let's start planning our meals. We've set out a series of menus, one for a week in the spring or summer, another for a week in the fall or winter, and then some menus you can use for special occasions such as the Fourth of July, the Super Bowl, and Christmas.

At the end of this section, we'll take a more detailed look at a few of these meals to demonstrate how to use the Pyramid Equivalents to plan menus.

Weekday Breakfasts:

Jogger's Sunrise Shake (p.84)
Whole wheat toast (two slices)
   with jam
Coffee or tea

Breakfast Rice Pudding (p. 77)
Toast
Orange juice
Coffee or tea

Oat-Bran Banana-Raisin
   Muffins
Honeydew melon
Lowfat cottage cheese
Coffee or tea

Toasted Banana Oatbread
   (p. 103) (two slices) with
   fat-free cream cheese
Nonfat or lowfat yogurt
Orange juice
Coffee or tea

The Guilt-Free "Comfort Food" Cookbook

Brown-Bag Lunches:

Roasted Eggplant Dip (p. 52)
(½ cup) plus pita bread (cut
into triangles) and a cut-up
red pepper for dipping
An apple
Nonfat yogurt

Cornmeal Flatbread wedge
(p. 94)
Tomatoes Stuffed with Tuna
Tabbouleh (p. 58)
Lowfat frozen yogurt for
dessert
Kiwifruit

Pocket Bread (p. 98) with
Chicken Salad Remoulade
(p. 135)
Raw carrot sticks
Nonfat frozen fruit sorbet with
banana slices

Texas "BLT" (p. 60) with
crudites and extra-fat-free
Ranch dressing for dipping
A plum or two

Roast beef sandwiches with
mustard on slices of Country
Sesame Rye Loaves (p. 88)
An apple

Snacks:

Tamale Pizza Cups (p. 56)
Fresh Corn Clam Chowder (p. 116)

Best Waldorf Salad (p. 136)

Weekday Dinners:

Baja Mahi-Mahi with Fresh
Mango Chutney (p. 194) (two
servings)
Orange-Barbecued Limas (p. 247)
Two slices of bread
Fresh blueberries

Posole Bean Chili (p. 216)
Mixed green salad
Fruit Compote with Lemon
Yogurt Cream (p. 284)

Grilled Peppercorn-Marinated
Steak (p. 141)
Spicy Crispy Fries (p. 236)
Mint Peas (p. 254)
Dinner rolls
Mixed green salad with Creamy
Pepper Ranch Salad
Dressing (p. 127)
Peaches

Creamy Broccoli, Chicken, and
Rice Casserole (p. 172)
Steamed carrots
Whole wheat roll or bread (two
pieces)
Lemon Sherbet (p. 287)

Capellini with Scallops and
Pesto "Cream Sauce" (p. 206)
Tex-Mex Corn Saute (p. 239)
Wilted Spinach Salad (p. 126)
Old-Fashioned Oatmeal-Raisin
Cookies (p. 288)
Lowfat or skim milk

The Guilt-Free "Comfort Food" Cookbook

Saturday Breakfast:

Sparkling Tropical Slush Punch (p. 66)
Vegetable-Barley Omelet (p. 80)

Ham Biscuits with Baked Berry Jam (p. 54)

Saturday Lunch:

Salmon Salad Melts (p. 64)
Lowfat or nonfat yogurt
Iced coffee

Saturday Snack:

A bagel

Saturday Dinner Party:

Island-Grilled Shrimp with
    Peach Salsa (p. 199)
(or Seared Tuna with Corn
    Relish [p. 192])
Garden Zucchini Skillet (p. 240)
(or Asparagus with Warm
    Citrus Vinaigrette [p. 255])

Mixed Greens with Raspberry
    Vinaigrette (p. 124)
Pepper-Parmesan Herb Bread
    (p. 92) (two slices)
Meringue Fruit Tart (p. 278) a
    la mode with ice milk

Spring/Summer Menus

Or perhaps you fancy a more carnivorous dinner party. You favor your health, but you haven't given up the ingrained American culinary preference for a well-seasoned piece of red meat. You don't have to. This Saturday serve:

Grilled Lamb Chops Marinated
    in Orange Juice, Garlic, and
    Rosemary (p. 155)
Herbed Quinoa Pilaf (p. 234)
Warm Roasted Vegetable Salad
    with Oriental Dressing (p. 128)

High-Rise Buttermilk
    Biscuits (p. 102)
Chocolate Sorbet with Cinna-
    mon and Vanilla (p. 286)

If you're in the mood for barbecued chicken when your friends come over in the summer, you won't miss with:

Grilled Chili-Lime Chicken with
    Tomato Chutney (p. 171)
Kasha Pilaf with Dates and
    Walnuts (p. 233)

Wilted Spinach Salad (p. 126)
Grilled yellow squash
Banana Cream Pie (p. 271)

Sunday Brunch:

Blueberry-Orange Coffee Cake
(p. 104)
Bayou Shrimp with Grits (p. 200)

Peach-Raspberry Aspic (p. 138)
Piña Colada Shakes (p. 67)

Sunday Dinner:

Sunday dinner is often the one time a week when people who live together get to sit down together. Here's a menu to stimulate the conversation:

Molasses-Barbecued Chicken
(p. 164)
Ranch Pasta and Vegetable
Salad (p. 132)

Potato Focaccia (p. 96) (two
slices)
Apple Crumb Pie (p. 272) with a
cup of lowfat milk

Fall/Winter Menus

Weekday Breakfasts:

Oat and Wheat Muesli (p. 76)
with half a cup of lowfat or
skim milk
Orange juice
Tea or coffee

Hearty Multi-Grain Buttermilk
Pancakes (p. 73)
Orange juice
Lowfat or skim milk
Tea or coffee

Pumpkin Spice Bran Muffins
(p. 108) with one ounce
fat-free cream cheese
Lowfat or nonfat yogurt
Orange juice
Tea or coffee

Whole Wheat Walnut Bread
(p. 87), toasted
Lowfat cheese
Apple slices
Tea or coffee

Overnight French Toast with
Spiced Apple Compote (p. 74)
Cup of lowfat or skim milk
Juice
Tea or coffee

The Guilt-Free "Comfort Food" Cookbook

Brown-Bag Lunches:

Pocket Bread (p. 98) with five
 ounces sliced turkey breast
 and Sweet-and-Tangy
 Pineapple Slaw (p. 137)
A banana

Sesame Wheat Crispbreads
 (p. 101) with Creole Bean
 Soup (p. 118)
An apple

Sweet-and-Sour Vegetable Beef
 Soup (p. 113)
A bagel
Lowfat or nonfat yogurt
An apple

Tuna Capri Sandwich (p. 62)
Lowfat or nonfat yogurt
Grapes

Marinated Bean Salad with
 Honey-Mustard Vinaigrette
 (p. 133)
Lowfat or nonfat milk
Crusty roll
An apple

Snacks:

Quick Turkey Nachos (p. 55)
Creamy Mint Cocoa (p. 70)
Black Bean "Gazpacho" (p. 119)

Weekday Dinners:

Vegetable-Barley Casserole
 (p. 225)
Mixed green salad
Crusty whole wheat bread
Vanilla ice milk

Low-Country Gumbo (p. 208)
Roasted Orange, Carrots, and
 Parsnips (p. 245)
Crusty whole wheat bread (two
 slices)
Nonfat or lowfat frozen yogurt

Chicken and Dumplings (p. 174)
Streusel Acorn Squash and
 Apples (p. 242)
Kale with Spicy Relish (p. 258)
Whole wheat bread (two slices)

Ice milk
Miami Rice and Beans (p. 214)
Kale with Spicy Relish (p. 258)
Whole wheat bread (two slices)
Fresh pineapple

Steamed Greek Fish (p. 193)
Mashed Root Vegetables (p. 237)
Green salad
Black-Tie Dinner Rolls (p. 100)
 (two rolls)
Marbled Chocolate-Raspberry
 Cheesecake (p. 269)

The Guilt-Free "Comfort Food" Cookbook

Saturday Breakfast:

Cantaloupe
Real Scrambled Eggs (p. 82)
Country-Style Sausage Patties
(p. 83)

Creamy Cheese Grits (p. 78)
Whole wheat toast

Saturday Lunch:

Greens and Beans over Grilled
Polenta (p. 220)
Lowfat or nonfat yogurt
A pear

Saturday Snack:

Baked (lowfat) tortilla chips
with salsa

Saturday Dinner Party:

Sweet Potato Chips with Blue
Cheese Dip (p. 45)
Cajun-Roasted Pork
Tenderloins (p. 154)
Angel-Hair Pasta with Roasted
Tomato Sauce (p. 230)

Mixed Greens with Raspberry
Vinaigrette (p. 124)
Whole Wheat Walnut Bread
(p. 87)
Magnolia Buttermilk Pie (p. 280)
Fruit salad

Sunday Brunch:

Grapefruit and orange slices
Breakfast Enchiladas (p. 79)
Green salad

Rich-and-Fudgy Brownies
(p. 290)
Lowfat or skim milk

Sunday Dinner:

Pot Roast with Plum-Peach
Ketchup (p. 144)
Sweet Potato Souffles (p. 243)
Cool Broccoli Salad with
Yogurt-Basil Dressing
(p. 123)

Toasted Oat and Wheat Bread
(p. 90) (two slices)
Carrot Cake (p. 264)

The Guilt-Free "Comfort Food" Cookbook

Special Occasion Menus

Finally, here are some menus designed around special occasions:

July 4th Celebration:

Chunky Guacamole with
  crudites (p. 46)
Grilled Sweet-and-Tangy
  Cornish Hens (p. 180)
Sweet-and-Tangy Pineapple
  Slaw (p. 137)

Picnic Potato, Corn, and Butter
  Bean Salad (p. 130)
Buttermilk Cornmeal Cake with
  Strawberry-Mint Sauce
  (p. 266)
Raspberry Lemonade (p. 68)

Super Bowl Buffet:

Crispy Potato Skins with
  Corn-Zucchini Salsa (p. 50)
Whole Wheat Lavash (p. 95)
Southwest Hoppin' John (p. 229)
Gourmet Burritos (p. 146)

Posole Bean Chili (p. 216)
Cornmeal Pizza with Chicken
  and Feta Cheese (p. 57)
Hummingbird Cake (p. 262)

Christmas Dinner Party:

Rich Vanilla Eggnog (p. 69)
Apricot-Stuffed Turkey Breast
  (p. 182)
Green Beans with Caramelized
  Onion and Tomato Relish
  (p. 257)

Creamed Peas and Onions (p. 256)
Mashed Root Vegetables (p. 237)
Toasted Oat and Wheat Bread
  (p. 90)
Pumpkin Spice Pie (p. 274)

New Year's Eve "Tapas" Buffet:

Mushrooms Stuffed with Pecans
  and Parmesan (p. 48)
Potato Focaccia (p. 96), Sesame
  Wheat Crispbreads (p. 101)
Crispy Battered Shrimp (p. 202)
Hominy Grits, Eggplant, and
  Tomato Casserole (p. 223)

Herbed Mustard Chicken-and-
  Vegetable Skewers (p. 175)
Old-Fashioned Poundcake
  (p. 261) with fruit

Building Balance

Each of these meals is fairly well balanced in terms of Pyramid
Equivalents. Let's explore how we use the information in this book to

The Guilt-Free "Comfort Food" Cookbook

build these meals. We'll start with the first breakfast: Jogger's Sunrise Shake (p. 84), two slices of whole wheat toast with jam, and coffee or tea. Toast gives us 2 Breads, and the shake provides 2 Fruits and 1 Dairy. So we start the day with a nice beginning:

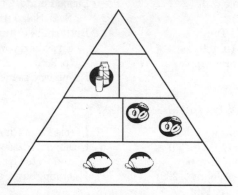

For lunch, let's say we have Pocket Bread (p. 98) with Chicken Salad Remoulade (p. 135), a half cup of raw carrot sticks, and nonfat frozen fruit sorbet with banana slices. The pocket bread will give us 2 Breads servings, the chicken salad ½ Vegetable and 1 Meat, the carrots 1 Vegetable, and let's call the fruit sorbet with a banana 1½ Fruits and Extras. Now our Pyramid looks like this:

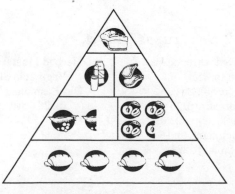

How are we doing? Pretty well, although we could use a few more vegetables. We'll make sure to include some with dinner: Capellini with Scallops and Pesto "Cream Sauce" (p. 206), Tex-Mex Corn Saute (p. 239), Wilted Spinach Salad (p. 126), and for dessert, Old-Fashioned

The Guilt-Free "Comfort Food" Cookbook

Oatmeal-Raisin Cookies (p. 288) with a cup of lowfat or skim milk. The capellini and scallops gives us 2 Breads, 1⅓ Vegetables, and 1 Meat. The corn saute provides 2 Vegetables (now we're talking!), the spinach salad another 1⅓ Vegetables, the oatmeal cookies yield 1 Bread and Extras, and the milk 1 Dairy. Now let's look at our Pyramid:

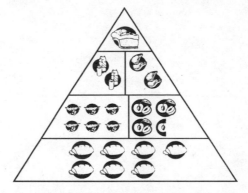

That's a complete Pyramid. Now let's look at the nutritional information:

1,800 Calories, 26 g Fat (3 g Saturated), 100 mg Cholesterol, 1,450 mg Sodium, 85 g Protein, 280 g Carbohydrates, Fiber (21 g), Vitamin C (310%), Folic Acid (80%), Calcium (105%), Iron (54%)

Not a bad day. The calorie level is basic and appropriate for many women. Many men will need to eat more, as will women who are particularly active. The more you exercise, the more you can eat while maintaining your weight, and the more you can eat, the more nutrients you'll take in. Even at this modest calorie level, this menu, which is quite low in fat and sodium and particularly low in saturated fat, is not perfect, but that's not how nutrition works. For example, today we took in more than three times the USRDA for vitamin C but only a little over half the iron. One reason is that we didn't eat any red meat or beans, both of which are good sources of iron. Tomorrow we will.

Eating right and well is a pattern, not an event. Understanding how each kind of food fits into a healthful pattern makes it easier to plan meals that provide taste, nutrition, and comfort without guilt.

It all begins with delicious recipes!

The Guilt-Free "Comfort Food" Cookbook

LIGHT MEALS: SANDWICHES, SNACKS, PARTY FOODS, AND BEVERAGES

We Americans are great snackers. We'll eat anything anytime. Sometimes that gets us into trouble. We get hungry in the afternoon and eat a whole bag of chips. We go to a party, or throw one, and eat piece after piece of creamy, buttery, caloric foods.

But snacking, and even party foods, can be healthful. Eating several small meals is actually easier on your body than skipping meals and overeating at one or two big meals. Such an eating pattern helps regulate blood sugar and blood cholesterol better than one or two big meals. A well-timed, well-planned mid-afternoon snack can assuage hunger without too much fat and keep us from raiding the cookie jar!

When family adults come home from work and kids come home from school, have something at hand that is delicious, nutritious, light, and memorable. Something like Quick Turkey Nachos (p. 55), or Chunky Guacamole (p. 46), or Roasted Eggplant Dip (p. 52), with fresh cut-up vegetables. When you entertain, a spread that includes light foods such as Sweet Potato Chips with Blue Cheese Dip (p. 45), Mushrooms Stuffed with Pecans and Parmesan (p. 48), Crispy Potato Skins with Corn-Zucchini Salsa (p. 50), or Crab Mousse Hors d'Oeuvres (p. 49) will give your guests a treat without loading them down with fat or calories. Whether it's an afternoon snack or a Saturday

The Guilt-Free "Comfort Food" Cookbook

night party, don't forget beverages: colorful, nonalcoholic drinks can make even a Tuesday afternoon feel special.

Light meals can also be used for lunch or dinner. It's easy to build a meal around a Tuna Capri Sandwich (p. 62) or Vegetable Gyro Sandwiches (p. 59). Many of the foods in this chapter can double as snacks, party foods, or light meals.

Start eating lighter, and you may find *yourself* getting lighter too!

The Guilt-Free "Comfort Food" Cookbook

Time: 20 minutes prep
2 hours chilling
45 minutes baking
Yield: 4 servings

Sweet Potato Chips with Blue Cheese Dip

*C*an't call them *fries*. Have to call them *bakes*. But they're thin and crispy, delicious and nutritious. Sweet potatoes are so rich in vitamin A (in the form of beta-carotene) that one serving of this snack provides more than twice one's daily needs!

*1/4 cup reduced-fat cream
   cheese, softened*
1/2 cup nonfat sour cream
1/4 cup crumbled blue cheese
1 clove garlic, crushed
1 tablespoon minced fresh basil
*1 tablespoon minced fresh
   parsley*

*2 tablespoons reduced-fat tub
   margarine, melted*
1 tablespoon skim milk
1/4 teaspoon salt
*2 (8-ounce) sweet potatoes,
   peeled*

Combine cream cheese, sour cream, blue cheese, garlic, basil, and parsley in a small bowl; beat until well blended. Cover and refrigerate 2 hours.

Preheat oven to 300°. Combine margarine, skim milk, and salt in a small saucepan; melt over medium heat.

Cut sweet potato into 1/8-inch slices. Place wire cooling racks on baking sheets; arrange sweet potato slices in a single layer on racks. Brush margarine mixture on rounds; bake for 35 to 45 minutes or until crispy and browned, removing chips as they cook.

Serve at room temperature with blue cheese dip.

Per Serving (dip by itself, one quarter of recipe): 85 Calories, 5 g Fat (3 g Saturated), 15 g Cholesterol, 185 mg Sodium, 5 g Protein, 5 g Carbohydrates
A Good Source of: Vitamin A (10%)
Pyramid Equivalent(s): 1/2 Dairy

Per Serving (chips with dip): 225 Calories, 8 g Fat (4 g Saturated), 15 mg Cholesterol, 350 mg Sodium, 7 g Protein, 32 g Carbohydrates
A Great Source of: Vitamin A (256%), Vitamin C (50%)
A Good Source of: Fiber (3 g), Vitamin B2 (17%), Vitamin B6 (16%), Pantothenic Acid (10%), Vitamin E (10%), Calcium (10%), Copper (12%), Potassium (460 mg)
Pyramid Equivalent(s): 1 Vegetable, 1/2 Dairy, Extras

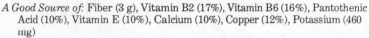

The Guilt-Free "Comfort Food" Cookbook

Time: 20 minutes prep
Yield: 2¹/₄ cups

Chunky Guacamole

*M*ost of us have gotten the lowfat message. Perhaps too well! Some high-fat foods, such as nuts and seeds, are quite nutritious. Avocados too. Their fat is mostly monounsaturated, which is a healthful substitute for saturated fat found in red meat and dairy products. Avocados are rich in vitamin A (as beta-carotene), vitamin C, folic acid, vitamin B6, potassium, and minerals such as copper.

So we have a better idea than total fat avoidance: moderation. In this recipe, we cut total fat by mixing in nonfat ricotta, and serving it with fresh vegetables. Each tablespoon has only 1.5 grams of fat.

So, enjoy—in moderation!

1 medium-sized ripe avocado
2 teaspoons lime juice
¹/₂ cup nonfat ricotta cheese
3 tablespoons Creamy Pepper
   Ranch Salad Dressing
   (p. 127) or commercial
   reduced-fat alternative
¹/₄ teaspoon ground cumin
¹/₄ teaspoon garlic powder
1 cup seeded, finely diced plum
   tomato
¹/₂ cup finely diced red pepper

¹/₄ cup minced green onion
¹/₄ cup minced fresh cilantro
2 tablespoons minced and
   seeded jalapeno pepper
   (optional)
crudites such as sliced
   cucumber, yellow squash,
   hollowed cherry tomatoes,
   carrot slices, radicchio,
   Belgian endive leaves
salt (optional)

Peel, seed, and mash avocado with lemon juice in a medium bowl. Place ricotta cheese in a fine wire-mesh sieve; press through sieve into bowl. Add dressing, cumin, and garlic powder, mixing well; stir in tomato, green pepper, green onion, cilantro, and jalapeno, if desired. Salt to taste, if desired.

Serve with cucumber and squash rounds, or spoon into tomatoes or lettuce leaves.

Per Serving (two tablespoons): 36 Calories, 3 g Fat (1 g Saturated), 3 mg Cholesterol, 50 mg Sodium, 1 g Protein, 2 g Carbohydrates
A Good Source of: Vitamin C (14%)
(No Pyramid Equivalents.)

Note: Served on vegetables, such as cherry tomatoes or cucumber and carrot slices: Vitamin C (21%); Pyramid Equivalent of ⅔ Vegetable.

The Guilt-Free "Comfort Food" Cookbook

Time: 20 minutes prep and
broiling
Yield: 2 dozen

Mushrooms Stuffed with Pecans and Parmesan

*F*inger foods are great at gatherings, formal or informal.

24 large fresh mushrooms
olive oil-flavored cooking spray
1 tablespoon olive oil
²/3 cup minced green onion
¹/2 teaspoon dried thyme
1 cup soft (or fresh) bread
*   crumbs*
¹/4 cup plus 2 tablespoons
*   freshly grated Parmesan*
*   cheese, divided*

2 tablespoons minced toasted
*   pecans*
2 tablespoons reduced-fat sour
*   cream*
¹/2 teaspoon freshly ground
*   pepper*

Clean mushrooms with damp cloth or paper towels; remove stems, reserving for other uses, if desired.

Coat a large nonstick skillet with cooking spray; place over medium-high heat until hot. Add mushroom caps; saute 5 minutes. Remove from skillet; drain and pat dry with towels.

Add olive oil to skillet; heat over medium heat. Add green onion and thyme; saute 2 minutes. Remove from heat and stir in bread crumbs, 2 tablespoons cheese, pecans, reduced-fat sour cream, and pepper.

Spoon bread-crumb mixture evenly into mushroom caps; mound ½ teaspoon Parmesan cheese on each. Place mushrooms on rack of a broiler pan coated with cooking spray; broil 4 to 6 inches from heat for 2 to 3 minutes or until lightly browned.

Per Mushroom: 30 Calories, 2 g Fat (1 g Saturated), 2 mg Cholesterol, 40 mg Sodium, 1 g Protein, 3 g Carbohydrates
(Not a significant source of vitamins or minerals. No Pyramid Equivalents.)

The Guilt-Free "Comfort Food" Cookbook

Time: 35 minutes prep
1 hour chilling
Yield: 2¹/₄ cups
(36 appetizers)

Crab Mousse Hors d'Oeuvres

*T*hese may be prepared up to four hours in advance. Refrigerate until
ready to serve.

1 envelope unflavored gelatin
*¹/₂ cup canned reduced-sodium
    chicken broth, undiluted*
*²/₃ cup fat-free salad dressing
    (such as Miracle Whip), or
    reduced-fat mayonnaise
    (such as Hellman's)*
2 tablespoons ketchup
1 tablespoon lemon juice
*2 tablespoons minced fresh
    parsley*

*¹/₂ teaspoon hot sauce (such as
    Tabasco)*
*6 ounces flaked fresh crabmeat,
    with cartilage removed*
*¹/₄ cup finely minced sweet red
    pepper*
*¹/₂ cup reduced-fat ricotta
    cheese*
18 slices party rye bread
18 Belgian endive leaves

Combine gelatin and chicken broth in a small saucepan; let stand 5
minutes. Cook over low heat, stirring constantly until gelatin dissolves.
Combine salad dressing, ketchup, lemon juice, parsley, and hot sauce in a
large bowl; mix well, and stir in gelatin-broth mixture. Chill until mixture
is the consistency of unbeaten egg white.

Fold crabmeat and red pepper into mixture. Press ricotta cheese
through a fine wire-mesh sieve into bowl. Stir well; chill just until mixture
mounds.

Cut shapes from bread using hors d'oeuvre cutters. Arrange bread
slices and endive leaves on a serving platter. Spoon crabmeat mixture into
a pastry bag fitted with a large round or star tip; pipe mousse on bread
slices and endive leaves, dividing evenly. Cover carefully with plastic wrap
and chill until mousse is firm (up to 1 hour) before serving.

Per Serving (two pieces): 62 Calories, 3 g Fat (1 g Saturated), 13 mg Cholesterol,
    165 mg Sodium, 4 g Protein, 6 g Carbohydrates
(Not a significant source of vitamins or minerals. No Pyramid Equivalents.)

The Guilt-Free "Comfort Food" Cookbook

Time: 25 minutes prep
1¹/₄ hours cooking
Yield: 16 potato skins
   (16 servings)

Crispy Potato Skins with Corn-Zucchini Salsa

*T*he potato skin appetizers you get in restaurants are deep-fried, probably in yesterday's oil. These crispy baked "fries" are fresher and more satisfying. Just make sure your potato skins are free of green spots or eyes, which contain chemicals that can make you sick. (If a potato has an eye or green spot, cut it out, scoop out about a half inch of the potato underneath, and proceed with this recipe.)

4 large baking potatoes (about two pounds)
1 tablespoon reduced-fat soft margarine or olive oil
1 cup finely diced zucchini
¹/₂ cup finely diced sweet red pepper
1 cup fresh or frozen corn kernels
¹/₂ cup sliced green onion
1 teaspoon chili powder

¹/₂ cup nonfat sour cream
¹/₄ cup minced fresh cilantro butter-flavored vegetable cooking spray
1 teaspoon chili powder
¹/₂ teaspoon salt
¹/₄ teaspoon ground red pepper
2 cups (8 ounces) shredded reduced-fat Monterey Jack cheese

Preheat oven to 450°. Scrub potatoes, and prick several times with a fork. Bake for 45 minutes to 1 hour or until tender. Let stand until cool enough to handle.

Meanwhile, melt margarine in a medium skillet over medium-high heat; add zucchini and red pepper; saute until zucchini is tender. Add corn, green onion, and 1 teaspoon chili powder; saute 3 minutes or until tender. Remove from heat; cool to room temperature. Stir in sour cream and cilantro.

Cut potatoes lengthwise into quarters; carefully scoop out pulp, leaving 1/8-inch shells. (Reserve pulp for other purposes, such as mashed potatoes.) Place potato skins on a baking sheet, and coat lightly with cooking spray.

Combine 1 teaspoon chili powder, salt, and pepper; sprinkle over potato skins. Bake at 425° for 12 to 15 minutes or until crisp. Spoon corn

The Guilt-Free "Comfort Food" Cookbook

mixture evenly in skins; sprinkle each with 2 tablespoons cheese. Broil until cheese melts. Serve hot.

Per Potato Skin: 115 Calories, 4 g Fat (2 g Saturated), 10 mg Cholesterol, 130 mg Sodium, 6 g Protein, 16 g Carbohydrates

A Good Source of: Fiber (2 g), Vitamin B6 (10%), Vitamin C (24%), Potassium (280 mg)

Pyramid Equivalent(s): 1 Bread, ½ Dairy

The Guilt-Free "Comfort Food" Cookbook

Time: 30 minutes prep
1¹/₄ hours baking
Yield: 2¹/₂ cups

Roasted Eggplant Dip

*T*his nutritious dip is nice to have in your refrigerator when your kids
come home from school ravenous. Or try it at your next party. Peel
and slice some carrots, and keep them in a bowl of water in the fridge.
Pull the dip and carrots out, and put them on the kitchen table when
you hear the doorbell.

Undercooked eggplant can sometimes be bitter, but this dish is
sweet and sumptuous. Even the garlic, long-cooked, becomes sweet
and nutty. Here's a tip: Chilling the cooked garlic makes it much easier to peel. The cloves pop right out of their papery shells.

1 large garlic bulb
1 tablespoon reduced-sodium
  soy sauce
1 tablespoon olive oil
1 (1-pound) eggplant, ends
  trimmed and cut in ¹/₂-inch
  slices
vegetable cooking spray
1 medium onion, cut into
  ¹/₂-inch slices

2 ripe tomatoes, cored, halved,
  and seeded
2 tablespoons lemon juice
2 tablespoons minced fresh mint
¹/₂ teaspoon freshly ground
  pepper
1 tablespoon toasted sesame
  seeds

Preheat oven to 400°. Remove papery skin from garlic; carefully
slice off stem end, using a small sharp knife. Stand garlic on the stem
side on a piece of heavy-duty aluminum foil. Combine soy sauce and olive oil; mix well and drizzle 1 teaspoon mixture on top of the cut side of
garlic. Wrap foil around garlic, sealing edges tightly. Bake for 40 minutes. Remove garlic. When completely cooled, peel shell from each
clove. (It should come off easily.)

Meanwhile, arrange eggplant and onion slices on nonstick baking
sheets coated with cooking spray; brush tops with half of remaining soy
sauce mixture. Bake at 425° for 10 minutes. Turn slices; brush with remaining soy sauce mixture, and continue baking 10 minutes or until
lightly browned and tender. Cool.

The Guilt-Free "Comfort Food" Cookbook

Arrange tomatoes, cut sides down, on a baking sheet coated with cooking spray; bake 10 to 15 minutes at 425° or until vegetables are soft.

Finely chop eggplant, onion, tomato, and garlic; place in a bowl. Add remaining ingredients, and mix well. Cover and refrigerate 1 hour before serving. (Mixture may be refrigerated up to 3 days.)

Serve on toasted pita triangles, crackers, sliced zucchini or cucumbers, carrots, pepper triangles, or as a pizza topping.

Per Serving (two tablespoons): 25 Calories, 1 g Fat (0 g Saturated), 0 mg Cholesterol, 35 mg Sodium, 1 g Protein, 3 g Carbohydrates
(Not a significant source of vitamins or minerals.)
Pyramid Equivalent(s): ½ Vegetable

The Guilt-Free "Comfort Food" Cookbook

Time: 45 minutes
plus 35 minutes to make biscuits
Yield: 12 servings

Ham Biscuits with Baked
Berry Jam

*M*ore irresistible finger food! If you like the Baked Berry Jam, try it over bread, on cottage cheese, or as a dessert topping on angel food cake, ice milk, or frozen yogurt.

12 High-Rise Buttermilk Biscuits (see p. 102)
Baked Berry Jam (recipe follows)
6 ounces shaved turkey ham, cut into 2-inch pieces

Split biscuits; spread 2 teaspoons jam on each biscuit bottom and top with ½ ounce turkey ham. Replace biscuit tops.

Baked Berry Jam
Yield: about 1½ cups

8 cups fresh raspberries, blackberries, or sliced strawberries
1 cup sugar
2 tablespoons lemon juice

Preheat oven to 375°. Rinse berries and dry on paper towels. Gently toss berries, sugar, and lemon juice. Spread in a nonstick 15- x 10- x 1-inch jelly-roll pan (or line a regular pan with aluminum foil and coat with vegetable cooking spray). Bake uncovered for 10 minutes or until berries are juicy; reduce oven temperature to 325° and continue baking, stirring gently every 15 minutes, until mixture forms a soft ball when a half-teaspoon is dropped in ice water. Spoon into a bowl or small jars; serve warm, or refrigerate (up to 2 weeks) and serve chilled.

Per Serving (one biscuit with ham and jam): 250 Calories, 5 g Fat (1 g Saturated), 10 mg Cholesterol, 450 mg Sodium, 7 g Protein, 45 g Carbohydrates
A Great Source of: Vitamin C (37%)
A Good Source of: Fiber (4 g), Vitamin B1 (13%), Vitamin B2 (16%), Vitamin B3 (13%), Vitamin E (12%), Calcium (14%), Iron (11%), Potassium (290 mg)
Pyramid Equivalent(s): 1 Fruit, Extras

The Guilt-Free "Comfort Food" Cookbook

Quick Turkey Nachos

*M*ake these mini-nachos in advance—they'll stay fresh in the refrigerator for two days—so they're waiting when you and your family come home. Just take out as many tortilla chips as you want, spoon on the topping, and broil. Makes a nice afternoon snack, a great appetizer, great party finger food, or healthful snack (for a change!) while watching the ball game on TV.

2 ounces reduced-fat cream cheese, softened
2 (5-ounce) cans of chunk turkey, drained (or 10 ounces shredded fresh cooked turkey)
1/3 cup commercial chunky taco sauce
1/4 cup minced green onion
1/4 cup minced fresh cilantro
1/4 teaspoon garlic powder
24 large fat-free tortilla chips
3/4 cup seeded and finely diced tomato
3/4 cup (3 ounces) shredded reduced-fat Cheddar or Monterey Jack cheese

Mash cream cheese in a bowl until smooth; add turkey, and shred with a fork. Stir in taco sauce, green onion, cilantro, and garlic powder. Cover and refrigerate.

To serve, arrange tortilla chips on a baking sheet; spoon 1½ tablespoons turkey mixture on each chip. Sprinkle each with ½ tablespoon tomato and ½ tablespoon cheese; broil 6 inches from heat source 1 minute or until cheese melts.

Per Nacho: 40 Calories, 4 g Protein, 2 g Carbohydrates, 0 g Fiber, 2 g Fat (1 g Saturated), 11 mg Cholesterol, 56 mg Potassium, 113 mg Sodium
(Not a significant source of vitamins or minerals. No Pyramid Equivalents.)

Per Four-Nacho Serving: 160 Calories, 8 g Fat (4 g Saturated), 45 mg Cholesterol, 450 mg Sodium, 16 g Protein, 8 g Carbohydrates
A Good Source of: Vitamin B3 (16%), Vitamin B6 (12%), Vitamin C (16%)
Pyramid Equivalent(s): 1 Bread, ½ Dairy, 1 Meat

The Guilt-Free "Comfort Food" Cookbook

Time: 20 minutes prep
17 minutes baking
Yield: 1 dozen

Tamale Pizza Cups

*3/4 cup plus 2 tablespoons
    cornmeal, divided*
3/4 cup all-purpose flour
2 teaspoons baking powder
1/4 teaspoon salt
*1/3 cup egg substitute (or 1
    large whole egg and 1 egg
    white)*
3/4 cup skim milk
2 tablespoons olive oil
vegetable cooking spray

*1 (14 1/2-ounce) can
    Mexican-style stewed
    tomatoes, drained*
*3/4 cup cooked kidney beans,
    drained*
*1/2 cup frozen whole kernel
    corn, thawed*
1/2 cup diced green pepper
1 teaspoon chili powder
*1 1/2 cups (6 ounces) shredded
    reduced-fat Cheddar cheese*

Preheat oven to 400°. Stir together ¾ cup cornmeal, flour, baking powder, and salt in a large bowl. Combine egg substitute, milk, and oil; add to dry ingredients, and stir until smooth. Coat a muffin pan with cooking spray; sprinkle remaining 2 tablespoons cornmeal in muffin cups, and tilt pan to coat bottoms. Tap out excess cornmeal.

Chop tomatoes; mix with beans, corn, green pepper, and chili powder.

Spoon batter evenly in muffin cups; spoon tomato mixture evenly on top of batter in centers of cups. Bake at 400° for 15 minutes or until cornbread is set. Sprinkle with cheese and bake 2 minutes or until cheese melts. Let cool 10 minutes before removing from muffin pan.

Per Serving (one pizza cup): 165 Calories, 6 g Fat (2 g Saturated), 11 mg Cholesterol, 330 mg Sodium, 9 g Protein, 21 g Carbohydrates
A Good Source of: Fiber (3 g), Vitamin B1 (10%), Vitamin C (15%), Calcium (22%)
Pyramid Equivalent(s): ½ Bread, ½ Vegetable, ½ Dairy

The Guilt-Free "Comfort Food" Cookbook

Time: 25 minutes prep
15 minutes baking
Yield: 6 servings

Cornmeal Pizza with Chicken and Feta Cheese

ℐf you can't find feta flavored with basil, simply add a half teaspoon of dried basil to regular feta. If you're buying imported feta, there's usually Greek, Bulgarian, and French. If you can find the French kind, it's likely to be lower in salt. There are also some fine domestic fetas available. Fetas are made with goat milk, so many people who have trouble digesting cow's milk find them more digestible.

*1/4 cup reduced-fat ricotta
   cheese
2 tablespoons Dijon mustard
2 teaspoons dried thyme
1 recipe Cornmeal Flatbread
   (p. 94), prepared for pizza
   crust
1 tablespoon olive oil
1/2 pound boneless, skinless
   chicken breasts, cut into
   1- x 1/4-inch strips*

*1 tablespoon lemon juice
1 cup seeded and finely diced
   tomatoes
2 tablespoons sliced ripe olives
1 (4-ounce) package crumbled
   feta cheese flavored with
   basil and tomato*

Mix together ricotta, mustard, and thyme; spread over Cornmeal Flatbread to within 1 inch from edge. Place on a baking sheet.

Preheat oven to 400°. Heat olive oil in a nonstick skillet over medium-high heat; add chicken, and saute until cooked. Sprinkle lemon juice over chicken; saute until liquid evaporates. Arrange chicken on tart; sprinkle with tomato, olives, and cheese. Bake for 15 minutes.

Per Serving (one slice): 350 Calories, 14 g Fat (5 g Saturated), 45 mg Cholesterol, 545 mg Sodium, 20 g Protein, 40 g Carbohydrates
A Great Source of: Fiber (4 g), Vitamin B2 (30%), Vitamin B3 (37%)
A Good Source of: Vitamin B1 (24%), Vitamin B6 (21%), Folic Acid (14%), Pantothenic Acid (11%), Vitamin C (12%), Vitamin E (16%), Calcium (21%), Iron (19%), Magnesium (15%), Zinc (13%), Potassium (390 mg)
Pyramid Equivalent(s): 1 Bread, 1 Dairy, 1 Meat

The Guilt-Free "Comfort Food" Cookbook

Time: 35 minutes prep
up to 24 hours refrigeration
Yield: 4 servings

Tomatoes Stuffed with Tuna Tabbouleh

3 cups water
1 cup bulgur wheat (or cracked wheat)
1 tablespoon olive oil
2 tablespoons lemon juice
³/4 cup finely minced parsley
2 tablespoons minced fresh mint
1/4 teaspoon salt
1/2 teaspoon freshly ground pepper

1 (6¹/2-ounce) can solid white tuna (packed in water), drained and flaked
1 cup seeded and finely diced cucumber
1/2 cup thinly sliced green onion
4 large lettuce leaves
4 large, ripe tomatoes

Bring water to a boil in a medium saucepan over medium-high heat; stir in bulgur. Cover, reduce heat, and simmer 15 to 20 minutes or until bulgur is tender. Drain well; place in a large bowl, and let cool to room temperature.

Add olive oil, lemon juice, parsley, mint, salt, and pepper to bulgur; stir well. Stir in tuna, cucumber, and green onion. Cover and refrigerate (up to 24 hours) before serving.

To serve, arrange lettuce leaves on serving plates. Using a small sharp knife, remove cores from tomatoes. Starting from top of tomato, make 6 vertical cuts to form even wedges, stopping knife about ¼ inch from bottom to keep tomato intact. Spoon tuna mixture into tomatoes.

Per Serving: 265 Calories, 6 g Fat (1 g Saturated), 20 mg Cholesterol, 195 mg Sodium, 19 g Protein, 38 g Carbohydrates

A Great Source of: Fiber (9 g), Vitamin B3 (30%), Vitamin B6 (25%), Vitamin C (99%), Vitamin E (25%), Magnesium (27%), Potassium (850 mg)

A Good Source of: Vitamin A (22%), Vitamin B1 (15%), Vitamin B2 (11%), Vitamin B12 (17%), Folic Acid (20%), Pantothenic Acid (11%), Copper (20%), Iron (17%)

Pyramid Equivalent(s): 1 Bread, 2 Vegetables, ½ Meat

The Guilt-Free "Comfort Food" Cookbook

Vegetable Gyro Sandwiches

*2 medium zucchini, cut into
1/2-inch slices
2 large sweet red peppers, cut
into 1/2-inch slices
12 large mushrooms, halved
olive oil-flavored vegetable
cooking spray
1 tablespoon olive oil
2 tablespoons balsamic or red
wine vinegar
1 tablespoon Dijon mustard*

*2 tablespoons fresh oregano or
thyme, minced
1 clove garlic, crushed
10 cherry tomatoes, quartered
6 large pitted ripe olives,
quartered
3 (7-inch) pita breads
2 cups (8 ounces) part-skim
mozzarella cheese (or
reduced-fat Jarlsberg)*

Combine squash, pepper, and mushrooms in a bowl; coat with cooking spray and toss well. Arrange vegetables in a 15- x 10- x 1-inch jelly-roll pan; broil 6 inches from heat source for 10 minutes or until vegetables are browned but crisp-tender, turning occasionally.

Toss cooked vegetables with olive oil, vinegar, mustard, oregano, and garlic in a large bowl. Stir in tomatoes and olives. Cover and refrigerate until ready to make sandwiches (up to 2 days).

Preheat oven to 350°. Cut each pita in half to form 2 rounds; stack rounds on a piece of aluminum foil, sprinkling each with about ½ teaspoon water. Seal tightly. Bake for 10 minutes or until hot.

Arrange vegetables in centers of bread rounds; sprinkle evenly with cheese. Roll up; secure with wooden picks. Place on a baking sheet; bake at 350° for 5 to 10 minutes or until vegetables are hot.

Per Serving: 250 Calories, 10 g Fat (5 g Saturated), 20 mg Cholesterol, 440 mg Sodium, 15 g Protein, 26 g Carbohydrates

A Great Source of: Vitamin B2 (25%), Vitamin C (56%), Calcium (35%)

A Good Source of: Fiber (3 g), Vitamin A (13%), Vitamin B1 (20%), Vitamin B3 (17%), Vitamin B6 (10%), Pantothenic Acid (11%), Vitamin E (11%), Copper (17%), Iron (15%), Magnesium (11%), Zinc (13%), Potassium (455 mg)

Pyramid Equivalent(s): ½ Bread, 2 Vegetables, 1 Dairy

The Guilt-Free "Comfort Food" Cookbook

Time: 20 minutes prep
3 hours chilling
Yield: 3 servings

Texas "BLT"

*H*ere's a colorful layered sandwich. Try it for lunch. How about brown bagging it to work? Start with one day a week. You'll save money, avoid high-fat temptations, and eat fresher foods. For a portable sandwich, wrap each serving individually in plastic wrap.

For a party, double the recipe and make two whole sandwiches. Cut into thirds. Then cut each serving in half or into thirds again. You'll have twelve or eighteen sandwiches. That's how many toothpicks you'll need. As a variation, you can make a very thin layer of avocado mixture, spinach, tomatoes, and black bean on one tortilla, roll it, and cut into pinwheels.

*1 cup black beans, cooked and
   drained*
*1/2 cup commercial picante
   sauce, divided*
1 clove garlic, crushed
1 teaspoon ground cumin
1/2 cup diced avocado
1 teaspoon lemon juice

1/3 cup nonfat cream cheese
2 tablespoons minced onion
3 (8-inch) flour tortillas
*6 large fresh spinach leaves or
   romaine lettuce leaves,
   trimmed*
1 tomato, thinly sliced

Combine beans, 2 tablespoons picante sauce, garlic, and cumin; mash mixture coarsely.

Combine avocado and lemon juice; toss. Add cream cheese and minced onion; mash mixture until smooth.

Place one tortilla on a plate; spread avocado mixture on tortilla to edges. Top with half of spinach leaves and another tortilla. Arrange remaining spinach leaves and tomato slices on tortilla stack. Spread bean mixture evenly on remaining tortilla; place, bean side down, on tomato slices. Wrap well in plastic wrap; refrigerate 3 hours.

To serve, cut stack into thirds; serve each piece with 2 tablespoons remaining picante sauce.

The Guilt-Free "Comfort Food" Cookbook

Per Serving: 310 Calories, 7 g Fat (1 g Saturated), 9 mg Cholesterol, 690 mg Sodium, 17 g Protein, 44 g Carbohydrates

A Great Source of: Fiber (8 g), Vitamin A (26%), Vitamin B1 (28%), Folic Acid (37%), Vitamin C (28%), Vitamin E (25%), Potassium (650 mg)

A Good Source of: Vitamin B2 (20%), Vitamin B3 (13%), Vitamin B6 (11%), Copper (19%), Iron (21%), Magnesium (19%), Zinc (10%)

Pyramid Equivalent(s): 1 Bread, 2 Vegetables, 1 Meat

The Guilt-Free "Comfort Food" Cookbook

Time: 25 minutes prep
Overnight chilling
Yield: 6 servings

Tuna Capri Sandwich

*3/4 pound eggplant, unpeeled
    and cut into 1/2-inch slices
1 medium purple onion, cut into
    1/4-inch slices
olive oil-flavored vegetable
    cooking spray
freshly ground pepper
1 (12-ounce) round loaf crusty
    Italian bread
1 (9-ounce) can white albacore
    tuna (packed in water),
    drained*

*3 tablespoons balsamic vinegar
2 tablespoons olive oil
16 large basil leaves, divided
2 canned or fresh-roasted red
    peppers, drained and cut
    into wide strips
4 ounces very thinly sliced
    part-skim mozzarella cheese*

Arrange eggplant and onion slices on a large nonstick baking sheet
coated with cooking spray; coat both sides of vegetables with cooking
spray and sprinkle with pepper. Broil 1 to 2 minutes on each side or until
browned and tender.

Cut bread in half horizontally; remove soft crumb from each half, leaving a 1-inch shell. Coat bottom half of bread with cooking spray; separate
tuna into chunks, and arrange in bottom half. Drizzle with half of vinegar
and olive oil; top evenly with eggplant and half of basil leaves. Arrange onion slices, cheese, remaining basil leaves, and red pepper strips on top;
drizzle with remaining balsamic vinegar and olive oil. Coat cut side of
bread top with cooking spray; place on sandwich.

Wrap loaf tightly with plastic wrap, then with heavy-duty aluminum
foil. Place on a platter with a baking pan on top; place in refrigerator and
weigh down the top with a milk jug or other weight overnight. Cut into
wedges, and serve chilled or at room temperature.

The Guilt-Free "Comfort Food" Cookbook

Per Serving: 330 Calories, 11 g Fat (4 g Saturated), 600 mg Sodium, 28 mg Cholesterol, 23 g Protein, 36 g Carbohydrates
A Great Source of: Vitamin B3 (27%), Vitamin C (82%)
A Good Source of: Fiber (4 g), Vitamin A (20%), Vitamin B1 (22%), Vitamin B2 (17%), Vitamin B6 (18%), Vitamin B12 (19%), Folic Acid (10%), Vitamin E (15%), Calcium (20%), Copper (13%), Iron (13%), Magnesium (12%), Zinc (10%), Potassium (410 mg)
Pyramid Equivalent(s): 2 Breads, 2 Vegetables, ½ Dairy, 1 Meat

The Guilt-Free "Comfort Food" Cookbook

Time: 15 minutes
Yield: 4 servings

Salmon Salad Melts

*S*almon is an excellent source of protein, low in saturated fat and rich in heart-healthful fish oils. Canned salmon with the bones is also rich in calcium, as are dairy foods, of course, so this dish is a great source of calcium.

It's a tad high in sodium. You can cut the sodium by a few hundred milligrams by omitting the capers, using low-sodium Thousand Island (if you can find it), and rinsing the salmon briefly under cold water. Keep a light hand on the salt shaker in the other foods you serve with it as well. For example, for lunch or a quick weekday dinner, serve this with spinach sauteed in a nonstick skillet with a teaspoon of olive oil, a splash of fresh lemon juice, and a salad of sliced fresh tomatoes with freshly ground pepper and, if it's in season, fresh basil.

You can make these into sixteen canapes for your next party or get-together: Before placing the bread on the baking sheet, cut each piece into quarters, and proceed with the recipe. You'll have sixteen "mini-melts."

*1/2 cup commercial nonfat
    Thousand Island salad
    dressing
1/4 cup nonfat sour cream
1 tablespoon chopped fresh dill
    or 1/2 teaspoon dried dill
1 1/2 teaspoons lemon juice
2 teaspoons drained capers
1/2 teaspoon freshly ground
    pepper
1 (14-ounce) can red salmon
    (packed in water), drained*

*1 cup finely chopped celery
4 slices pumpernickel or dark
    rye bread, lightly toasted
1/3 large purple onion, sliced
    paper-thin
1 small cucumber, peeled and
    very thinly sliced
3/4 cup (3 ounces) shredded
    reduced-fat Jarlsberg
    cheese*

Combine dressing, sour cream, dill, lemon juice, capers, and pepper in a large bowl; mix well. Measure out and reserve 2 tablespoons mixture. Stir in salmon and celery.

Place bread slices on a baking sheet; spread reserved salad dressing

The Guilt-Free "Comfort Food" Cookbook

mixture evenly on bread slices. Arrange onion slices and cucumber slices on bread.

Spoon salmon mixture evenly on sandwiches; sprinkle evenly with cheese. Broil 4 to 6 inches from heat source until cheese melts.

Per Serving: 320 Calories, 9 g Fat (3 g Saturated), 50 mg Cholesterol, 1,050 mg Sodium, 30 g Protein, 28 g Carbohydrates

A Great Source of: Vitamin B3 (33%), Calcium (48%), Potassium (630 mg)

A Good Source of: Fiber (3 g), Vitamin A (10%), Vitamin B2 (23%), Vitamin B6 (20%), Vitamin B12 (12%), Vitamin C (11%), Vitamin E (20%), Iron (12%), Magnesium (14%), Zinc (15%)

Pyramid Equivalent(s): 1 Bread, 1 Vegetable, ½ Dairy, 2 Meats

The Guilt-Free "Comfort Food" Cookbook

Time: 15 minutes prep
3-4 hours freezing
Yield: 9 cups (9 servings)

Sparkling Tropical Slush
Punch

*T*his makes a pretty, nonalcoholic punch for entertaining. But you can also keep it in the freezer and have a refreshing nonalcoholic "cocktail" every night! Just scoop out a half cup of the frozen mixture into a glass, add a half cup chilled seltzer or mineral water, stir, and enjoy.

1 (16-ounce) package frozen
   peaches, thawed
1 medium banana, peeled and
   sliced
1 cup peach or apricot nectar
2 (6-ounce) cans limeade
   concentrate, thawed and
   undiluted

$4^1/_3$ cups sparkling
   orange-flavored carbonated
   water, chilled

Process peaches, banana, and nectar in an electric blender until smooth. Pour through a fine wire-mesh sieve into a container. Stir in lime-ade concentrate, mixing well. Cover and freeze 3-4 hours or until slushy.

To serve, transfer juice mixture to a small punch bowl; stir in mineral water, and serve immediately.

Per Serving: 140 Calories, 0 g Fat (0 g Saturated), 0 mg Cholesterol, 8 mg Sodium, 0 g Protein, 37 g Carbohydrates
A Great Source of: Vitamin C (95%)
Pyramid Equivalent(s): 2 Fruits

The Guilt-Free "Comfort Food" Cookbook

Piña Colada Shake

*C*ool, cool, cool. Nonfat dry milk powder adds body, plus calcium, without fat.

1 cup canned unsweetened (or fresh, cubed) pineapple tidbits, drained
$^1/_2$ (12-ounce) can frozen pineapple-orange-banana juice concentrate

$^1/_4$ cup instant nonfat dry milk powder
1 (8-ounce) container nonfat vanilla-flavored yogurt
1 teaspoon coconut extract
crushed ice

Spread pineapple tidbits in a baking pan; cover and freeze 1 hour or until firm.

Combine pineapple and remaining ingredients, except ice, in an electric blender; cover and process until smooth. Add enough crushed ice to reach 4 cups; cover and process until slushy. Pour into glasses, and serve immediately.

Per Serving: 120 Calories, 0 g Fat (0 g Saturated), 2 mg Cholesterol, 80 mg Sodium, 6 g Protein, 24 g Carbohydrates
A Great Source of: Vitamin C (29%)
A Good Source of: Vitamin B2 (15%), Vitamin B12 (10%), Calcium (20%), Potassium (380 mg)
Pyramid Equivalent(s): 1 Fruit, ½ Dairy

The Guilt-Free "Comfort Food" Cookbook

Time: 10 minutes
Yield: 6 cups (6 servings)

Raspberry Lemonade

*H*ere's a nice change of pace for lemonade. If you like, substitute frozen strawberries for raspberries and fresh lime juice for lemon to make strawberry limeade. Of course, if you have fresh berries, that's fine too.

1 (12-ounce) package frozen unsweetened raspberries, thawed
3¹/₂ cups water, divided
³/₄ cup sugar
1 cup fresh lemon juice (about 6 to 8 lemons)

Process raspberries and 1 cup water in an electric blender until smooth; press through a fine wire-mesh sieve into a pitcher. Add remaining water, sugar, and lemon juice, stirring until sugar dissolves. Pour into glasses filled with ice cubes.

Per Serving: 165 Calories, 0 g Fat (0 g Saturated), 0 mg Cholesterol, 6 mg Sodium, 0 g Protein, 43 g Carbohydrates
A Great Source of: Vitamin C (47%)
A Good Source of: Fiber (3 g)
Pyramid Equivalent(s): 1 Fruit, Extras

The Guilt-Free "Comfort Food" Cookbook

Time: 20 minutes prep
2 hours chilling
Yield: 7 cups (7 servings)

Rich Vanilla Eggnog

*Y*ou won't believe this eggnog is nearly fat-free. We tested it with Edy's fat-free frozen vanilla yogurt, which is a wonderful product, but it would work with any good nonfat frozen yogurt or ice milk. Each shake provides about half the calcium a woman needs in an entire day, and more than half of the calcium a man needs.

5¹/₂ cups water
1²/₃ cups nonfat dry milk
   powder
¹/₂ cup sugar
1 (4-inch) piece vanilla bean,
   split lengthwise
¹/₂ cup egg substitute

¹/₂ teaspoon freshly grated
   nutmeg
2 cups fat-free frozen vanilla
   yogurt (or vanilla ice milk),
   softened
freshly grated nutmeg or
   cinnamon sticks (optional)

Stir together water, milk powder, and sugar until smooth in a large saucepan. Add vanilla bean; bring to a boil over medium heat, stirring constantly until sugar melts. Gradually stir about one-fourth of the hot mixture into egg substitute; add to remaining hot mixture, stirring constantly. Stir in ½ teaspoon nutmeg. Cook over low heat, stirring constantly, until thickened.

Remove from heat; let cool. Cover and chill thoroughly. Just before serving, remove and discard vanilla bean; stir in frozen yogurt. Sprinkle each serving with nutmeg or add a cinnamon stick, if desired.

Per Serving (one cup): 225 Calories, 1 g Fat (0 g Saturated), 7 mg Cholesterol, 230 mg Sodium, 15 g Protein, 40 g Carbohydrates

A Great Source of: Vitamin B2 (36%), Vitamin B12 (25%), Calcium (47%), Potassium (700 mg)

A Good Source of: Vitamin A (23%), Pantothenic Acid (16%), Magnesium (11%), Zinc (13%)

Pyramid Equivalent(s): 1 Dairy, Extras

Time: 20 minutes
Yield: 3 cups (3 servings)

Creamy Mint Cocoa

*H*ere's a flavorful twist on hot cocoa: mint and vanilla. Make this for your kids when they come home from school, and no one will bug you about dinner being ready. They'll also be getting some extra calcium without fat; marshmallow cream is fat-free.

Or make it for yourself in the evening. If you're concerned about calories, you can replace the quarter cup of sugar with a sugar substitute, which will bring calories down to 200 per serving. Or try a hot cup after dinner—as dessert.

3 cups skim milk
1/4 cup packed fresh mint
    leaves or 2 tablespoons
    dried mint

1/4 cup unsweetened cocoa
1/4 cup sugar
1/3 cup marshmallow cream
2 teaspoons vanilla extract

Bring milk and mint just to a boil in a medium saucepan over medium heat, stirring occasionally. Immediately remove from heat; let cool 15 minutes. Strain though a wire-mesh sieve; discard mint leaves. Return milk to saucepan.

Stir together cocoa and sugar until blended; add to milk mixture. Stir in marshmallow cream. Cook over medium heat, stirring constantly with a wire whisk, until smooth and hot. Remove from heat, and stir in vanilla; serve immediately.

Per Serving: 275 Calories, 1 g Fat (1 g Saturated), 4 mg Cholesterol, 140 mg Sodium, 10 g Protein, 59 g Carbohydrates

A Great Source of: Calcium (31%)

A Good Source of: Vitamin A (15%), Vitamin B2 (21%), Vitamin B12 (15%), Copper (17%), Magnesium (16%), Zinc (10%), Potassium (520 mg)

Pyramid Equivalent(s): 1 Dairy, Extras

The Guilt-Free "Comfort Food" Cookbook

ᗪown-Home BREAKFASTS

$\mathscr{E}$at breakfast like a king, lunch like a prince, dinner like a pauper." It's an old saying that reflects the nutritional wisdom of consuming most of our calories in the morning and afternoon. That's when our bodies need the most energy—during the day. It's when most of us are most active.

A good breakfast is particularly important. After all, we are *breaking* the *fast*—we may not have eaten in ten or twelve hours. The best breakfast is rich in complex carbohydrates to help fuel our bodies, with some protein, vitamins such as A and C, and calcium. Children who eat breakfast do better at school, and adults who eat a healthful breakfast tend to eat less fat and more fiber over the course of the day.

What constitutes a good breakfast? A good Pyramid rule of thumb is to try to eat 2 Grains, 1 Dairy, and 1 or 2 Fruits at the morning meal. This can be as simple as a large bowl of cereal with a cup of lowfat milk, and a three-quarter-cup glass of juice, a cup of yogurt, and a piece of fruit and/or a glass of juice. Or start with lowfat muffins such as Oat-Bran Banana-Raisin Muffins (p. 108), Double Corn Muffins (p. 106), or Cranberry Orange Muffins (p. 107), with a cup of lowfat or skim milk and a piece of fruit or a glass of juice or both.

When you have time, make a memorable breakfast, such as our Hearty Multi-Grain Buttermilk Pancakes (p. 73). It provides 2 Breads and 1 Dairy; have them with juice and/or fruit and you'll be there. Overnight French Toast with Spiced Apple Compote (p. 74), with 1 Bread, 1 Fruit, and 1 Meat, would do well with a cup of lowfat or skim

The Guilt-Free "Comfort Food" Cookbook

milk and a glass of orange juice. Breakfast Rice Pudding (p. 77) gives you 1 Bread, 2 Fruits, and 1 Dairy. Oat and Wheat Muesli (p. 76) is 2 Breads and 2 Fruits; have it with a glass of milk or lowfat or nonfat yogurt. Jogger's Sunrise Shake (p. 84), with 2 Fruits and 1 Dairy, would get your there with two pieces of whole wheat toast.

On occasion, perhaps the weekend, try Real Scrambled Eggs (p. 82), with 1 Meat, and Country-Style Sausage Patties (p. 83), also with 1 Meat, and Creamy Cheese Grits (p. 78), with ¾ Bread, 1 Dairy, and ½ Meat, along with some toast and fruit, for a lower-fat version of an old-fashioned breakfast. You'll already have nearly your day's maximum from the Meat group, though, so go light over the next meal or two. Similarly, Breakfast Enchiladas (p. 79), with 2 Breads and 2 Meats, needs some fruit, and a glass of lowfat milk; Vegetable-Barley Omelet (p. 80), with 2 Breads and 1½ Meats, would do well with some juice and a glass of milk.

A hearty breakfast, rich in fiber-rich complex carbohydrates, with lowfat dairy foods for protein and calcium, and fruit or fruit juice for fiber and vitamins A and C, will give your body the tools it needs to build a day of energy for you. Eggs are also good sources of protein, especially low-cholesterol egg substitutes or whole eggs combined with egg whites. Even lowfat sausages are fine, although on most days, with only two or three servings from the Meats group, you might want to save your meat for lunch or dinner. Perhaps you'll want to serve sausages only on the weekend.

There are many paths to a healthful diet. Most such paths, though, start with a delicious, hearty breakfast. Why not start today?

Time: 10 minutes prep
15 minutes standing
10 minutes cooking
Yield: 2 dozen pancakes (6 servings)

Hearty Multi-Grain Buttermilk Pancakes

𝒫lan ahead for convenience by doubling this recipe. Make enough for your family, enjoy breakfast, then make the rest of the pancakes. Let cool, wrap in stacks of three in heavy duty plastic wrap, and freeze for up to a month. When you want a quick breakfast, put each bundle in the microwave on medium-high for forty-five to ninety seconds, or until hot.

1 cup regular rolled oats, uncooked
1/2 cup whole wheat flour
1/2 cup all-purpose flour
1/2 cup cornmeal
1 tablespoon baking powder
1/4 teaspoon salt

3 egg whites, lightly beaten
2 1/4 cups nonfat buttermilk
1 tablespoon honey
2 tablespoons canola oil
1 teaspoon vanilla extract
vegetable cooking spray

Combine oats, whole wheat flour, all-purpose flour, cornmeal, baking powder, and salt in a large bowl; mix well and set aside. Combine egg whites, buttermilk, honey, oil, and vanilla extract; blend well. Make a well in the center of the dry ingredients; gradually pour buttermilk mixture into center, stirring just until dry ingredients are moistened. Cover and let stand at room temperature at least 15 minutes.

Coat a griddle or nonstick skillet with cooking spray; heat over medium heat. Cook pancakes in batches, pouring about 2 tablespoons batter for each pancake onto hot griddle. Turn pancakes when top is covered with bubbles and edges look cooked.

Per Serving (four pancakes): 260 Calories, 7 g Fat (1 g Saturated), 3 mg Cholesterol, 400 mg Sodium, 10 g Protein, 40 g Carbohydrates
A Great Source of: Calcium (28%)
A Good Source of: Vitamin B1 (20%), Vitamin B2 (20%), Iron (12%), Magnesium (16%), Potassium (300 mg)
Pyramid Equivalent(s): 2 Breads, 1 Dairy

The Guilt-Free "Comfort Food" Cookbook

Time: 30 minutes for compote
2 hours or overnight chilling
25 minutes cooking
Yield: 8 servings

Overnight French Toast with Spiced Apple Compote

*O*n Saturday afternoon, soak the bread, make the compote, and stick them in the refrigerator. Then, for Sunday morning, you can have a really special breakfast on the table in less than half an hour.

8 (1-inch) slices Italian bread
1 cup frozen egg substitute,
    thawed (or 2 whole eggs
    and 4 whites)
1 cup nonfat buttermilk
1/4 cup plus 2 tablespoons
    sugar, divided
2 teaspoons vanilla extract

vegetable cooking spray
6 medium-size Granny Smith
    apples, peeled, cored, and
    very thinly sliced
2/3 cup water
1 teaspoon ground cinnamon
3 tablespoons powdered sugar
3 tablespoons powdered sugar

Arrange bread slices in an 11- x 7- x 2-inch square baking dish. Combine egg substitute, buttermilk, 1/4 cup sugar, and vanilla; stir until sugar dissolves. Pour over bread slices, and turn bread to coat. Cover and refrigerate at least two hours, or overnight, turning bread occasionally.

Combine apples, water, cinnamon, and remaining 2 tablespoons sugar in a heavy, medium saucepan; bring to a boil over medium heat, stirring until sugar melts. Reduce heat to low; simmer 15 to 20 minutes or until apples are soft. Cover and refrigerate overnight.

In the morning, preheat oven to 425°. Place soaked bread slices on a 15- x 10- x 1-inch jelly-roll pan coated with cooking spray. Bake for 15 minutes; turn and bake an additional 10 minutes or until toasted. Meanwhile, warm apple mixture on the stove.

Transfer French toast to serving plates; sift powdered sugar evenly over toast. Spoon apple mixture evenly beside each serving.

The Guilt-Free "Comfort Food" Cookbook

Per Serving: 250 Calories, 5 g Fat (1 g Saturated), 2 mg Cholesterol, 270 mg Sodium, 7 g Protein, 44 g Carbohydrates

A Good Source of: Fiber (3 g), Vitamin B1 (14%), Vitamin B2 (15%), Vitamin E (10%), Potassium (255 mg)

Pyramid Equivalent(s): 1 Bread, 1 Fruit, 1 Meat

The Guilt-Free "Comfort Food" Cookbook

Time: 20 minutes prep and cooking
4 hours or overnight chilling
Yield: 6 cups (6 servings)

Oat and Wheat Muesli

his homey, hearty breakfast stores well in a covered container in the refrigerator for up to two days. So if you cook up some on Sunday night, you'll have a homemade breakfast Monday and Tuesday mornings. Tuesday night, you might want to make some more!

1/2 cup whole wheat berries, uncooked
1 1/2 cups Irish oatmeal (not quick-cooking), uncooked
1/2 cup raisins
2 cups unsweetened apple juice
1 cup nonfat plain yogurt

1/4 cup honey
2 cups coarsely grated, unpeeled apple
1/4 cup toasted wheat germ
3 tablespoons toasted slivered almonds

Cook wheat berries in boiling water, just enough to cover, 15 minutes; drain and cool.

Combine wheat berries, oatmeal, raisins, and apple juice in a heavy medium saucepan; bring to a boil, stirring constantly. Remove from heat and let cool to room temperature. Stir in yogurt, honey, apples, wheat germ, and almonds; refrigerate 4 hours or overnight before serving. Serve hot or cold.

Per Serving: 300 Calories, 3 g Fat (0 g Saturated), 1 Cholesterol, 40 mg Sodium, 7 g Protein, 65 g Carbohydrates
A Great Source of: Fiber (5 g)
A Good Source of: Vitamin B1 (15%), Vitamin B2 (12%), Vitamin E (21%), Calcium (11%), Iron (10%), Magnesium (14%), Zinc (12%), Potassium (460 mg)
Pyramid Equivalent(s): 2 Breads, 2 Fruits

The Guilt-Free "Comfort Food" Cookbook

Breakfast Rice Pudding

1 (15¹/₄-ounce) can unweetened
crushed pineapple,
undrained
2 cups cooked short- or
medium-grain rice, cooked
without salt or fat

1 (12-ounce) can evaporated
skim milk
¹/₄ cup sugar
¹/₄ teaspoon salt
¹/₃ cup raisins
¹/₂ cup nonfat vanilla-flavored
yogurt

Drain pineapple in a wire-mesh sieve, reserving pineapple and juice separately.

Combine juice, rice, milk, sugar, salt, and raisins in a heavy, medium saucepan; cook over low heat, stirring frequently, until mixture is thick and creamy, about 20 to 30 minutes. Stir in pineapple, and cook until hot.

Spoon into bowls; top each serving with 2 tablespoons yogurt.

Per Serving (¼ of recipe): 375 Calories, 1 g Fat (0 g Saturated), 4 mg Cholesterol, 250 mg Sodium, 11 g Protein, 83 g Carbohydrates

A Great Source of: Calcium (33%)

A Good Source of: Vitamin A (10%), Vitamin B1 (23%), Vitamin B2 (22%), Vitamin B3 (12%), Vitamin B6 (11%), Pantothenic Acid (13%), Vitamin C (20%), Copper (10%), Iron (13%), Magnesium (15%), Zinc (11%), Potassium (600 mg)

Pyramid Equivalent(s): 1 Bread, 2 Fruits, 1 Dairy

Note: As 6 servings: 250 Calories; ⅔ Pyramid Equivalents for Bread, Fruit, and Dairy.

The Guilt-Free "Comfort Food" Cookbook

Time: 30 minutes prep
35 minutes cooking
Yield: 6 servings

Creamy Cheese Grits

3 cups skim milk
3/4 cup regular (not quick-
  cooking) grits, uncooked
dash of salt
1/2 cup finely minced
  reduced-fat Canadian
  bacon (about a quarter
  pound)
1/2 cup reduced-fat ricotta
  cheese

4 egg whites, beaten
1 tablespoon stick margarine
  (or butter), melted
1 cup (4 ounces) shredded
  reduced-fat Cheddar
  cheese, divided
vegetable cooking spray

Preheat oven to 325°. Bring milk to a boil in a heavy, medium sauce-pan; gradually stir in grits and salt. Return to a boil; cover, reduce heat, and simmer 10 to 15 minutes or until very thick, stirring occasionally. Let cool. Stir in Canadian bacon, ricotta cheese, egg whites, margarine, and ½ cup Cheddar cheese until well blended.

Pour mixture in a 1-quart casserole coated with cooking spray; bake for 35 to 40 minutes or until set. Sprinkle with cheese; continue baking 2 minutes.

Per Serving: 250 calories, 8 g Fat (4 g Saturated), 33 mg Cholesterol, 530 mg So-dium, 21 g Protein, 24 g Carbohydrates
A Great Source of: Vitamin B2 (25%), Calcium (38%)
A Good Source of: Fiber (2 g), Vitamin A (13%), Vitamin B1 (22%), Vitamin B3 (12%), Vitamin B12 (12%), Vitamin C (10%), Potassium (375 mg)
Pyramid Equivalent(s): 3/4 Bread, 1 Dairy, 1/2 Meat, Extras

The Guilt-Free "Comfort Food" Cookbook

Time: 20 minutes prep
10 minutes cooking
Yield: 6 servings

Breakfast Enchiladas

*1¼ cups cooked black beans,
    drained*
*1 cup commercial chunky salsa,
    divided*
*1½ cups frozen egg substitute,
    thawed, or 3 whole eggs and
    3 egg whites*
¼ teaspoon salt
½ teaspoon ground cumin
1/8 teaspoon ground red pepper
vegetable cooking spray

*½ cup fresh or frozen corn
    kernels*
½ cup sliced green onion
*6 (7-inch) flour tortillas,
    warmed*
*½ cup (2 ounces) shredded
    reduced-fat Monterey Jack
    cheese*
*½ cup plus 1 tablespoon nonfat
    sour cream*

Combine black beans and ¼ cup salsa in a bowl; mix with a fork, mashing beans coarsely. Set aside.

Combine egg substitute and spices in a bowl; mix well. Coat a large nonstick skillet with cooking spray; place over medium heat. Add corn and green onion; saute 2 minutes. Pour egg mixture evenly in skillet; cook, stirring occasionally, until set.

Spoon bean mixture evenly down centers of tortillas; spoon egg mixture evenly on top of bean mixture. Sprinkle evenly with cheese. Roll up; place seam side down in a 12- x 8- x 2-inch baking dish; cover with foil and bake at 350° for 10 to 15 minutes or until hot.

To serve, top each enchilada with 2 tablespoons remaining salsa and 1½ tablespoons nonfat sour cream.

Per Serving: 320 Calories, 11 g Fat (2 g Saturated), 5 mg Cholesterol, 580 mg Sodium, 18 g Protein, 39 g Carbohydrates

A Great Source of: Fiber (5 g), Vitamin B2 (27%), Vitamin B1 (26%), Vitamin C (28%)

A Good Source of: Vitamin A (21%), Vitamin B3 (10%), Folic Acid (21%), Pantothenic Acid (15%), Vitamin E (20%), Calcium (11%), Copper (11%), Iron (20%), Magnesium (14%), Potassium (425 mg)

Pyramid Equivalent(s): 2 Breads, 2 Meats

Time: 10 minutes prep
30 minutes cooking
Yield: 8 servings

Vegetable-Barley Omelet

A heart-healthy breakfast for egg lovers. This omelet has a contribution from every food group except fruit. There's barley from the Breads, cottage cheese from Dairy, eggs and beans from the Meats group, corn and peppers and salsa from the Vegetables group. Try this for a Sunday brunch.

But don't stop there. With some crusty bread and a green salad, it's a wonderful light supper. If you have fruit for dessert, you've got an entire Eating Right Pyramid (see illustration in Introduction) on your plate!

2 teaspoons olive oil
7 large eggs (or 1³/4 cups egg substitute or 3 whole large eggs plus 8 large egg whites)
1 cup 1% lowfat cottage cheese
1/2 teaspoon salt
1/2 teaspoon freshly ground pepper
2 cups cooked medium barley

1¹/4 cups canned and drained black or red kidney beans (or dry beans soaked, cooked, and drained)
³/4 cup fresh-cut or frozen whole kernel corn, thawed
1/2 cup finely chopped green or red pepper
1/4 cup minced fresh cilantro

Toppings:

1 medium ripe avocado, peeled, diced, and tossed with 1 teaspoon lemon juice
1 cup commercial salsa
1/2 cup nonfat sour cream

Preheat oven to 400°. Brush a 9-inch cast-iron or ovenproof skillet with olive oil; set aside.

Combine eggs or egg substitute, cottage cheese, salt, and pepper in container of an electric blender; process until smooth.

Layer barley, beans, corn, green pepper, and cilantro in skillet; pour

The Guilt-Free "Comfort Food" Cookbook

egg mixture evenly over surface, allowing mixture to seep through layers. Bake uncovered for 30 minutes or until puffed and set. Let stand 5 minutes before cutting into wedges.

Top each serving evenly with avocado, 2 tablespoons salsa, and 1 tablespoon sour cream.

Variation: 1½ cups sliced and cooked new potatoes may be substituted for the beans and corn.

Per Serving: 270 Calories, 11 g Fat (2 g Saturated), 190 mg Cholesterol, 435 mg Sodium, 16 g Protein, 30 g Carbohydrates, 8 g Fiber, 435 mg Sodium
A Great Source of: Fiber (8 g), Vitamin C (43%)
A Good Source of: Vitamin A (21%), Vitamin B1(14%), Vitamin B2 (22%), Vitamin B6 (13%), Vitamin B12 (11%), Folic Acid (24%), Pantothenic Acid (12%), Vitamin C (43%), Vitamin E (16%), Copper (16%), Iron (13%), Magnesium (14%), Zinc (10%), Potassium (485 mg)
Pyramid Equivalent(s): 2 Breads, 1½ Meats

The Guilt-Free "Comfort Food" Cookbook

Time: 10 minutes
Yield: 2 servings

Real Scrambled Eggs

$\mathcal{T}$hese cost less than egg substitutes and cook up much fluffier.

> *4 egg whites*
> *1 egg yolk*
> *2 teaspoons water*
> *butter-flavored vegetable cooking spray*

Beat together egg whites, yolk, and water. Coat a nonstick skillet with cooking spray, and heat over medium-high heat. Pour half of egg mixture into pan; let cook, without stirring, until set on top around edges; drag a spatula gently through eggs as they continue to cook. Repeat with second half of mixture.

Per Serving: 65 Calories, 3 g Fat (1 g Saturated), 100 mg Cholesterol, 115 mg Sodium, 8 g Protein, 1 g Carbohydrate
A Good Source of: Vitamin B2 (21%)
Pyramid Equivalent(s): 1 Meat

The Guilt-Free "Comfort Food" Cookbook

Country-Style Sausage Patties

*F*or a nice change of pace, make these in the Italian style, with a slight variation in the spices. Instead of the quantities of rubbed sage, thyme, and marjoram, substitute one teaspoon dried thyme, one teaspoon fennel seeds, and a half teaspoon rubbed sage. You might also want to increase the amount of red ground pepper from a fourth to a half teaspoon.

10 ounces lean ground pork
10 ounces lean ground turkey
1 slice bacon, minced
1 clove garlic, finely chopped
2 teaspoons rubbed sage
1/2 teaspoon dried thyme

1/2 teaspoon dried marjoram
1/2 teaspoon salt
1/2 teaspoon freshly ground
pepper
1/4 teaspoon ground red pepper
vegetable cooking spray

Combine all ingredients except cooking spray in food processor fitted with knife blade; cover and pulse until well blended.

Moisten hands with cold water and shape mixture into 16 (3/8-inch thick) patties.

Coat a large nonstick skillet with cooking spray; place over medium heat until hot. Cook patties in batches 10 to 15 minutes or until browned and cooked, turning frequently.

Per Serving: 65 Calories, 4 g Fat (2 g Saturated), 26 mg Cholesterol, 30 mg Sodium, 7 g Protein, 0 g Carbohydrates
(Not a significant source of vitamins or minerals.)
Pyramid Equivalent(s): 1 Meat

The Guilt-Free "Comfort Food" Cookbook

Time: 5 minutes prep
30 minutes freezing
Yield: 3 cups
(1 large or 2 smaller servings)

Jogger's Sunrise Shake

*H*ere's the game plan: Slice the bananas, and pop them in the freezer. Then go for a jog. While you're gliding over the macadam, think of this refreshing shake—cool and sweet and thick, rich in potassium that will keep your muscles cramp-free, calcium for your bones, vitamin C to help wounds heal faster, and protein to help muscles repair themselves. When you walk in the door, hot from your workout, cool down in the shower, and then relax for a moment with this shake.

Helpful hint: This plan works as well for brisk walks, walking the dog, bicycling, swimming, and gardening. To be honest, you can enjoy our Sunrise Shake even if you just got out of bed. Take your walk afterwards!

1 small banana
1 tablespoon fresh lemon or lime juice
1 cup nonfat strawberry-banana yogurt
3 tablespoons frozen orange juice concentrate
1/4 cup water
ice cubes

Slice banana; toss with lemon juice. Spread slices on a baking sheet, and freeze until solid. (No need to cover if you are making the shake now; if you're fixing the fruit for later, cover with aluminum foil.)

Just before serving, process banana slices, yogurt, orange juice concentrate, and water in an electric blender until smooth. Add ice cubes to the 3-cup level; cover and process until smooth and slushy. Serve immediately.

Per Serving (for entire shake): 300 Calories, 1 g Fat (0 g Saturated), 3 mg Cholesterol, 145 mg Sodium, 13 g Protein, 67 g Carbohydrates

A Great Source of: Vitamin C (195%)

A Good Source of: Vitamin B2 (36%), Vitamin B6 (42%), Folic Acid (36%), Calcium (39%), Potassium (1380 mg)

Pyramid Equivalent(s): 2 Fruits, 1 Dairy

The Guilt-Free "Comfort Food" Cookbook

BREADS, BISCUITS, AND MUFFINS

There is something marvelous about fresh-baked bread. The ingredients are so simple: flour, water, salt, sometimes yeast, perhaps a smidgeon of sugar. Yet the results are so varied: crusty yeast breast, soft flatbreads, crackers, soft muffins, quick biscuits.

Breads, and the grains they are made with, are literally the foundation of a healthful diet, forming the base of the Pyramid. Complex carbohydrates, the kind found in grains (rather than sugars), are the body's best source of energy. Each of us should get between six and eleven servings of foods from the Breads group—which includes breads, rice, pasta, crackers, and popcorn—each day. Improving the balance of your diet can be as simple as making a sandwich with a little less meat, more vegetables, and slightly thicker slices of delicious home-baked bread.

Whole grains provide more fiber, vitamins, and minerals than refined white flours, but you don't have to go all the way to whole to enjoy these benefits. Many of the breads in this chapter combine the nutty taste and good nutrition of whole wheat flour with the lightness that comes from white flour. That's the Guilt-Free "Comfort Food" approach—good food that emphasizes taste in the pursuit of health. A good example is Toasted Oat and Wheat Bread (p. 90), which combines oats, whole wheat flour, and all-purpose flour to create a tasty, flavorful, light loaf.

In our hurried lives, it may seem that there's no time to make

The Guilt-Free "Comfort Food" Cookbook

yeast breads that take hours to rise. There are plenty of quick breads and muffins here, such as Sesame Wheat Crispbreads (p. 101), High-Rise Buttermilk Biscuits (p. 102), and Banana Oatbread (p. 103). But there are wonderful yeast breads too. Give them a chance. Making bread doesn't take much time in the kitchen. It just takes patience while you let the yeast turn wheat flour into dough, its elastic gluten expanding to contain the gases created by growing yeast. It's a living food. All you have to do is mix it up, pound it down, and set it out while you make dinner or go for a walk or read a book. Then pop it in the oven. In a little while, you'll have a fresh, aromatic loaf, an invitation to good taste and good health—bread, the very staff of life.

Time: 20 minutes
2 hours 15 minutes rising
35 minutes baking
Yield: 18 servings

Whole Wheat Walnut Bread

1 package active dry yeast
2 cups warm water (110°),
divided
2 tablespoons olive oil
2 tablespoons honey
1/2 teaspoon salt

4 to 5 cups whole wheat flour,
divided
3/4 cup finely chopped toasted
walnuts
vegetable cooking spray

Sprinkle yeast over ½ cup warm water in a small bowl; let stand 5 minutes.

Blend oil, honey, salt, remaining 1½ cups water, and yeast mixture in a large mixing bowl. Add 3 cups flour; with an electric mixer, beat 1 minute at low speed to blend. Stir in walnuts and enough remaining flour until dough becomes too difficult to stir. Knead on a floured surface about 10 minutes or until dough is smooth and slightly elastic, working in enough flour to prevent sticking. Place in a large bowl coated with cooking spray; coat dough evenly with cooking spray.

Cover with cloth or plastic wrap and let rise in a warm place 1½ hours, or until almost doubled in bulk. Knead briefly to expel air bubbles; place in a 9-inch springform pan coated with cooking spray. Cover loosely and let rise 45 to 55 minutes or until almost doubled. Preheat oven to 375°.

Remove cover. Bake in lower third of oven at 375° for 35 to 40 minutes or until crust is browned and a wooden skewer inserted in center comes out clean. Remove from pan and cool completely on a wire rack.

Per Serving: 145 Calories, 5 g Fat (0 g Saturated), 0 mg Cholesterol, 62 mg Sodium, 5 g Protein, 22 g Carbohydrates

A Good Source of: Fiber (3 g), Vitamin B1 (10%), Vitamin B3 (10%), Magnesium (12%)

Pyramid Equivalent(s): 1 Bread

The Guilt-Free "Comfort Food" Cookbook

Time: 20 minutes prep
2 hours to rise
25 minutes to bake
Yield: 4 loaves (16 quarter-loaf servings)

Country Sesame Rye Loaves

*T*he combination of bread flour and rye makes a rich yet light loaf.

1¹/₂ cups warm water (110°)
1 teaspoon sugar
1 package active dry yeast
2 teaspoons toasted sesame oil
1¹/₂ teaspoons toasted sesame
  oil

1¹/₂ teaspoons salt
3 to 3¹/₂ cups bread flour,
  divided
2 cups rye flour, divided
vegetable cooking spray
1 tablespoon sesame seeds

Combine water and sugar in a large mixing bowl; sprinkle yeast over water and let stand 5 minutes. Stir until dissolved. Stir in oil. Mix in salt, 1 cup bread flour, and 1 cup rye flour, one cup at a time, with an electric mixer on low speed, until blended. Stir in remaining 1 cup rye flour and 1½ cups bread flour, one cup at a time, until dough becomes difficult to stir.

Turn dough out on a well-floured surface and knead, gradually incorporating more bread flour as necessary to prevent sticking, about 10 minutes or until dough is smooth and slightly elastic. Place dough in a large bowl coated with cooking spray, and coat evenly with cooking spray. Cover with cloth or plastic wrap and let rise 1½ hours in a warm place, until about doubled in volume.

Preheat oven to 400°.

Punch dough down; divide into four parts. Shape each part into a seven-inch loaf; place on two baking sheets, and make a ½-inch-deep slash down center of each loaf, beginning two inches from ends of each loaf. Coat with cooking spray, and sprinkle evenly with sesame seeds. Cover loosely and let rise in a warm place 30 to 45 minutes, or until almost doubled.

Liberally mist loaves with water before placing in lower third of oven. Bake 10 minutes; open oven door and mist bread again. Reduce oven temperature to 375° and continue baking 12 to 20 minutes or until loaves sound hollow when tapped on bottom. Let cool on a wire rack.

The Guilt-Free "Comfort Food" Cookbook

Per Serving (¹/₄ a loaf): 140 Calories, 1 g Fat (0 g Saturated), 0 mg Cholesterol, 170 mg Sodium, 4 g Protein, 28 g Carbohydrates
A Good Source of: Fiber (3 g), Vitamin B1 (14%)
Pyramid Equivalent(s): 2 Breads

The Guilt-Free "Comfort Food" Cookbook

Time: 30 minutes prep
1½ hours rising
25 minutes baking
Yield: 34 to 36 (½-inch) slices

Toasted Oat and Wheat Bread

1 cup regular oats, uncooked
2½ cups whole wheat flour
3½ cups all-purpose flour,
   divided
½ teaspoon salt
2 packages active dry yeast
1 cup evaporated skimmed milk

1 cup water
½ cup honey
3 tablespoons stick margarine
   (or butter)
1 large egg
vegetable cooking spray

Preheat oven to 375°. Spread oats in a single layer in a shallow baking pan. Bake for 8 to 10 minutes or until lightly toasted, stirring occasionally. Let cool. Turn off oven.

Combine whole wheat flour, salt, yeast, and ½ cup all-purpose flour in a large mixing bowl. Combine evaporated skim milk, water, honey, and margarine in a medium saucepan; heat until very warm (120° to 130°). With electric mixer running at low speed, gradually add honey mixture to dry ingredients, beating just until blended. Increase speed to medium; beat 2 minutes, scraping bowl occasionally. Beat in egg and 1 cup all-purpose flour to make a thick batter; continue beating 2 minutes, scraping bowl often. Stir in oats and 1½ cups all-purpose flour to make a soft dough.

Knead dough on a lightly floured surface about 10 minutes or until smooth and elastic, working in remaining ½ cup all-purpose flour. Shape dough into a ball, and place in a large bowl coated with cooking spray; coat dough evenly with cooking spray. Cover with cloth or plastic wrap and let rise in a warm place 45 minutes to 1 hour, or until doubled in bulk.

Punch dough down; divide dough in half. Roll one portion of dough into a 10- x 6-inch rectangle on a lightly floured surface. Roll up, starting at short end, pressing firmly to expel air; pinch ends to seal. Place, seam side down, on a baking sheet coated with cooking spray. Shape remaining dough and place on same baking sheet, spacing loaves 4 to 6 inches apart.

Cover and let rise in a warm place, free from drafts, 45 minutes or until doubled in bulk. Preheat oven to 350°.

Using a sharp knife, cut 3 to 5 crisscross slashes across top of each loaf. Bake for 25 to 30 minutes or until loaves sound hollow when tapped. Cool on wire racks.

The Guilt-Free "Comfort Food" Cookbook

Per Serving (one slice): 115 Calories, 2 g Fat (0 g Saturated), 6 mg Cholesterol, 25 mg Sodium, 4 g Protein, 22 g Carbohydrates
A Good Source of: Fiber (2 g), Vitamin B1 (11%)
Pyramid Equivalent(s): 1 Bread

The Guilt-Free "Comfort Food" Cookbook

Time: 20 minutes prep
1³/₄ hours rising
50 minutes baking
Yield: 15 (¹/₂-inch) slices

Pepper-Parmesan Herb Bread

*F*estive, healthy, and delicious. Finely chopped roasted red peppers add color and taste . . . aromas of dill and rosemary bloom in the oven . . . a small amount of Parmesan cheese adds flavor with little fat. Parmesan cheese is high in fat and salt, but it's so intensely flavored that even a small amount enlivens bread, pasta, or vegetables. In this bread, for example, each slice has about a tablespoon baked into it; that contributes only 1.5 grams of fat per slice. Pregrated Parmesan may have fillers and extra salt; instead, buy a hunk of the good stuff—imported (Parmesan Reggiano, Pecorino) or domestic—keep it tightly wrapped in plastic in your refrigerator, and grate it when you need it.

3¹/₂ to 4¹/₂ cups all-purpose flour, divided
1 package active dry yeast
1 tablespoon finely crushed dried rosemary or dill
1 teaspoon freshly ground pepper
³/₄ cup water

¹/₂ cup evaporated skimmed milk
2 tablespoons olive oil
¹/₂ teaspoon salt
3 ounces freshly grated Parmesan cheese
2 finely chopped canned roasted sweet red peppers
vegetable cooking spray

Combine 1 cup flour, yeast, rosemary, and pepper in a large mixing bowl; stir well.

In a small saucepan, heat milk, water, oil, and salt to 120° to 130°. Add to flour mixture, and, with an electric mixer, beat at low speed for 30 seconds, scraping bowl. Increase speed to high and beat 3 minutes. Using a wooden spoon, stir in cheese, peppers, and enough of the remaining flour until dough becomes difficult to stir. Knead on a lightly floured surface, working in enough remaining flour to make a smooth, moderately stiff dough. Shape into a ball; place in a large bowl coated with cooking spray. Coat dough evenly with cooking spray; cover with cloth or plastic wrap and let rise 1 to 1½ hours, or until doubled in bulk.

The Guilt-Free "Comfort Food" Cookbook

Punch dough down; shape into a 14-inch-long loaf on a baking sheet coated with cooking spray. Cover loosely and let rise 45 minutes to 1 hour or until almost doubled in bulk. After a half hour, preheat oven to 375°.

Position oven rack in lower third of oven; bake at 375° for 30 to 35 minutes or until golden. Cover loosely with aluminum foil after 20 minutes to prevent overbrowning. Let cool on a wire rack.

Per Serving: 85 Calories, 2 g Fat (0 g Saturated), 2 mg Cholesterol, 90 mg Sodium, 3 g Protein, 13 g Carbohydrates
A Good Source of: Vitamin C (15%)
Pyramid Equivalent(s): 1 Bread

The Guilt-Free "Comfort Food" Cookbook

Time: 30 minutes prep and
  standing
1 hour to rise
10 minutes to bake
Yield: 8 servings

Cornmeal Flatbread

*F*latbreads have many uses. Try this one with soup and salad or as the foundation for an open-faced sandwich or a healthy pizza!

vegetable cooking spray
cornmeal
1 cup all-purpose flour
$1/_2$ cup whole wheat flour
$1/_2$ cup cornmeal
1 package active dry yeast

1 cup warm water (110°)
1 tablespoon sugar
$1/_2$ teaspoon salt
$1/_2$ cup evaporated skim milk
2 tablespoons olive oil

Coat a large baking sheet with cooking spray; dust with cornmeal. Draw a circle 10 inches in diameter on the center of the sheet with a toothpick or wooden skewer; set aside.

Combine flour and cornmeal; mix well. Combine yeast, warm water, and ½ cup flour mixture in a large bowl; let stand 10 minutes. Stir in remaining flour mixture and remaining ingredients, mixing thoroughly. Knead on a floured surface 10 minutes or until soft but still moist. Place in a large bowl coated with cooking spray; coat dough with cooking spray. Cover with cloth or plastic wrap and let rise in a warm place, free from drafts, 1 hour or until doubled in size.

Preheat oven to 450°. Turn dough out onto baking sheet. Dust hands with cornmeal, and press dough out to edge of circle, smoothing into an even layer. Prick surface all over with a fork. Bake for 10 to 12 minutes or until lightly browned. Serve warm.

Note: To make a pizza crust, press to a 12-inch circle, and bake at 450° for 8 minutes.

Per Serving: 160 Calories, 4 g Fat (0 g Saturated), 1 mg Cholesterol, 155 mg Sodium, 5 g Protein, 27 g Carbohydrates
A Good Source of: Fiber (2 g), Vitamin B1 (14%), Vitamin B2 (12%), Vitamin B3 (10%)
Pyramid Equivalent(s): 2 Breads

The Guilt-Free "Comfort Food" Cookbook

Time: 25 minutes prep
3 hours rising
25 minutes baking
Yield: 8 breads

Whole Wheat Lavash

*L*avash is a large, round, thin Middle Eastern bread that is soft when warm and almost cracker-like when completely cooled and eaten the next day. To soften the breads, sprinkle lightly with water and wrap in foil before heating. Roll up sandwich fillings in wedges of warm bread.

1 tablespoon sugar
1/2 teaspoon active dry yeast
1 1/2 cups lukewarm water (105° to 115°)

1 1/2 cups whole wheat flour
1 teaspoon salt
2 to 2 1/2 cups all-purpose flour
vegetable cooking spray

Sprinkle sugar and yeast over water in a large mixing bowl; stir until dissolved. Gradually stir in whole wheat flour and salt at low speed in an electric mixer fitted with dough hook until incorporated; continue to beat 30 seconds. Add bread flour, ½ cup at a time, until dough is stiff. Transfer to a lightly floured work surface; knead 5 to 7 minutes or until smooth and elastic, adding more flour only if dough feels sticky.

Shape dough into a ball; place in a large bowl coated with cooking spray. Coat dough with cooking spray. Cover with cloth or plastic wrap, and let rise in a warm place, free from drafts, 3 hours, or until doubled in bulk.

Heat oven to 500°. Position oven racks in lower half of oven. Coat 2 large baking sheets with cooking spray.

Punch down dough; let rest 10 minutes. Turn dough out onto a lightly floured surface; divide into 8 equal pieces. Working with 2 pieces at a time, keep remaining dough pieces loosely covered with plastic wrap. Flatten each piece into a disc; alternately roll each piece on prepared baking sheets into a very thin rectangle 1/8-inch thick, allowing each round to rest briefly while continuing to roll the other.

Bake dough 1½ to 2 minutes. Using tongs, carefully flip lavash and cook 45 seconds to 1 minute. Transfer each to a kitchen towel; fold in half and keep warm, or allow to cool on wire racks. Repeat with remaining dough.

Per Serving (one lavash): 200 Calories, 1 g Fat (0 g Saturated), 0 mg Cholesterol, 270 mg Sodium, 6 g Protein, 42 g Carbohydrates

A Good Source of: Fiber (4 g), Vitamin B1 (23%), Vitamin B2 (12%), Vitamin B3 (17%), Iron (13%), Magnesium (10%)

Pyramid Equivalent(s): 2 Breads

The Guilt-Free "Comfort Food" Cookbook

Time: 30 minutes prep
3 hours rising
20 minutes baking
Yield: 25 pieces

Potato Focaccia

*F*ocaccia, or Italian flatbread, usually stales quickly, but not this one. It will still taste fine the next day, thanks to potatoes, which add staying power as well as a mildly sweet taste and moistness. You can use this for pizza, or serve it as the Italians do, with a small bowl of heated olive oil, flavored with crushed rosemary and dried red pepper, for dipping or drizzling. Just remember: Even heart-healthy olive oil has 120 calories per tablespoon!

1/3 pound peeled and chopped *red potatoes*	*1 package active dry yeast* *1 teaspoon sugar*
1/3 cup water	*3 tablespoons olive oil*
1 cup nonfat buttermilk, *warmed to 110°*	*1 teaspoon salt* *5 to 5 1/2 cups bread flour*

Combine potatoes and water in a small saucepan; cover and bring to a boil. Reduce heat and cook 10 minutes or until potatoes are tender. Transfer mixture to a food processor and process until smooth. Add water to mixture to measure 1 cup, if necessary.

Combine warm buttermilk and sugar in a large mixing bowl; sprinkle yeast over buttermilk and let stand 5 minutes. Stir in olive oil, salt, potato puree, and 3 cups flour, beating well at medium speed in electric mixer fitted with dough hook. Stir in remaining flour, 1 cup at a time; transfer to a bowl coated with cooking spray. Coat hands with cooking spray; knead 2 minutes or until it is soft and slightly sticky. Form it into a ball, and coat evenly with cooking spray. Cover with cloth or plastic wrap and let dough rise in a warm place, free from drafts, 1½ to 2 hours or until doubled in bulk.

Press dough into a 15- x 10- x 1-inch jelly-roll pan coated with cooking spray; cover loosely, and let rise in a warm place 1½ to 2 hours or until almost doubled in bulk.

Preheat oven to 400°. Make ¼-inch deep indentations at 2-inch intervals on top of dough with the tip of a wooden spoon handle or fingertip; coat with cooking spray. Bake in bottom third of oven at 400° for 20 to 25

The Guilt-Free "Comfort Food" Cookbook

minutes or until golden. Let cool in pan on a wire rack; serve warm or at room temperature. Cut into 3- x 2-inch rectangles.

Per Serving (one piece): 125 Calories, 2 g Fat (0 g Saturated), 0 mg Cholesterol, 97 mg Sodium, 4 g Protein, 22 g Carbohydrates
(Not a significant source of vitamins or minerals.)
Pyramid Equivalent(s): 1 Bread

The Guilt-Free "Comfort Food" Cookbook

Time: 25 minutes prep
1 hour rising
20 minutes baking
Yield: 12 pockets

Pocket Bread

*S*team makes the hollow in the middle of this Middle Eastern bread.
That's where you can stuff a meal: Cool Broccoli Salad (p.123),
Chicken Salad Remoulade (p.135), Marinated Bean Salad (p.133), or
sliced turkey breast with Sweet-and-Tangy Pineapple Slaw (p.138).

1 package active dry yeast
1½ cups warm water (110°)
½ teaspoon salt
2 tablespoons olive oil

1½ cups whole wheat flour
2½ to 3 cups all-purpose flour,
  divided
vegetable cooking spray

Sprinkle yeast over water in a large mixing bowl; let stand 5 minutes,
then stir until dissolved. Add salt, olive oil, whole wheat flour, and 1 cup
all-purpose flour; with an electric mixer fitted with dough hook, beat at
low speed until blended. Beat at high speed 3 to 5 minutes or until dough
is stretchy. Stir in 1½ cups remaining all-purpose flour until evenly moistened.

Sprinkle about ¼ cup remaining flour on a work surface; scrape
dough onto surface, and roll to coat lightly with the flour. Knead until
dough is no longer sticky and feels satiny, about 8 to 10 minutes; add just
enough remaining flour as you knead to keep dough from sticking. Transfer to a large bowl coated with cooking spray; coat dough evenly with cooking spray. Cover with cloth or plastic wrap and let dough rise in a warm
place, free from drafts, 1 hour or until doubled in bulk. (Dough has risen
enough when a hole poked in dough springs back.) Knead dough briefly to
expel air bubbles.

Preheat oven to 500°. Divide dough into 12 equal pieces. On a lightly
floured work surface, roll 1 piece into a ⅛-inch-thick round; repeat with 2
additional pieces. Place rounds, at least 2 inches apart, on a large baking
sheet coated with cooking spray. Bake on lowest oven rack for 5 to 6 minutes or until rounds are puffed and speckled brown. Transfer to a wire
rack; cool 1 minute, then seal in a large heavy-duty plastic bag to soften.
Repeat rolling, baking, and cooling process with remaining rounds.

The Guilt-Free "Comfort Food" Cookbook

Per Serving (one pocket): 165 Calories, 3 g Fat (0 g Saturated), 0 mg Cholesterol, 92 mg Sodium, 5 g Protein, 31 g Carbohydrates
A Good Source of: Fiber (3 g), Vitamin B1 (19%), Vitamin B2 (11%), Vitamin B3 (14%), Iron (11%)
Pyramid Equivalent(s): 2 Breads

The Guilt-Free "Comfort Food" Cookbook

Time: 20 minutes prep
1 hour and 5 minutes rising
12 minutes baking
Yield: 3 dozen

Black-Tie Dinner Rolls

*B*efore you make dinner, make this dough, and let it rise. Just before dinner, pop dough balls in the oven, and you'll have nutritious, elegant, delicious dinner rolls.

*3¹/₄ cups all-purpose flour,
   divided
3 cups whole wheat flour,
   divided
¹/₂ teaspoon salt
2 packages active dry yeast
1 cup skim milk*

*³/₄ cup water
¹/₄ cup honey
¹/₄ cup stick margarine (or
   butter)
1 large egg
2 large egg whites
vegetable cooking spray*

Preheat oven to 375°. Combine 2 cups all-purpose flour, 1 cup whole wheat flour, salt, and yeast in a large mixing bowl; blend well.

Combine milk, water, honey, and margarine in a small saucepan; cook over medium heat until mixture reaches 120° to 130°. Add to flour mixture, and beat at low speed in an electric mixer for 30 seconds, scraping bowl. Increase speed to high and beat 3 minutes. Add egg and egg whites, and beat until blended. Using a wooden spoon, stir in remaining whole wheat flour and enough of the remaining all-purpose flour until dough becomes difficult to stir.

Knead on a lightly floured surface about 10 minutes, working in enough of the remaining all-purpose flour to make a smooth, elastic dough. Place dough in a bowl coated with cooking spray; coat dough evenly with cooking spray. Cover with cloth or plastic wrap and let rise in a warm place until doubled in bulk (about 45 to 60 minutes).

Preheat oven to 375°. Punch dough down, and divide into 36 equal portions. Shape into balls, and place on large baking sheets coated with cooking spray. Cover and let rise in a warm place 20 minutes or until doubled in bulk. Bake for 12 minutes or until golden. Remove from baking sheets, and let cool on wire racks.

Per Serving (one roll): 100 Calories, 2 g Fat (0 g Saturated), 6 mg Cholesterol, 54
   mg Sodium, 3 g Protein, 18 g Carbohydrates
A Good Source of: Fiber (2 g), Vitamin B1 (10%)
Pyramid Equivalent(s): 1 Bread

The Guilt-Free "Comfort Food" Cookbook

Time: 15 minutes prep
30 minutes chilling
40 minutes baking
Yield: 4 crispbreads (16 servings)

Sesame Wheat Crispbreads

*S*tore-bought crispbreads are okay, but nothing beats these fresh little beauties, just cooled. Whole wheat flour, wheat germ, and yogurt give them more nutritional value to boot.

1¼ cups all-purpose flour
1 cup whole wheat flour
¼ cup toasted wheat germ
1 tablespoon sugar
¼ teaspoon garlic powder
¼ teaspoon salt
⅓ cup stick margarine (or butter), cut into pieces

1 (8-ounce) carton plain nonfat yogurt
vegetable cooking spray
2 tablespoons plus 2 teaspoons sesame seeds, lightly toasted

Combine dry ingredients in a large bowl; mix well. Cut in margarine with a pastry blender until mixture resembles coarse meal. Make a well in center of mixture; add yogurt and stir just until moistened. Shape into a ball; cover and chill 30 minutes.

Preheat oven to 425°. Divide dough into 4 equal portions. (Keep remaining portions chilled while working with one.) Roll one portion of dough out on a baking sheet coated with cooking spray into a very thin 12- x 10-inch rectangle; brush lightly with water. Sprinkle with 2 teaspoons sesame seeds, and roll lightly into dough using rolling pin. Bake for 10 to 12 minutes or until edges are lightly browned. Remove from baking sheet and cool on a wire rack. Repeat with remaining portions of dough and sesame seeds. Break crispbread into pieces.

Per Serving (¼ a crispbread): 120 Calories, 5 g Fat (1 g Saturated), 0 mg Cholesterol, 90 mg Sodium, 15 g Protein, 64 g Carbohydrates
A Good Source of: Fiber (2 g), Vitamin B1 (10%), Vitamin E (10%)
Pyramid Equivalent(s): 2 Breads

The Guilt-Free "Comfort Food" Cookbook

High-Rise Buttermilk Biscuits

1¹/₂ cups all-purpose flour
¹/₂ cup whole wheat flour
¹/₄ cup nonfat dry milk powder
2 teaspoons baking powder
³/₄ teaspoon baking soda

¹/₂ teaspoon salt
¹/₄ cup stick margarine (or
butter), cut into bits
1 cup nonfat buttermilk
vegetable cooking spray

Preheat oven to 425°. Combine all dry ingredients in a fine wire-mesh sieve; sift into a large bowl. Cut in margarine until mixture forms coarse crumbs. Make a well in center of mixture; stir in buttermilk until mixture forms a ball.

Knead dough on a lightly floured surface 4 or 5 times; pat into a rectangle about 1 inch thick. Cut biscuits with a 2-inch round cutter; place on a baking sheet and bake for 10 to 11 minutes or until golden. Serve warm.

Note: If desired, 2 cups all-purpose flour may be used instead of 1½ cups all-purpose flour and ½ cup whole wheat flour.

Per Serving: 125 Calories, 4 g Fat (1 g Saturated), 1 mg Cholesterol, 300 mg Sodium, 4 g Protein, 18 g Carbohydrates
A Good Source of: Vitamin B1 (11%), Calcium (12%)
Pyramid Equivalent(s): 1 Bread

The Guilt-Free "Comfort Food" Cookbook

Banana Oatbread

*W*hen your bananas are too ripe to slice into cereal, bake them into this delicious bread. If you don't have oat bran cereal, substitute regular whole oats, ground in a food processor until fine.

*1/3 cup firmly packed light
    brown sugar*
1/3 cup sugar
1/3 cup nonfat buttermilk
*1 1/2 cups mashed overripe
    bananas*
1 large egg
1 large egg white
3 tablespoons canola oil

1 teaspoon vanilla extract
1 1/2 cups all-purpose flour
1/2 cup oat bran cereal
1 1/4 teaspoons baking powder
1/2 teaspoon baking soda
1/2 teaspoon salt
1 teaspoon ground cinnamon
vegetable cooking spray

Preheat oven to 350°. Combine sugars and buttermilk in a large bowl; mix until sugar dissolves. With a wire whisk, stir in bananas, egg, egg white, canola oil, and vanilla extract.

Combine dry ingredients in a fine wire-mesh sieve; sift over banana mixture. Stir just until dry ingredients are moistened.

Pour into a 9- x 5- x 3-inch baking pan; bake for 40 to 50 minutes or until a wooden pick inserted in center comes out clean. Let cool in pan 10 minutes; remove from pan and cool completely on a wire rack.

Per Serving: 165 Calories, 4 g Fat (1 g Saturated), 18 mg Cholesterol, 210 mg So-
    dium, 3 g Protein, 29 g Carbohydrates
A Good Source of: Vitamin B1 (10%), Vitamin E (10%)
Pyramid Equivalent(s): 1 Bread

The Guilt-Free "Comfort Food" Cookbook

Time: 15 minutes prep
30 minutes baking
Yield: 12 servings

Blueberry-Orange
Coffee Cake

A traditional sour-cream coffee cake can have thirty or even forty grams
of fat per serving. Ours has six. Try it and you'll discover that good
taste doesn't have to mean high fat. As an option, substitute blueberries with sliced strawberries.

2 cups fresh blueberries
1 tablespoon sugar
2 teaspoons grated orange rind
1/4 cup stick margarine (or
*   butter), softened*
1/2 cup sugar
1/2 cup egg substitute (or 1
*   whole egg and 1 egg white,*
*   beaten)*
1 1/2 cups sifted cake flour

3/4 teaspoon baking powder
1/2 teaspoon baking soda
1/4 teaspoon salt
1/3 cup vanilla lowfat yogurt
3 tablespoons frozen, thawed
*   orange juice concentrate*
1 teaspoon vanilla extract
vegetable cooking spray
Crumb Topping (recipe follows)

Preheat oven to 350°. Combine blueberries, sugar, and orange rind;
toss and set aside.

Beat margarine at medium speed with an electric mixer until creamy;
gradually add ½ cup sugar, beating well. Beat in egg substitute.

Combine flour, baking powder, baking soda, and salt. Combine yogurt, orange juice concentrate, and vanilla, mixing well. Add flour mixture
alternately with yogurt mixture, beginning and ending with dry ingredients, beating at low speed just until blended after each addition.

Pour batter into an 8-inch square baking pan coated with cooking
spray; top with blueberry mixture. Sprinkle with crumb topping; bake for
30 to 35 minutes or until a wooden pick inserted in center comes out clean.
Cool slightly on a wire rack; serve warm.

The Guilt-Free "Comfort Food" Cookbook

Crumb Topping
Yield: 1/2 cup

3 tablespoons Grape Nuts cereal
2 tablespoons cake flour
2 tablespoons light brown sugar

1/2 teaspoon ground cinnamon
2 tablespoons stick margarine
(or butter), softened

Combine dry ingredients in a small bowl; add butter, and mix until crumbly.

Per Serving: 180 Calories, 6 g Fat (1 g Saturated), 0 mg Cholesterol, 225 mg Sodium, 3 g Protein, 29 g Carbohydrates
A Good Source of: Vitamin A (12%), Vitamin B1 (12%), Vitamin C (16%), Vitamin E (12%)
Pyramid Equivalent(s): 2 Breads

The Guilt-Free "Comfort Food" Cookbook

Time: 10 minutes prep
20 minutes baking
Yield: 12 muffins

Double Corn Muffins

*W*hen corn is in season, peel an ear, cut off one end, stand it up over a plate, and—carefully!—slice off the kernels with a sharp knife. If fresh corn is out of season, frozen works fine. Just thaw it first.

1¹/₂ cups yellow cornmeal
¹/₂ cup all-purpose flour
1 tablespoon sugar
1¹/₂ teaspoons baking powder
¹/₂ teaspoon baking soda
¹/₂ teaspoon salt
1 cup nonfat buttermilk
¹/₂ cup evaporated skim milk

¹/₄ cup egg substitute (or 1 large egg, beaten)
3 tablespoons stick margarine (or butter), melted
1 cup corn kernels, fresh or frozen, thawed
vegetable cooking spray

Preheat oven to 400°. Combine cornmeal, flour, sugar, baking powder, baking soda, and salt in a large bowl; mix well. Process buttermilk, evaporated skim milk, egg substitute, and margarine in an electric blender until combined; add corn and pulse until corn mixture is coarsely pureed.

Coat a muffin pan with cooking spray; divide batter evenly among cups. Bake for 20 to 25 minutes or until a wooden pick inserted in centers comes out clean. Cool in pan on a wire rack 5 minutes; remove from pan and serve warm.

Note: To make cornbread, pour batter into a 9-inch square baking pan coated with cooking spray. Bake at 400° for 18 to 20 minutes or until a wooden pick inserted in center comes out clean.

Per Serving: 135 Calories, 4 g Fat (1 g Saturated), 1 mg Cholesterol, 270 mg Sodium, 4 g Protein, 22 g Carbohydrates
A Good Source of: Fiber (2 g), Vitamin B1 (10%), Calcium (10%)
Pyramid Equivalent(s): 1 Bread

The Guilt-Free "Comfort Food" Cookbook

Time: 15 minutes to soften
dried cranberries
8 minutes prep
15 minutes baking
Yield: 1 dozen

Cranberry Orange Muffins

*1/3 cup chopped dried
   cranberries*
*1/3 cup plus 2 tablespoons
   sugar, divided*
*3 tablespoons boiling orange
   juice or water*
1³/4 cups all-purpose flour
*1/2 cup yellow cornmeal (or 1/3
   cup more all-purpose flour)*
2¹/2 teaspoons baking powder

1/2 teaspoon baking soda
1/2 teaspoon salt
*1/2 cup egg substitute (or 1
   whole egg and 1 egg white,
   beaten)*
*1 cup plus 2 tablespoons nonfat
   buttermilk*
2 tablespoons canola oil
*2 teaspoons freshly grated
   orange rind*

Combine cranberries and 2 tablespoons sugar in a small bowl, mixing well. Stir in boiling orange juice or water; set aside for 15 minutes to soften cranberries.

Preheat oven to 400°. Combine flour, cornmeal, remaining ⅓ cup sugar, baking powder, baking soda, and salt. In another bowl, combine egg substitute, buttermilk, oil, and orange rind, mixing well. Add cranberry mixture, stirring just until combined.

Spoon batter evenly into muffin cups coated with cooking spray. Bake for 15 minutes or until golden. Let cool in pan 2 or 3 minutes; serve warm.

Per Serving: 165 Calories, 3 g Fat (0 g Saturated), 1 mg Cholesterol, 260 mg Sodium, 4 g Protein, 31 g Carbohydrates
A Good Source of: Vitamin B1(13%), Vitamin B2 (10%), Calcium (11%)
Pyramid Equivalent(s): 2 Breads

The Guilt-Free "Comfort Food" Cookbook

Time: 10 minutes prep
20 minutes baking
Yield: 2 dozen

Oat-Bran Banana-Raisin Muffins

*T*hat "healthy" bran muffin you buy on the way to work may have as many as 500 calories and 25 grams of fat. Bake up a dozen of these instead. As a variation, try substituting a cup of mashed-fruit baby food for the bananas.

2 cups oat bran cereal (such as Mother's Hot Oat Bran Cereal)
1 cup whole wheat flour
1 cup cake flour, sifted
2¹/₂ teaspoons baking powder
1 teaspoon baking soda
¹/₂ teaspoon salt
1 teaspoon ground cinnamon
¹/₂ cup firmly packed brown sugar

¹/₂ cup sugar
1 cup raisins
1³/₄ cups nonfat buttermilk
1 cup mashed overripe bananas
¹/₂ cup egg substitute (or 2 eggs, beaten)
¹/₄ cup canola oil
1 teaspoon vanilla extract
vegetable cooking spray

Preheat oven to 400°. Combine oat bran cereal, whole wheat flour, cake flour, baking powder, baking soda, salt, and cinnamon in a large bowl; stir in sugar and raisins, mixing well.

Combine buttermilk, banana, egg substitute, oil, and vanilla; mix until smooth. Add to dry ingredients, stirring until moistened. Spoon evenly into muffin pans coated with cooking spray. Bake for 20 minutes or until a wooden pick inserted in center comes out clean.

Note: For Pumpkin Spice Bran Muffins, substitute pumpkin pie spice for the cinnamon and canned mashed pumpkin for banana.

Per Serving: 125 Calories, 3 g Fat (0 g Saturated), 1 mg Cholesterol, 230 mg Sodium, 3 g Protein, 23 g Carbohydrates
(Not a significant source of vitamins or minerals.)
Pyramid Equivalent(s): 1 Bread

The Guilt-Free "Comfort Food" Cookbook

Cinnamon Orange Scones

2¹/₂ cups sifted cake flour
1¹/₄ cups quick-cooking oats
¹/₃ cup sugar
2¹/₂ teaspoons baking powder
¹/₂ teaspoon baking soda
¹/₂ teaspoon salt
2 teaspoons grated orange rind
1 teaspoon ground cinnamon

¹/₄ cup stick margarine (or
    butter), cut into pieces and
    frozen
1 cup nonfat buttermilk
3 egg whites
1 tablespoon sugar
¹/₄ teaspoon ground cinnamon
vegetable cooking spray

Preheat oven to 400°. Combine flour, oats, ⅓ cup sugar, baking powder, baking soda, salt, orange rind, and 1 teaspoon cinnamon in a food processor; cover and process until oats are ground. Sprinkle margarine pieces evenly over mixture; pulse until mixture forms coarse crumbs. With a spatula or spoon, turn mixture out into a bowl.

Combine buttermilk and egg whites; beat until smooth. Make a well in center of flour mixture; add buttermilk mixture and stir just until moistened. Turn out onto a lightly floured surface; pat dough to 1-inch thickness. Cut into 12 rounds using a 2-inch cutter, re-rolling scraps as needed.

Arrange rounds on a baking sheet coated with cooking spray. Coat tops of scones with cooking spray. Combine 1 tablespoon sugar and ¼ teaspoon ground cinnamon; sprinkle evenly on scones. Bake for 15 minutes or until golden brown. Serve warm.

Per Serving: 180 Calories, 5 g Fat (1 g Saturated), 1 mg Cholesterol, 300 mg Sodium, 5 g Protein, 30 g Carbohydrates

A Good Source of: Vitamin B1 (17%), Vitamin B2 (10%), Calcium (11%), Iron (11%)

Pyramid Equivalent(s): 2 Breads

The Guilt-Free "Comfort Food" Cookbook

$\mathscr{S}$OUPS

$\mathscr{S}$oup starts many a meal. The word *soup* itself originated thousands of years ago in Greece, with the word for water—literally translated, "rain." It is related to the German and Old English words for "to drink," "to dunk bread in broth" *(sop),* and "to soak" or "to steep." Whatever its origins, soup is a wonderful invention. In the winter, it warms; in the summer, cool soups refresh. On hot nights, for example, try our cool, nutritious Black Bean "Gazpacho" (p. 119).

Even a simple broth, at the beginning of the meal, sets the tone for a relaxed experience. You can't rush eating hot soup! Slowing down has many benefits in our harried world. One is taste. Soup is meant to be tasted, not wolfed. Slowing us down also helps us control appetite. Even before we eat, when we smell the aromas of food, and even when we start to think about food, our brains begin to prepare our stomachs for the food that's on its way. As we eat, the signals travel from the tongue to the brain to the stomach and back up to the brain. After a while, our brains get the message that we've eaten—that we've consumed plenty of calories, and don't need any more. That's when we feel "full," and stop feeling hungry.

Soup, by slowing our consumption, gives the body enough time to start sending those messages to the brain. So our hunger begins to diminish. By the time the main course arrives, we're not so ravenous.

Soups can also be a wonderful way to get more vegetables into our day. That's true whether the soup has beef, chicken, seafood, or only

The Guilt-Free "Comfort Food" Cookbook

beans and vegetables. Every soup in this chapter provides at least 1 Vegetable serving. Most have 2 Vegetables. Some have 3 or 4 Vegetables.

Soup can start a meal—or be a meal. Most of the soups in this chapter have enough protein to serve as the main dish for a light dinner. All you'll need is a salad and a whole-grain bread. That way, when you are using your bread to "sop" up the savory flavors that remain after your spoon has done its best, you can feel good that you are participating in a practice as ancient as soup itself.

Time: 30 minutes prep and cooking
1 hour simmering
Yield: 9 cups (6 servings)

Sweet-and-Sour Vegetable Beef Soup

*A*nother super-nutritious dish, thanks to the combination of lean flank steak and all those vegetables. You'll love the sweet-and-sour sensation.

*1 (8-ounce) can unsweetened
    pineapple tidbits,
    undrained*
2 teaspoons cornstarch
vegetable cooking spray
*3/4 pound lean, beef flank steak,
    trimmed and cut into
    1-inch cubes*
*1 (14 1/2-ounce) can unsalted
    stewed tomatoes, undrained*
*1 (14 1/2-ounce) can reduced-
    sodium vegetable broth,
    undiluted*

1 tablespoon chili powder
1 tablespoon paprika
*3 tablespoons brown sugar,
    firmly packed*
3 tablespoons cider vinegar
1/2 teaspoon salt
1 1/2 cups chopped onion
*1 1/2 cups sliced carrots (1/2-inch
    thick)*
3 cups sliced cabbage
2 cups cauliflowerets

Drain pineapple, reserving tidbits and juice separately. Stir together juice and cornstarch until smooth; set aside.

Coat a Dutch oven (or, if you don't have one, any large heavy saucepan) with cooking spray; heat over medium heat. Add beef, and saute 2 minutes; increase heat to medium-high and saute until beef browns. Stir in tomatoes, broth, chili powder, paprika, brown sugar, vinegar, and salt; add onion and carrots; bring to a boil. Cover, reduce heat, and simmer 40 minutes.

Stir in cabbage, cauliflower, and pineapple tidbits; cover and simmer 20 minutes. Stir cornstarch mixture; add to soup, and cook just until thickened, stirring constantly.

Per Serving: 240 Calories, 7 g Fat (3 g Saturated), 38 mg Cholesterol, 420 mg Sodium, 20 g Protein, 27 g Carbohydrates
A Great Source of: Fiber (5 g), Vitamin A (83%), Vitamin B3 (26%), Vitamin B12 (32%), Vitamin C (76%), Potassium (900 mg)
A Good Source of: Vitamin B1 (15%), Vitamin B2 (15%), Vitamin B6 (21%), Folic Acid (14%), Vitamin E (13%), Copper (14%), Iron (19%), Magnesium (13%), Zinc (22%)
Pyramid Equivalent(s): 3 Vegetables, 1 Meat

The Guilt-Free "Comfort Food" Cookbook

Time: 30 minutes prep and cooking
45 minutes simmering
Yield: 13 cups (8 or 9 servings)

Granny's Soulful Chicken Soup

*W*as Granny's ever this good?

*4 (6-ounce) skinned chicken
    breast halves
2 cups sliced carrot
1 cup chopped onion
1 cup sliced celery
2 medium red potatoes, peeled
    and quartered*

*8 cups fat-free, reduced-sodium
    chicken broth
1 bay leaf
1/2 teaspoon pepper
1 cup broken dried fettucini
    noodles, uncooked
11/2 cups fresh or frozen peas*

Combine chicken, carrot, onion, celery, potatoes, broth, bay leaf, pepper, and noodles in a Dutch oven (or, if you don't have one, any large heavy saucepan); bring to a boil. Cover, reduce heat, and simmer 25 minutes or until chicken is tender. Cool to room temperature.

Remove chicken and bay leaf from Dutch oven. Remove bones and shred chicken. Mash potatoes coarsely in Dutch oven.

Return chicken to Dutch oven; add fettucini. Bring to a boil; cover and simmer 10 minutes. Stir in peas; cover and simmer 10 additional minutes.

Per Serving (11/2 cups): 270 Calories, 4 g Fat (1 g Saturated), 46 mg Cholesterol, 670 mg Sodium, 24 g Protein, 33 g Carbohydrates

A Great Source of: Vitamin A (61%), Vitamin B3 (56%), Vitamin B6 (32%), Vitamin C (28%)

A Good Source of: Fiber (4 g), Vitamin B1 (21%), Vitamin B2 (12%), Pantothenic Acid (10%), Copper (11%), Iron (12%), Magnesium (14%), Zinc (10%), Potassium (525 mg)

Pyramid Equivalent(s): 1 Bread, 1 Vegetable, 1 Meat

The Guilt-Free "Comfort Food" Cookbook

Time: 1 hour and 15 minutes prep
and cooking
Yield: 4 (1¹/₂-cup) servings

Boston Fish Chowder

*M*ake this extraordinarily nutritious soup the center of a meal. It's got enough protein to serve as a main course. All it needs is some good bread for dipping!

1 tablespoon canola oil
1¹/₂ cups finely chopped celery
1 cup chopped onion
¹/₂ cup finely chopped green pepper
4 cloves garlic, minced
6 cups finely chopped green cabbage
3¹/₂ cups skim milk
1 medium russet potato, peeled and cut in half

1 bay leaf
1 teaspoon sugar
¹/₂ teaspoon Old Bay seasoning
¹/₂ teaspoon salt
¹/₄ teaspoon white pepper
2 tablespoons all-purpose flour
1 pound firm white-fleshed fish fillets, such as scrod, cod, orange roughy, or halibut, cut into 1-inch pieces

Heat oil in a Dutch oven (or any large heavy pan) over medium heat; add celery, onion, green pepper, and garlic, and saute until tender. Add cabbage; cook, stirring occasionally, 5 minutes or until cabbage is just tender. Add milk and next 5 ingredients; bring to a boil. Cover, reduce heat; simmer for 30 minutes.

Strain mixture through a fine wire-mesh sieve, reserving liquid. Transfer potato, 1½ cups liquid, and flour to an electric blender; process until smooth. Return vegetables, reserved liquid, and potato mixture to Dutch oven; stir in fish. Bring to a simmer over medium heat, stirring constantly; simmer, uncovered, 15 minutes, stirring occasionally.

Per Serving (1¹/₂ cups): 325 Calories, 5 g Fat (1 g Saturated), 50 mg Cholesterol, 500 mg Sodium, 32 g Protein, 40 g Carbohydrates

A Great Source of: Fiber (5 g), Vitamin B2 (28%), Vitamin B6 (40%), Vitamin B12 (31%), Vitamin C (105%), Vitamin E (32%), Calcium (37%), Magnesium (26%), Potassium (1,535 mg)

A Good Source of: Vitamin A (17%), Vitamin B1 (24%), Vitamin B3 (21%), Folic Acid (23%), Pantothenic Acid (15%), Copper (13%), Iron (11%), Zinc (13%)

Pyramid Equivalent(s): 4 Vegetables, 1 Dairy, 1¹/₃ Meats

The Guilt-Free "Comfort Food" Cookbook

Time: 45 minutes prep and cooking
Yield: 4 or 5 servings

Fresh Corn Clam Chowder

e like creamy soups too. But instead of cream and butter, we made this soup unctuous by pureeing corn and potatoes with a little flour. Be careful to wash leeks carefully; trim the ends, then slice lengthwise, and run each half under cold running water.

2 cups sliced leeks (about 2, trimmed)
1 tablespoon canola oil
1 medium green pepper, diced
1 medium red pepper, diced
3 cups canned low-sodium chicken broth
2 medium red-skinned potatoes, diced (about 1¹/₂ cups)

3 cups fresh or frozen corn kernels
2 tablespoons all-purpose flour
1 (6.5-ounce) can chopped clams, undrained
2 teaspoons paprika
¹/₂ teaspoon salt
1¹/₂ teaspoons hot sauce (such as Tabasco)

Heat oil in a large saucepan over medium-high heat; add leeks and peppers, and saute until tender. Remove vegetables from saucepan; set aside. Add chicken broth to saucepan, and bring to a boil. Add potatoes and corn; cover, reduce heat, and simmer 10 to 15 minutes or until potatoes are tender.

Using a slotted spoon, transfer half of potatoes and corn to an electric blender; add flour, and process until smooth. Return to saucepan; stir in clams, paprika, salt, hot sauce, and reserved vegetable mixture. Bring to a boil; cover, reduce heat, and simmer 15 minutes.

Per Serving (1¹/₂ cups): 285 Calories, 6 g Fat (1 g Saturated), 15 mg Cholesterol, 760 mg Sodium, 12 g Protein, 48 g Carbohydrates
A Great Source of: Fiber (6 g), Vitamin A (25%), Vitamin B6 (25%), Vitamin B12 (356%), Vitamin C (116%), Copper (26%), Iron (47%), Potassium (880 mg)
A Good Source of: Vitamin B1 (24%), Vitamin B2 (14%), Folic Acid (23%), Pantothenic Acid (15%), Vitamin E (18%), Magnesium (20%), Zinc (10%)
Pyramid Equivalent(s): 2 Breads, 2 Vegetables, 1 Meat

The Guilt-Free "Comfort Food" Cookbook

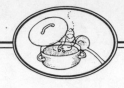

Curried Squash Soup

*H*ere's a lovely, lively, low-calorie soup. It's a good source of vitamin A, mostly in the form of beta-carotene, an antioxidant found in green and yellow fruits and vegetables, which may help protect against cancer and heart disease. It has a moderate amount of fat, mostly in the form of healthful monounsaturates.

1 cup finely chopped onion
1 clove garlic, minced
2 tablespoons olive or canola oil
1 pound sliced yellow squash
1 medium carrot, finely chopped
2 teaspoons curry powder
$1/_4$ teaspoon ground ginger

$1^3/_4$ cups water
1 tablespoon vegetable-flavored
   bouillon granules
2 teaspoons lemon or lime juice
$1/_4$ cup plus 2 tablespoons plain
   lowfat yogurt

Saute onion and garlic in olive oil in a heavy, medium saucepan over medium heat until tender. Add squash and carrot; saute 10 minutes. Stir in curry powder and ginger; saute 1 minute. Add water and vegetable bouillon granules; bring to a boil, stirring constantly. Cover, reduce heat, and simmer 20 minutes or until vegetables are tender.

Process soup, in batches, in an electric blender until smooth. Return to saucepan; stir in lime juice. Cook over medium-low heat until hot, stirring constantly. Ladle into bowls; spoon 1½ tablespoons yogurt on each serving.

Per Serving (1½ cups): 225 Calories, 12 g Fat (2 g Saturated), 2 mg Cholesterol, 750 mg Sodium, 6 g Protein, 26 g Carbohydrates

A Great Source of: Fiber (6 g), Vitamin A (81%), Vitamin C (63%), Potassium (700 mg)

A Good Source of: Vitamin B1 (15%), Vitamin B2 (12%), Vitamin B6 (18%), Folic Acid (17%), Vitamin E (21%), Calcium (13%), Copper (12%), Iron (11%), Magnesium (18%)

Pyramid Equivalent(s): 2 Vegetables

The Guilt-Free "Comfort Food" Cookbook

Time: 55 minutes prep and cooking
Yield: 9 cups (6 servings)

Creole Bean Soup

*H*ardy and hot, this soup packs a wallop. It also nourishes. Beans are
healthful alternatives to meat, rich in protein and minerals. And they
have something meat lacks: fiber. Like the Black Bean "Gazpacho"
(p. 119), this dish is incredibly rich in fiber, providing nearly half a
day's worth in a single serving.

1 tablespoon olive oil
2 cloves garlic, minced
1 medium onion, chopped
1 medium green pepper, chopped
3/4 cup diced celery
1 teaspoon dried thyme
1 bay leaf, halved
4 cups canned reduced-sodium
  chicken broth
1 (14 1/2-ounce) can Cajun-style
  stewed tomatoes, undrained

2 cups sliced fresh or frozen
  okra
1 1/2 cups cooked, drained white
  kidney beans
1 1/2 cups cooked, drained red
  kidney beans
2 ounces smoked turkey
  sausage (or reduced-fat/
  sodium ham, diced)
3 cups hot cooked rice
hot sauce (such as Tabasco)

Heat olive oil in a large heavy saucepan over medium heat; add garlic,
onion, pepper, celery, thyme, and bay leaf, and saute 8 to 10 minutes or until vegetables are very tender. Stir in broth and tomatoes; bring just to a
boil. Cover and simmer for 15 minutes.

Stir in okra; cover and simmer another 15 minutes. Stir in beans and
sausage; cover and simmer 5 more minutes. Discard bay leaf; serve over
rice with hot sauce.

Per Serving: 360 Calories, 6 g Fat (1 g Saturated), 6 mg Cholesterol, 700 mg Sodium, 15 g Protein, 62 g Carbohydrates
A Great Source of: Fiber (10 g), Vitamin B1 (28%), Folic Acid (34%), Vitamin C
  (53%), Iron (31%), Magnesium (27%), Potassium (925 mg)
A Good Source of: Vitamin B3 (17%), Vitamin B6 (20%), Vitamin E (12%), Calcium (14%), Copper (24%), Zinc (16%)
Pyramid Equivalent(s): 1 Bread, 2 Vegetables, 1 Meat

The Guilt-Free "Comfort Food" Cookbook

Time: 25 minutes prep and cooking
4 hours chilling
Yield: 6 cups (4 servings)

Black Bean "Gazpacho"

*G*azpacho, a cold Spanish soup sometimes called "liquid salad," is made with tomatoes, cucumbers, peppers, and onions. Try this one when the weather's warm. The pureed black beans in this version add body, flavor, and plenty of nutrition: protein, B vitamins, minerals, cancer-protective substances, and soluble fiber, which helps lower blood cholesterol and regulate blood sugar. A serving of this soup provides more than half a day's worth of fiber. Serve this with a wilted spinach salad, some whole wheat bread, and fresh lemonade, and you have an *incredibly* nutritious meal.

*4 cups seeded, coarsely chopped
    ripe tomatoes*
*1 (12-ounce) can spicy hot
    vegetable juice cocktail
    (such as reduced-sodium
    Tangy V-8), divided*
*1 (15-ounce) can cooked black
    beans, rinsed and drained*
*1 cup seeded and finely diced
    cucumber*

*1 cup finely diced yellow or
    green pepper*
*1/2 cup finely chopped sweet
    onion*
2 tablespoons red wine vinegar
1 medium ripe avocado
1 tablespoon lemon juice
1/2 cup plain nonfat yogurt

Combine tomatoes and ½ cup vegetable juice in a food processor; process until coarsely pureed. Pour into a large bowl or container; stir in remaining vegetable juice, black beans, cucumber, pepper, onion, vinegar, and avocado. Cover and refrigerate 4 hours or overnight.

Just before serving, peel and slice avocado thinly; toss with lemon juice. Ladle soup into wide soup bowls; top evenly with slices of avocado and yogurt.

Per Serving: 320 Calories, 9 g Fat (2 g Saturated), 1 mg Cholesterol, 360 mg Sodium, 15 g Protein, 50 g Carbohydrates

A Great Source of: Fiber (15 g), Vitamin A (28%), Vitamin B1 (34%), Vitamin B6 (31%), Folic Acid (64%), Vitamin C (153%), Vitamin E (33%), Copper (36%), Magnesium (36%), Potassium (1,515 mg)

A Good Source of: Vitamin B2 (20%), Vitamin B3 (18%), Pantothenic Acid (18%), Calcium (13%), Iron (24%), Zinc (15%)

Pyramid Equivalent(s): 4 Vegetables, 1 Meat

The Guilt-Free "Comfort Food" Cookbook

$\mathcal{S}$ALADS

$\mathcal{A}$lmost anything becomes a salad. Greens, of course. But also fruit, vegetables, meat, chicken, fish, and cheese. Seasonal salads can be cold, cool, room temperature—even warm. This chapter demonstrates the full range of the salad. There are some simple green things, such as Mixed Greens with Raspberry Vinaigrette (p. 124), or Wilted Spinach Salad (p. 126), which provide a new way to "wilt" spinach leaves without greasy bacon fat.

Getting into the salad habit is a quick way of boosting your family's consumption of vegetables. The best bet is to look for darker greens such as romaine, red leaf, curly endive, watercress, and spinach. The darker the green, the more vitamins. That's not to say you should shy away from lighter greens, such as Boston (sometimes called Butter) and Bibb. The trick to a tasty salad is to combine sweeter lighter greens with tangier, spicier greens such as watercress. Then let the tastiness and freshness of the lettuces and greens shine through with a dressing that's low in fat, such as our Creamy Pepper Ranch Salad Dressing (p. 127). If you get into the habit of serving a simple mixed greens salad every night, you'll go a long way toward protecting yourself and your family from chronic illnesses.

Lettuce can be the salad, but it can also be the stage for more dramatic presentations. In the summer, when the weather is warm and the farmers' markets are brimming with fresh produce, throw some eggplant and yellow squash and fresh corn in the back of your car, and

The Guilt-Free "Comfort Food" Cookbook

treat your family to Warm Roasted Vegetable Salad with Oriental Dressing (p. 128). A single serving has only 130 calories, yet provides 3 Vegetables. Bring it to the next community barbecue, and your friends will be talking about it all year. Bavarian Slaw (p. 131), Southern Succotash Salad (p. 134), and Ranch Pasta and Vegetable Salad (p. 132) are similarly hardy vegetable salads.

With main dish salads such as Chicken Salad Remoulade (p. 135), you can move the salad bowl into the center of the dining room table.

Salad can even be dessert. That's the case with Best Waldorf Salad (p. 136), Sweet-and-Tangy Pineapple Slaw (p. 137), and Peach-Raspberry Aspic (p. 138). Each salad is fine to serve with a meal, or as a starter. But all three salads are fruity and a little sweet, so you will find they make a fitting end to a meal. When it comes to salads, the only limit is your imagination.

Cool Broccoli Salad with Yogurt-Basil Dressing

$1^1/_2$ pounds fresh broccoli
$1/_2$ pound sliced fresh
   mushrooms
1 (2-ounce) jar diced pimento,
   drained
$1/_2$ cup sliced green onion
$1/_4$ cup sliced ripe olives
1 cup plain nonfat yogurt

$1/_2$ cup grated Parmesan cheese
2 tablespoons balsamic or
   white wine vinegar
$1/_4$ cup fresh basil, minced (or 1
   teaspoon dried basil)
$1/_2$ teaspoon dried oregano
1 clove garlic, minced

Trim off large leaves of broccoli, and remove tough ends of lower stalks.

Wash and cut into 1-inch pieces. Combine broccoli, mushrooms, pimento, green onion, and olives in a large bowl.

Combine yogurt and remaining ingredients; stir well. Stir into broccoli mixture; mix well. Cover and refrigerate 4 hours before serving.

Per Serving: 85 Calories, 3 g Fat (1 g Saturated), 6 mg Cholesterol, 200 mg Sodium, 8 g Protein, 10 g Carbohydrates
A Great Source of: Vitamin A (30%), Vitamin C (147%)
A Good Source of: Fiber (3 g), Vitamin B6 (11%), Folic Acid (19%), Pantothenic Acid (13%), Calcium (20%), Copper (11%), Potassium (500 mg)
Pyramid Equivalent(s): 2 Vegetables

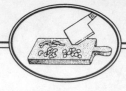

Time: 15 minutes
1 hour chilling
Yield: 6 servings

Mixed Greens with Raspberry Vinaigrette

*T*here's no easier way to add fresh vegetables to your family's diet than serving salads. Fresh salad greens are good sources of fiber, vitamin C, iron, calcium, vitamin A (in the form of beta-carotene), and B vitamins, especially folic acid. That makes sense—folic acid gets its name from the Latin word for "leaf" (*folia*, as in "foliage"). Folic acid is a wonder vitamin. It protects DNA, helps to prevent the most common form of birth defect (neural tube defects such as spina bifida), and protects against cancer and heart disease. It may even help prevent depression. It's widely distributed in fruits and vegetables. Many Americans, though, don't get enough.

We would if we got into the salad habit. To save time, you can purchase prewashed, mixed salad greens in the supermarket (sometimes called *mesclun*). If fresh berries are in season, they add a surprising yet fitting flavor accent.

1 cup fresh or frozen
  raspberries, thawed
3 tablespoons raspberry vinegar
3 tablespoons orange juice
2 teaspoons sugar
2 tablespoons olive oil
1 tablespoon minced fresh basil
  or 1 teaspoon dried basil
¹/₄ teaspoon salt
8 cups mixed salad greens
  (curly endive, red leaf
  lettuce, romaine,
  watercress, or arugula)

1 cup red onion, sliced thinly
  into rings
1 cup fresh berries: blueberries,
  sliced strawberries,
  raspberries (optional)
2 ounces goat cheese (or feta),
  crumbled
freshly ground pepper

Process raspberries, vinegar, orange juice, sugar, olive oil, basil, and salt in electric blender until smooth. Press through a fine wire-mesh sieve into a bowl. Cover and refrigerate at least 1 hour.

Toss salad greens, onion, and ½ cup salad dressing in a large bowl; di-

The Guilt-Free "Comfort Food" Cookbook

vide evenly among 6 salad plates. Arrange berries, if desired, on plates; crumble goat cheese evenly over salads, and sprinkle with pepper. Refrigerate remaining salad dressing up to 1 week.

Per Serving: 125 calories, 8 g Fat (3 g Saturated), 10 mg Cholesterol, 140 mg Sodium, 5 g Protein, 10 g Carbohydrates
A Great Source of: Vitamin A (26%), Folic Acid (25%), Vitamin C (38%)
A Good Source of: Fiber (3 g), Vitamin B2 (12%), Vitamin E (13%), Calcium (14%), Potassium (335 mg)
Pyramid Equivalent(s): 1½ Vegetables, 1 Fruit

The Guilt-Free "Comfort Food" Cookbook

Wilted Spinach Salad

*H*ere, we "wilt" the spinach with a sauce of cranberry sauce, vinegar, olive oil, honey, thyme, salt, and pepper instead of bacon grease. Spinach is rich in iron, and the vitamin C in the orange sections helps makes this iron more available to the body. That's true any time you combine a vegetable source of iron (beans, greens) with a food rich in vitamin C (many fruits and vegetables). The acidity of the vinegar helps too.

8 cups torn fresh spinach leaves (about a pound)
1/2 cup fresh orange sections
1/3 cup snipped fresh chives or minced green onion
1/4 cup whole-berry cranberry sauce

2 tablespoons balsamic or red wine vinegar
2 tablespoons olive oil
1 tablespoon honey
1 teaspoon dried thyme
1/4 teaspoon salt
1/2 teaspoon freshly ground pepper

Combine spinach, oranges, and chives in a salad bowl; set aside.
Combine remaining ingredients in a small saucepan; bring to a boil.
Pour over spinach mixture, and toss. Serve immediately.

Per Serving: 95 Calories, 5 g Fat (1 g Saturated), 0 mg Cholesterol, 150 mg Sodium, 3 g Protein, 12 mg Carbohydrates
A Great Source of: Vitamin A (52%), Folic Acid (38%), Vitamin C (51%)
A Good Source of: Fiber (3 g), Vitamin E (19%), Iron (14%), Magnesium (16%), Potassium (470 mg)
Pyramid Equivalent(s): 1⅓ Vegetables

The Guilt-Free "Comfort Food" Cookbook

Time: 10 minutes
Yield: 1²/₃ cups

Creamy Pepper Ranch Salad Dressing

*C*reamy without being fatty? You bet. Wash out a commercial salad dressing bottle, pour this in, recap, and make a new batch when you need a refill! Try it on spinach salad, in potato salads, or as a dip for raw vegetables.

1 medium clove garlic
1 to 1¹/₂ teaspoons coarse
  ground pepper
¹/₂ teaspoon salt
³/₄ cup nonfat buttermilk
¹/₂ cup plain nonfat yogurt
¹/₂ cup reduced-fat mayonnaise

2 teaspoons lemon juice
1 teaspoon white wine vinegar
¹/₂ teaspoon Worcestershire
  sauce
2 tablespoons finely minced
  parsley or cilantro

Combine garlic, pepper, and salt in a mortar; mash with pestle until mixture forms a paste and pepper is finely ground. Combine pepper mixture and remaining ingredients; whisk until smooth. Cover and refrigerate 2 hours for flavors to blend.

Per Serving (two tablespoons): 35 Calories, 2 g Fat (0 g Saturated), 3 mg Cholesterol, 155 mg Sodium, 1 g Protein, 3 g Carbohydrates
(Not a significant source of vitamins and minerals.)
Pyramid Equivalent(s): Extras

The Guilt-Free "Comfort Food" Cookbook

Time: 20 minutes prep
25 minutes roasting
Yield: 6 servings

Warm Roasted Vegetable
Salad with Oriental Dressing

*M*ost of us think of salads as cold. But warm salads can be delicious. This one, for instance. Each serving of this salad provides three servings of vegetables in the Pyramid. That's your minimum for vegetables in one fell swoop!

1/4 cup balsamic vinegar
1/4 cup reduced-sodium teriyaki sauce
1 tablespoon canola oil
2 1/2 teaspoons Oriental sesame oil
1 1/2 tablespoons grated fresh gingerroot (about a 2-inch piece)
1 1/2 tablespoons crushed garlic
3/4 cup plain nonfat yogurt
1 large onion, cut vertically into thin slices (about 1 1/2 cups)

3 cups cubed eggplant (1-inch cubes)
3 cups cubed yellow squash (1-inch cubes)
1 large sweet red pepper, cut into 1-inch squares
1 cup fresh corn kernels (about 2 ears corn)
1 head romaine lettuce
vegetable cooking spray

Preheat oven to 450°. Combine vinegar, teriyaki sauce, canola and sesame oils, ginger, and garlic in a jar; shake to blend. Stir ¼ cup of this dressing into yogurt. Cover and refrigerate yogurt mixture. Reserve remaining mixture.

Combine onion, eggplant, and squash on a nonstick baking sheet coated with cooking spray; sprinkle with half of remaining vinegar mixture, and toss well. Combine pepper and corn on another nonstick baking sheet coated with cooking spray; sprinkle with remaining vinegar mixture, and toss well. Bake at 450° until vegetables are browned and tender, about 35 minutes for onion mixture and about 25 to 30 minutes for corn mixture. Stir every 15 minutes.

To serve, arrange lettuce on plates; top with vegetable mixture. Spoon yogurt mixture evenly on salads.

The Guilt-Free "Comfort Food" Cookbook

Per Serving: 130 Calories, 5 g Fat (1 g Saturated), 1 mg Cholesterol, 440 mg Sodium, 6 g Protein, 18 g Carbohydrates

A Great Source of: Folic Acid (25%), Vitamin C (78%)

A Good Source of: Fiber (4 g), Vitamin A (20%), Vitamin B1 (12%), Vitamin B2 (10%), Vitamin B6 (12%), Vitamin E (10%), Calcium (10%), Magnesium (12%), Potassium (570 mg)

Pyramid Equivalent(s): 3 Vegetables

The Guilt-Free "Comfort Food" Cookbook

Time: 25 minutes
Yield: 6 cups (6 servings)

Picnic Potato, Corn, and
Butter Bean Salad

*B*ring this creamy, spicy salad to your next picnic. You don't have to tell anyone it's low in fat! If you can't find butter beans, a Southern delicacy that is slowly making its way up North, try white kidney or lima beans.

2¹/₂ pounds medium-sized
red-skinned potatoes,
scrubbed
¹/₂ cup plain nonfat yogurt
¹/₂ cup reduced-fat sour cream
2 tablespoons Dijon mustard
¹/₂ teaspoon seasoned salt
¹/₂ teaspoon freshly ground
pepper

1 cup cooked fresh corn or
frozen corn, thawed
1 cup cooked fresh butter beans
or canned butter beans,
drained
¹/₂ cup thinly sliced green onion
3 tablespoons sliced pickled
jalapenos, drained

Place potatoes in a large saucepan; cover with water and bring to a boil. Reduce heat and simmer 20 minutes or until tender. Drain in a colander; let stand until cool enough to handle. Break potatoes into coarse chunks with a wooden spoon or fork.

Combine yogurt and next 4 ingredients; stir into potatoes, mixing well. Stir in corn, butterbeans, green onion, and jalapenos. Cover and refrigerate or serve at room temperature.

Per Serving: 280 Calories, 4 g Fat (2 g Saturated), 8 mg Cholesterol, 340 mg Sodium, 10 g Protein, 56 g Carbohydrates

A Great Source of: Fiber (7 g), Vitamin B6 (32%), Vitamin C (48%), Potassium (1,040 mg)

A Good Source of: Vitamin B1 (24%), Vitamin B2 (10%), Vitamin B3 (16%), Folic Acid (20%), Pantothenic Acid (16%), Copper (22%), Iron (12%), Magnesium (20%), Zinc (10%)

Pyramid Equivalent(s): 2 Vegetables

The Guilt-Free "Comfort Food" Cookbook

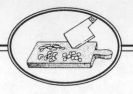

Bavarian Slaw

*I*f you love the flavor of bacon, use it as we do—for flavor. Even with the bacon in this salad, each serving still has only two grams of fat.

1 pound small (2-inch)
   red-skinned potatoes
1/2 cup nonfat plain yogurt
1/4 cup nonfat mayonnaise
2 tablespoons cider vinegar
2 teaspoons crushed caraway
   seeds

1 large Red Delicious apple
2 1/2 cups chopped green cabbage
1/2 cup chopped green onion
2 slices bacon, cooked and
   crumbled

Cook potatoes in boiling water to cover 15 to 20 minutes or until tender. Drain and cool; cut into 1-inch cubes.

Combine yogurt and next 3 ingredients in a large bowl. Core (but don't peel) apple, and cut into ½ inch cubes; add to yogurt mixture, and mix. Add potatoes, cabbage, green onion, and bacon; mix well. Cover and refrigerate 1 hour.

Per Serving: 150 Calories, 2 g Fat (0 g Saturated), 3 mg Cholesterol, 215 mg Sodium, 6 g Protein, 30 g Carbohydrates

A Great Source of: Fiber (6 g), Vitamin C (36%), Copper (43%), Iron (34%), Potassium (635 mg)

A Good Source of: Vitamin B6 (15%), Calcium (12%), Magnesium (11%)

Pyramid Equivalent(s): 2 Vegetables

The Guilt-Free "Comfort Food" Cookbook

Time: 25 minutes
2 hours chilling
Yield: 8 cups (8 servings)

Ranch Pasta and Vegetable
Salad

*T*ry this cool, crunchy salad with either the Marinated Bean Salad (p.
133) or the Chicken Remoulade (p. 135) for a complete meal.

  If you can find multicolored corkscrew macaroni, that will make
this dish even more colorful. A true feast for the eyes!

6 ounces corkscrew pasta,
  uncooked
1/4 pound fresh snow peas,
  trimmed (about 11/2 cups)
11/2 cups broccoli flowerets
1 cup sliced fresh mushrooms
1 cup cherry tomato halves
2 medium yellow squash,
  trimmed and cut into 2-x
  1/4-inch strips
3/4 cup nonfat buttermilk

1/2 cup 1% lowfat cottage cheese
2 teaspoons white wine vinegar
1 clove garlic, chopped
1/4 teaspoon salt
1 green onion, chopped (about
  1/3 cup)
1 jalapeno pepper, seeded and
  chopped (about 2
  tablespoons)
1/3 cup chopped fresh cilantro
  or parsley

  Cook pasta according to package directions, omitting salt and fat.
Drain; rinse under cold water, and drain again. Place in a large bowl.

  Blanch snow peas, broccoli, and squash in boiling water 30 seconds;
drain and rinse under cold water to stop cooking process. Drain well; add
to pasta.

  Process buttermilk and next 4 ingredients in an electric blender until
smooth; add green onion, jalapeno, and cilantro; process until minced.
Pour over pasta mixture, and toss. Cover and refrigerate at least 2 hours.

Per Serving: 125 Calories, 1 g Fat (0 g Saturated), 1 mg Cholesterol, 170 mg So-
  dium, 7 g Protein, 23 g Carbohydrates
A Great Source of: Vitamin C (58%)
A Good Source of: Fiber (3 g), Vitamin B1 (21%), Vitamin B2 (15%), Vitamin B3
  (13%), Folic Acid (11%), Iron (10%), Potassium (335 mg)
Pyramid Equivalent(s): 1 Bread, 2 Vegetables

The Guilt-Free "Comfort Food" Cookbook

Marinated Bean Salad with Honey-Mustard Vinaigrette

*F*or your next summer picnic, try this salad with corn-on-the-cob, new potatoes, snap peas, a sliced tomato salad, watermelon, and fresh lemonade. Or serve it as a side salad when the weather gets cool. A small half-cup serving provides good amounts of protein, vitamins, minerals, and fiber. A larger serving—a cup or a cup and a half—provides enough protein for a main dish.

1¹/₂ cups cooked kidney beans, drained
1¹/₂ cups cooked chick peas (garbanzo beans), drained
2 small carrots, thinly sliced
1 medium cucumber, peeled, seeded, and finely diced
1 large red or green pepper, chopped

¹/₂ cup minced onion
¹/₂ cup minced fresh cilantro or parsley
¹/₄ cup commercial honey mustard
¹/₄ cup white wine vinegar
1 tablespoon olive oil

Combine kidney beans, chick peas, carrots, cucumber, pepper, onion, and cilantro in a large bowl. Combine honey mustard, vinegar, and olive oil; mix well and pour over bean mixture. Stir well. Cover and refrigerate 3 to 4 hours or overnight.

Per Serving: 120 Calories, 3 g Fat (0 g Saturated), 0 mg Cholesterol, 45 mg Sodium, 5 g Protein, 20 g Carbohydrates
A Great Source of: Vitamin A (42%)
A Good Source of: Fiber (4 g), Folic Acid (21%), Vitamin C (18%), Iron (10%), Potassium (310 mg).

Pyramid Equivalent(s): 1 Vegetable, 1 Meat

Note: One-cup serving: 10% or more B1, B6, Vitamin E, Copper, Magnesium, and Zinc.

Time: 20 minutes
3 hours chilling
Yield: 4 cups (4 main-dish servings)

Southern Succotash Salad

*H*ere's a salad that could be a meal. It will serve two to four as a main course, six to eight as a side salad. The relatively small amounts of ham provide protein, B vitamins (especially B1), iron and other minerals, and of course, flavor, without much fat at all. There's a fair amount of sodium, though, so serve this with a side vegetable that doesn't require added salt, such as sweet potatoes. Salad with oil and vinegar is salt-free; so is fresh fruit. That's the *Guilt-Free "Comfort Food"* approach: Eat what you like—in the right proportions.

*1³/4 cups cooked fresh or frozen
   corn kernels, thawed*
*1³/4 cups cooked fresh or frozen
   baby lima beans, thawed*
*1 cup finely diced cooked lean
   ham*
³/4 cup finely chopped red onion
³/4 cup thinly sliced celery

*¹/4 cup minced fresh cilantro or
   parsley*
*¹/2 cup Creamy Pepper Ranch
   Salad Dressing (p. 127) or
   commercial nonfat ranch
   dressing (such as Kraft or
   Hidden Valley)*
2 tablespoons lime juice
¹/2 teaspoon ground cumin

Combine corn, limas, ham, onion, celery, and cilantro in a bowl. Combine salad dressing, lime juice, cumin, and red pepper; pour over salad, and toss well. Cover and chill at least 3 hours, stirring occasionally. Serve on lettuce leaves.

Per Serving: 310 Calories, 9 g Fat (1 g Saturated), 28 mg Cholesterol, 870 mg Sodium, 18 g Protein, 43 g Carbohydrates
A Great Source of: Fiber (9 g), Vitamin B1 (42%), Folic Acid (42%), Potassium (770 mg)
A Good Source of: Vitamin B6 (18%), Pantothenic Acid (12%), Vitamin C (18%), Copper (14%), Iron (16%), Magnesium (20%), Zinc (14%)
Pyramid Equivalent(s): 2½ Vegetables, 1 Meat

The Guilt-Free "Comfort Food" Cookbook

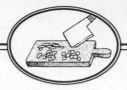

Chicken Salad Remoulade

*R*emoulade is a piquant mayonnaise sauce for cold poultry, meats, and shellfish. The name itself comes from the French (and earlier, Latin) name for "horseradish." This one leaves out nearly all the saturated fat and cholesterol that clog most versions, yet it remains spirited and satisfying.

For a cool summer menu, serve with Cool Broccoli Salad with Yogurt-Basil Dressing (p. 123), Bavarian Slaw (p. 131), bread, and fruit for dessert. Keep it cool!

2 tablespoons lemon juice
2 tablespoons Creole mustard
1 tablespoon olive oil
1 teaspoon paprika
1 teaspoon white wine vinegar
1¹/₂ teaspoons prepared
*   horseradish*

1 teaspoon Worcestershire sauce
2 cups shredded, cooked
*   white-meat chicken*
³/₄ cup thinly sliced celery
¹/₄ cup minced green onion
4 large red leaf lettuce leaves
12 cherry tomatoes

Combine lemon juice, mustard, olive oil, paprika, vinegar, horseradish, and Worcestershire sauce in a medium bowl; mix well. Add chicken, celery, and green onion; toss well. Cover and refrigerate at least 3 hours, stirring occasionally.

Line salad plates with lettuce leaves; spoon salad mixture over. Garnish each with 3 cherry tomatoes.

Per Serving: 130 Calories, 6 g Fat (1 g Saturated), 37 mg Cholesterol, 172 mg Sodium, 15 g Protein, 6 g Carbohydrates

A Great Source of: Vitamin B3 (32%), Vitamin C (31%)

A Good Source of: Fiber (2 g), Vitamin B6 (17%), Vitamin E (12%), Potassium (380 mg)

Pyramid Equivalent(s): ½ Vegetable, 1 Meat

The Guilt-Free "Comfort Food" Cookbook

Best Waldorf Salad

*T*ry this lowfat classic either as a salad at the beginning of the meal or as a light dessert!

3 large Red Delicious or Granny Smith apples

2 teaspoons lemon juice (about half a lemon)

1¹/2 cups seedless green grape halves

1 cup finely diced celery

¹/3 cup raisins

¹/4 cup finely chopped toasted walnuts or pecans

¹/4 cup nonfat salad dressing (Miracle Whip) or reduced-calorie mayonnaise

¹/4 cup nonfat buttermilk

2 teaspoons sugar

1 ounce blue cheese

Peel apples; dice. Toss with lemon juice in a large bowl. Add grapes, celery, raisins, and walnuts.

Combine salad dressing and remaining ingredients; stir into apple mixture.

Cover and refrigerate 1 hour.

Per Serving (one cup): 265 Calories, 10 g Fat (3 g Saturated), 5 mg Cholesterol, 210 mg Sodium, 4 g Protein, 44 g Carbohydrates

A Great Source of: Vitamin C (28%)

A Good Source of: Fiber (4 g), Vitamin B6 (11%), Vitamin E (21%), Copper (11%), Potassium (470 mg)

Pyramid Equivalent(s): 2 Fruits, Extras

The Guilt-Free "Comfort Food" Cookbook

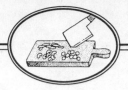

Sweet-and-Tangy Pineapple Slaw

*B*righten up your winter table with this colorful salad. When the days end early and lettuces are often wilted and expensive, red and green cabbage and fresh spinach can bring some seasonal cheer. But you needn't drown your coleslaw with saturated-fat-laden mayonnaise. This slaw, which is rich in fiber and folic acid and vitamin C, relies on lowfat sour cream for body, pineapple and almonds for flavor accents. Enjoy!

3 cups very thinly sliced green cabbage
3 cups very thinly sliced red cabbage
2$^1/_2$ cups very thinly sliced fresh spinach
1 (8-ounce) can unsweetened pineapple tidbits, drained (or 1 cup fresh pineapple, cubed)

$^1/_3$ cup reduced-fat sour cream
2 tablespoons frozen pineapple-orange juice concentrate, thawed
1 tablespoon cider vinegar
$^1/_4$ teaspoon salt
$^1/_4$ teaspoon red pepper
$^1/_4$ cup toasted slivered almonds

Combine cabbages, spinach, and pineapple tidbits in a large bowl, and set aside. Combine sour cream, juice concentrate, vinegar, salt, and red pepper; mix well, and stir into cabbage mixture. Cover and refrigerate 1 hour.

Just before serving, stir in almonds.

Per Serving: 100 Calories, 5 g Fat (1 g Saturated), 5 mg Cholesterol, 125 mg Sodium, 3 g Protein, 14 g Carbohydrates
A Great Source of: Vitamin C (77%), Vitamin E (30%)
A Good Source of: Fiber (3 g), Vitamin A (18%), Vitamin B6 (10%), Folic Acid (20%), Magnesium (14%), Potassium (420 mg)
Pyramid Equivalent(s): 1 Fruit, 1½ Vegetables

The Guilt-Free "Comfort Food" Cookbook

Peach-Raspberry Aspic

olded aspic salads have a rich tradition in our country. This one is delicious and low in fat. Try it as a cool side dish or even as a light dessert.

*1 (16-ounce) package frozen
    peach slices, thawed,
    drained, and divided*
1¹/₂ cups water, divided
*1 (3-ounce) package peach or
    apricot gelatin*
*1 (8-ounce) carton nonfat
    peach-flavored yogurt*

*1 (8-ounce) carton nonfat
    raspberry-flavored yogurt*
*¹/₂ cup no-sugar-added
    raspberry fruit spread,
    melted and cooled*
*2 cups fresh raspberries or
    frozen unsweetened
    raspberries, thawed
    (optional)*

Process half of peach slices and ¾ cup water in an electric blender until smooth. Bring remaining water and peach puree to a boil in a medium saucepan; remove from heat. Stir in gelatin until dissolved. Measure out ⅓ cup mixture, and set aside at room temperature.

Cool remaining gelatin; whisk in peach-flavored yogurt until smooth. Pour into a 2-quart serving dish; cover and chill until set.

Whisk raspberry yogurt and reserved ⅓ cup gelatin mixture until smooth; spread over peach gelatin mixture. Chill until just firm but not set. Spoon fruit spread evenly over gelatin layer by teaspoonfuls; drag tip of a sharp knife through spoonfuls to swirl fruit spread into topping mixture. Cover and refrigerate 4 hours or until firm.

Spoon into serving dishes; arrange remaining peach slices and raspberries evenly in serving dishes.

Per Serving: 220 Calories, 0 g Fat (0 g Saturated), 1 mg Cholesterol, 100 mg Sodium, 5 g Protein, 51 mg Carbohydrates
A Great Source of: Vitamin C (105%)
A Good Source of: Vitamin B2 (11%), Vitamin E (14%)
Pyramid Equivalent(s): 1 Fruit, 1 Dairy, Extras

The Guilt-Free "Comfort Food" Cookbook

BEEF, PORK, VEAL, AND LAMB

*R*ed meat arouses passionate discussion. Some health-oriented enthusiasts vow to give up red meat. Other people believe a life without steak is a sad, sad thing. Cheer up. Beef, pork, veal, and lamb can each be a part of a spectacularly healthful way of eating. The trick, as always, is to understand balance.

Red meat is a rich source of many nutrients: iron, zinc, trace minerals, B vitamins, and protein. The fat in red meat, however, is saturated—the kind that raises blood cholesterol. So the trick is to consume lean red meat in moderate amounts. That way you get the taste and nutrition without the fat. Most of the saturated fat we get from meat comes not from small servings of lean steak and stir-fries but from high-fat hamburgers and processed meats such as luncheon meats.

So if you like red meat, the first place to start is buying good lean cuts. For beef, leans cuts include flank steak, round roast, round steak, and sirloin steak. Each cut has fewer than ten grams of fat per three-and-a-half-ounce serving. For pork, lean cuts include fresh ham and pork loins; for lamb, leg shanks and loin chops; for veal, the leanest cuts are veal chops, veal cutlets, and blade steak.

The next step is to make sure your total weekly consumption is moderate. How you achieve balance is a personal matter. A serving of animal protein foods is two or three ounces per person. Most of our recipes provide that amount. But if you really want a thick, juicy, six-

The Guilt-Free "Comfort Food" Cookbook

ounce sirloin steak once in a while, let yourself have it. If you have a steak once a week, or once every two weeks, you'll be fine. Enjoy it.

If you want to enjoy red meat more often, though—a few times a week—you'll want to learn how to use more modest portions in filling, savory dishes. Our dishes take both approaches. If you like a nice slab of meat on occasion, you'll enjoy pork loin chops (Cherry-Teriyaki Pork, p. 153), lamb chops (Grilled Lamb Chops Marinated in Orange Juice, Garlic, and Rosemary, p. 155), sirloin steak (Grilled Peppercorn-Marinated Steak, p. 141), and veal chops (Veal Chops Stuffed with Apples, Walnuts, and Two Wheats, p. 156).

Red meats have such rich flavors, you can also use a smaller amount to impart delicious taste to grains, potatoes, and vegetables. For example in Gourmet Burritos (p. 146), lean ground beef meets black beans for a memorable dish. In Peppered Lamb Stir-Fry (p. 158), a pound of lean lamb, fried up with asparagus and peppers and shallots and served over rice, serves six. The better we understand beef, pork, lamb, and veal, the better we can enjoy it while keeping our intake of saturated fat low. Along the way, we can enjoy its unique tastes and take in a bounty of nutrients.

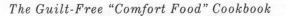

The Guilt-Free "Comfort Food" Cookbook

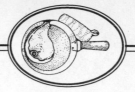

Time: 6 hours marinating
25 minutes prep and cooking
Yield: 7 (3-ounce) servings

Grilled
Peppercorn-Marinated Steak

*I*nstead of fatty hamburgers and hot dogs on your outdoor grill, try lean sirloin marinated overnight to stay tender. If you don't have a grill or hibachi, or if it's raining or snowing or hailing or too hot, you can broil the sirloinon high in a rack in the bottom third of the oven for about the same amount of time. (To save clean-up time when oven broiling, put three-fourths an inch of water in the bottom of the broiler pan; fat drippings will float rather than stick.)

*1 tablespoon drained green
 peppercorns
1 teaspoon dried marjoram
2 cloves garlic
3 tablespoons Dijon mustard*

*1 tablespoon canola oil
1 (1½ pounds) lean boneless
 top sirloin steak, cut 1½
 inches thick, trimmed*

Combine peppercorns, marjoram, and garlic in a mortar; crush with a pestle until mixture forms a coarse paste.

Place steak in a shallow dish; rub mustard mixture on both sides of steak. Cover with heavy-duty plastic wrap and refrigerate 6 hours or overnight.

Grill steak over hot coals (400° to 500°) 7 to 10 minutes on each side or until desired degree of doneness. To serve, slice thinly across grain into thin slices.

Per Serving: 145 Calories, 9 g Fat (3 g Saturated), 65 mg Cholesterol, 19 g Protein, 1 g Carbohydrates, 135 mg Sodium

A Great Source of: Vitamin B12 (45%)

A Good Source of: Vitamin B2 (11%), Vitamin B3 (15%), Vitamin B6 (19%), Iron (13%), Zinc (22%), Potassium (315 mg)

Pyramid Equivalent(s): 1 Meat

The Guilt-Free "Comfort Food" Cookbook

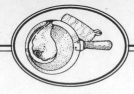

Time: 30 minutes standing time
15 minutes prep
15 minutes cooking
Yield: 4 servings

Salisbury Steak with
Mushroom Sauce

*H*ere's another way to make lean ground beef delicious. Mixing the beef with bulgur wheat not only improves the nutritional balance and adds fiber, but it makes a delicious patty. These are not lowfat entrees, however. Hamburger, even lean hamburger, is still high in fat, about nineteen grams in three-and-a-half cooked ounces. Our patty has only twelve grams. You can reduce that even more by pressing out the fat in the pan as the patties are cooking and discarding it.

The Mushroom Sauce, incidentally, is fat-free and very low in sodium. You can make it earlier in the day—perhaps in the morning—and refrigerate it until you are ready to cook dinner.

1/2 cup low-sodium beef broth
1/3 cup bulgur
3/4 pound lean ground beef
3/4 cup finely chopped onion

1 tablespoon reduced-sodium
* soy sauce*
1/4 teaspoon pepper
2 tablespoons all-purpose flour
vegetable cooking spray

Bring beef broth to a boil in a small bowl in the microwave or a saucepan on the stove. Pour into medium bowl; add bulgur; let stand 20 minutes or until liquid is absorbed.

Crumble ground beef in a food processor fitted with knife blade; add bulgur, onion, soy sauce, and pepper. Pulse until well mixed. Form into 4 (¾-inch thick) patties. Coat patties on both sides with flour.

Coat a large nonstick skillet with cooking spray; add oil, and heat over medium-low heat. Cook patties about 6 minutes on each side or until meat is no longer pink in the center. Add Mushroom Sauce to skillet, and cook 2 minutes or until hot.

The Guilt-Free "Comfort Food" Cookbook

Mushroom Sauce
Yield: 1¹/₂ cups

vegetable cooking spray
1 teaspoon canola oil
¹/₂ pound sliced fresh
 mushrooms
¹/₄ cup reduced-sodium beef
 broth

2 tablespoons all-purpose flour
1 cup evaporated skimmed milk
2 teaspoons Worcestershire
 sauce
¹/₄ teaspoon salt

Coat a large nonstick skillet with cooking spray; add oil, and heat over medium heat. Add mushrooms; cook until browned and tender, stirring frequently.

Meanwhile, combine broth and flour, stirring until smooth. Stir in milk, Worcestershire sauce, and salt. Add flour mixture to skillet; cook over low heat, stirring constantly until thickened.

Per Serving (two tablespoons Mushroom Sauce): 30 Calories, 1 g Fat (0 g Saturated), 0 mg Cholesterol, 80 mg Sodium, 2 g Protein, 4 g Carbohydrates
(Not a significant source of vitamins, minerals. No Pyramid Equivalents.)

Per Serving (one patty with two tablespoons sauce): 300 Calories, 12 g Fat (5 g Saturated), 65 mg Cholesterol, 465 mg Sodium, 25 g Protein, 26 g Carbohydrates
A Great Source of: Vitamin B2 (31%), Potassium (765 mg)
A Good Source of: Fiber (3 g), Vitamin B1 (12%), Vitamin B3 (21%), Pantothenic Acid (19%), Calcium (21%), Copper (18%), Iron (19%)
Pyramid Equivalent(s): 1 Vegetable, 1 Meat

The Guilt-Free "Comfort Food" Cookbook

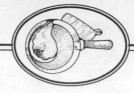

Time: 45 minutes prep
4$\frac{1}{2}$ hours cooking
Yield: 12 servings

Pot Roast with Plum-Peach
Ketchup

*H*ere's a guilt-free version of a favorite American comfort food. Good cooking techniques keep the meat moist, and an old-fashioned "ketchup," made with plums and peaches, perfectly complements the roast. Don't be put off by the long ingredients list—it's mostly spices. This is an easy recipe.

Start with a lean roast, such as a select-grade arm or bottom-round pot roast, which has only about seven grams of fat per three-and-a-half-ounce cooked serving. (By contrast, even extra-lean ground hamburger meat has sixteen grams of fat per three-and-a-half-ounce cooked serving—and you may have had to add some fat to the pan.)

You can make this recipe even lower in fat by refrigerating the liquid, then skimming off the fat. After the roast has cooked, remove it from the pan, pull out the onions with a slotted spoon, discard the spices and bay leaves, then pour off the liquid; refrigerate for a few hours, and skim the fat. Then proceed with the rest of the recipe directions, bringing the liquid to a boil to make the ketchup.

Here's another old trick: Pot roast always tastes better the second day, so make this the day *before* you want it—say, Saturday for Sunday dinner. That way, you can follow the directions above, skim off the fat, then proceed with the rest of the directions without having to wait around.

The ketchup, by the way, is so delicious you may want to try it over other meats such as grilled sirloin, grilled chicken, or turkey burgers. If preparing the ketchup without the roast, start with a third cup beef broth instead of the reduced cooking liquid. As an alternative, either for this recipe or others, you can make a Tomato Fruit Ketchup by substituting two (sixteen-ounce) cans of diced tomatoes for the plums.

The Guilt-Free "Comfort Food" Cookbook

1 (3 pounds) boneless beef pot
   roast
1 teaspoon dried thyme
1/4 teaspoon salt
1/2 teaspoon garlic powder
vegetable cooking spray
1 large onion, thickly sliced
12 whole peppercorns
12 whole allspice
2 bay leaves

2 cups water (or reduced-
   sodium beef broth)
2 (15-ounce) cans plums,
   drained and pitted
6 dried peaches
2 tablespoons white wine
   vinegar
2 tablespoons sugar
1/4 teaspoon salt

Preheat oven to 350°. Trim fat from roast. Combine thyme, ¼ teaspoon salt, and garlic powder; rub over surface of roast. Coat an ovenproof
Dutch oven with cooking spray; heat over medium-high heat. Add roast
and brown well on all sides (about 8 to 10 minutes). Remove from Dutch
oven. Arrange onion slices in bottom of Dutch oven; add peppercorns, allspice, bay leaves, and water, stirring well. Place roast on top of onion;
cover tightly and bake for 3½ to 4 hours, or until roast is tender. (If you
are cooking this Saturday for Sunday dinner, refrigerate now.)

Remove from pan; pour cooking liquid into a saucepan. Bring to a
boil; boil uncovered until reduced to ⅓ cup. Stir in plums, dried peaches,
vinegar, sugar, and ¼ teaspoon salt; reduce heat and simmer uncovered
for 15 minutes. Let cool; transfer to an electric blender container and process until smooth.

To serve, wrap roast in heavy-duty aluminum foil; bake at 350° for 30
minutes or until hot. Slice and serve with fruit ketchup.

Per Serving (with ketchup): 195 Calories, 5 g Fat (2 g Saturated), 58 mg Choles-
   terol, 182 mg Sodium, 20 g Protein, 19 g Carbohydrates
A Great Source of: Vitamin B12 (28%)
A Good Source of: Fiber (2 g), Vitamin A (10%), Vitamin B2 (16%), Vitamin B6
   (14%), Iron (17%), Zinc (15%), Potassium (375 mg)
Pyramid Equivalent(s): 1 Fruit, 1 Meat

The Guilt-Free "Comfort Food" Cookbook

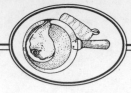

Gourmet Burritos

*G*round beef and black beans are old American friends. Together they create a delicious taste combination, low in cost, lower in fat, and more healthful than beef-only burritos. Spinach adds flavor and nutrition. So we get a one-dish supper that is not only moderately low in fat and sodium and calories, but rich in fiber, B vitamins, and a powerhouse of minerals. (A single serving provides eight grams of fiber, nearly half the twenty grams a day that we strive for.) Kids love these mouth-watering burritos—especially when they get to help in the kitchen and add their own toppings at the table!

1 pound lean ground beef
2 cloves garlic, minced
3 tablespoons ketchup, divided
2 tablespoons reduced-sodium
  soy sauce
1/3 cup minced green onions
1/3 cup minced fresh cilantro
1 tablespoon grated fresh ginger

1 (15-ounce) can black beans,
  drained and mashed
1/2 teaspoon ground cumin
1/4 teaspoon ground red pepper
6 (8-inch) flour tortillas, heated
12 to 18 spinach leaves,
  trimmed
vegetable cooking spray

Toppings

plain nonfat yogurt
diced tomatoes
shredded lettuce
cilantro leaves

Cook ground beef and garlic in a large skillet until browned, stirring to crumble. Drain in a colander; pat meat dry with paper towels. Return to skillet, and stir in 2 tablespoons ketchup, soy sauce, green onions, cilantro, and ginger; cook over medium heat, stirring frequently, until mixture is hot. Remove from heat; cover to keep warm.

Combine beans, remaining ketchup, cumin, and red pepper in a small saucepan; cook over medium-low heat, stirring constantly, until hot.

To serve, arrange 2 or 3 spinach leaves on each tortilla; spread evenly

The Guilt-Free "Comfort Food" Cookbook

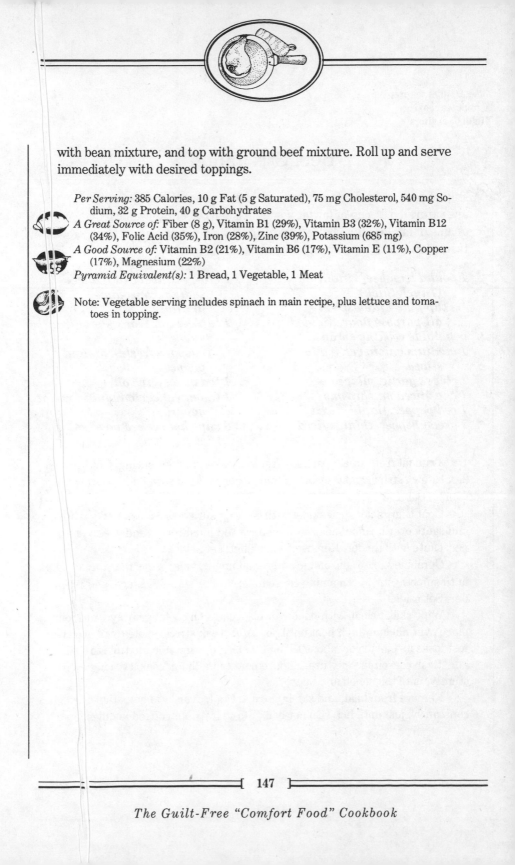

with bean mixture, and top with ground beef mixture. Roll up and serve immediately with desired toppings.

Per Serving: 385 Calories, 10 g Fat (5 g Saturated), 75 mg Cholesterol, 540 mg Sodium, 32 g Protein, 40 g Carbohydrates

A Great Source of: Fiber (8 g), Vitamin B1 (29%), Vitamin B3 (32%), Vitamin B12 (34%), Folic Acid (35%), Iron (28%), Zinc (39%), Potassium (685 mg)

A Good Source of: Vitamin B2 (21%), Vitamin B6 (17%), Vitamin E (11%), Copper (17%), Magnesium (22%)

Pyramid Equivalent(s): 1 Bread, 1 Vegetable, 1 Meat

Note: Vegetable serving includes spinach in main recipe, plus lettuce and tomatoes in topping.

Time: 20 minutes prep
20 minutes cooking
Yield: 6 servings

Beef Stroganoff

A cup of sour cream has forty grams of fat; more than half (twenty-six) are saturated. A cup of lowfat yogurt has only about three or four grams of fat; less than half are saturated. And yogurt has a tangy taste that works wonderfully in this classic dish.

*1 pound lean beef sirloin
    (1-inch thick)*
*1/4 cup plus 1 tablespoon
    all-purpose flour, divided*
vegetable cooking spray
*1 medium onion, vertically
    sliced*
2 cloves garlic, minced
1 cup sliced mushrooms
1 red pepper, thinly sliced
1 green pepper, thinly sliced

*1 (10^1/$_2$-ounce) can reduced-
    sodium consomme,
    undiluted*
*1 tablespoon Worcestershire
    sauce*
*1/2 teaspoon freshly ground
    pepper*
1 teaspoon olive oil
*1 (8-ounce) carton plain lowfat
    yogurt*
6 cups hot cooked noodles

Trim fat from steak; partially freeze steak for easier slicing. Cut into 2- x 1/4-inch strips, and toss with 2 tablespoons all-purpose flour, coating evenly. Set aside.

Coat a large nonstick skillet with cooking spray; add onion and garlic, and saute over medium heat until tender. Add mushrooms and green pepper; saute until tender. Remove from skillet; set aside.

Combine 1/4 cup consomme and remaining 2 tablespoons flour, mixing until smooth; stir in remaining consomme, Worcestershire sauce, and pepper. Set aside.

Wipe skillet clean with paper towels; coat with cooking spray. Add oil; place over medium-high heat until hot. Add steak strips; saute until meat just loses its pink color (about 15 minutes). Add vegetable mixture to skillet; stir in consomme mixture. Reduce heat to medium; cook, stirring constantly, until thickened and bubbly.

Remove from heat, and stir in yogurt. Cook over low heat, stirring constantly, just until hot. (Do not boil.) Serve over hot cooked noodles.

The Guilt-Free "Comfort Food" Cookbook

Per Serving: 415 Calories, 8 g Fat (3 g Saturated), 60 mg Cholesterol, 450 mg Sodium, 24 g Protein, 53 g Carbohydrates

A Great Source of: Vitamin B1 (32%), Vitamin B2 (29%), Vitamin B3 (33%), Vitamin B6 (25%), Vitamin B12 (37%), Vitamin C (62%), Iron (28%), Potassium (625 mg)

A Good Source of: Fiber (3 g), Pantothenic Acid (10%), Calcium (10%), Copper (21%), Magnesium (15%), Zinc (30%)

Pyramid Equivalent(s): 2 Breads, 1 Vegetable, 1 Meat

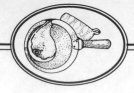

Time: 25 minutes prep
30 minutes cooking
Yield: 6 servings

Skillet Beef Puff

*T*he art of menu planning is combining high-fat and lowfat foods into meals that are low to moderate in fat. Consider this entree. Each serving has twelve grams of fat. That's a moderate amount. But if you're trying to stick to, say, sixty-five grams of fat a day, you don't want to load up the rest of dinner with high-fat side dishes, butter on the bread, high-fat salad dressings, and ice cream for dessert. So try balancing this delicious entree with a lighter side dish such as Mint Peas (p. 254) and a tossed green salad with a lowfat dressing (store-bought, or try our Creamy Pepper Ranch Dressing, p. 127). Finish with a lowfat dessert such as our Fruit Compote with Lemon Yogurt Cream (p. 284). Your entire dinner will be in the twenty to twenty-five grams of fat range and will be fit for a king. Not to mention your family.

*1 pound boneless top sirloin
   steak, trimmed
2/3 cup skim milk
1 whole egg
3 egg whites
2/3 cup plus 2 tablespoons
   all-purpose flour, divided
1/4 teaspoon salt
vegetable cooking spray*

*1 tablespoon olive oil
2 tablespoons reduced-sodium
   teriyaki sauce
2 medium red peppers, thinly
   sliced
1 small onion, thinly sliced
1 cup sliced fresh mushrooms
1 cup diced tomatoes*

    Partially freeze steak; slice diagonally across grain into 2- x ¼-inch strips. Set aside. Preheat oven to 450°.

    Combine milk, egg whites, ⅔ cup flour, and salt in a small bowl; whisk until well blended.

    Coat an ovenproof, nonstick, 9-inch skillet with cooking spray; place in oven for 2 minutes or until hot. Pour batter into skillet; bake 10 minutes. Reduce oven to 350°; bake 10 minutes or until golden. Transfer to a serving platter or individual plates.

    Meanwhile, toss steak slices with 2 tablespoons flour. Heat 1 tablespoon oil in a large, heavy skillet over medium-high heat; add steak slices, and saute until browned. Add teriyaki sauce, peppers, onion, and mush-

The Guilt-Free "Comfort Food" Cookbook

rooms; cook, stirring frequently, until vegetables are just tender. Stir in tomatoes; spoon into puffed shell. Serve immediately.

Per Serving: 265 Calories, 12 g Fat (4 g Saturated), 85 mg Cholesterol, 390 mg Sodium, 19 g Protein, 20 g Carbohydrates
A Great Source of: Vitamin C (90%)
A Good Source of: Fiber (2 g), Vitamin A (19%), Vitamin B1 (13%), Vitamin B2 (14%), Vitamin B3 (10%), Iron (18%), Potassium (500 mg)
Pyramid Equivalent(s): ½ Bread, 1½ Vegetables, 1 Meat

The Guilt-Free "Comfort Food" Cookbook

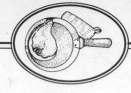

Pork Chops with Sweet-and-Sour Apples and Onions

vegetable cooking spray
4 (3-ounce) boneless pork chops
    (³/₄-inch thick), trimmed
salt (optional)
freshly ground pepper
2 teaspoons olive oil
2 medium red onions, thinly
    sliced
1 tablespoon light brown sugar

2 medium apples, cored and
    thinly sliced
2 cloves garlic, crushed
¹/₄ cup frozen apple juice
    concentrate
2 tablespoons red wine vinegar
2 tablespoons reduced-sodium
    teriyaki sauce

Coat a large nonstick skillet with cooking spray; heat over medium-high heat.

Sprinkle pork chops lightly on both sides with salt; season with pepper. Cook pork chops until browned on both sides (about 4 to 5 minutes total). Transfer pork chops to plate; cover with aluminum foil to keep warm.

Add oil to skillet. Add onions and sugar; saute until onions are tender but not brown. Add garlic and apples; saute 3 to 4 minutes. Stir in remaining ingredients; add pork chops and any accumulated juices to skillet. Cover, reduce heat, and simmer 5 to 6 minutes or until pork chops are done.

Per Serving: 250 Calories, 8 g Fat (2 g Saturated), 50 mg Cholesterol, 380 mg Sodium, 20 g Protein, 26 g Carbohydrates
A Great Source of: Vitamin B1 (59%), Vitamin B6 (29%)
A Good Source of: Fiber (2 g), Vitamin B2 (15%), Vitamin B3 (22%), Vitamin C (15%), Vitamin E (10%), Magnesium (10%), Zinc (12%), Potassium (600 mg)
Pyramid Equivalent(s): ½ Vegetable, ½ Fruit, 1 Meat

The Guilt-Free "Comfort Food" Cookbook

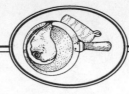

Cherry-Teriyaki Pork

*P*ork loin chops, sometimes labeled as center-cut pork chops, can be very lean. Here's a quick skillet entree that keeps them that way, while bringing out pork's natural sweetness.

4 (¹/₂-inch thick) lean boneless pork chops (3 to 4 ounces each), trimmed
freshly ground pepper
vegetable cooking spray
1 teaspoon olive oil
¹/₃ cup cherry preserves
1 clove garlic, minced

2 tablespoons reduced-sodium teriyaki sauce
1 tablespoon balsamic vinegar
¹/₂ teaspoon dried thyme
¹/₃ cup canned reduced-sodium chicken broth
2 teaspoons cornstarch

Flatten pork chops to ¼-inch thick between sheets of wax paper. Season both sides of chops with pepper. Coat a large nonstick skillet with cooking spray; add oil, and place over medium heat until hot. Add chops and cook until browned (about 4 or 5 minutes), turning once. Remove from skillet; keep warm by placing on a plate and covering with foil.

Add preserves and next four ingredients to skillet; bring to a boil over medium-low heat, stirring frequently. In a small bowl, stir chicken broth and cornstarch until smooth; stir into skillet. Cook, stirring constantly, until thickened. Return chops and any accumulated juices to skillet, turning to coat with sauce. Cook until hot.

Per Serving: 240 Calories, 7 g Fat (2 g Saturated), 60 mg Cholesterol, 410 mg Sodium, 22 g Protein, 22 g Carbohydrates
A Great Source of: Vitamin B1 (66%), Vitamin B3 (25%), Vitamin B6 (27%)
A Good Source of: Vitamin B2 (17%), Vitamin B12 (10%), Zinc (12%), Potassium (420 mg)
Pyramid Equivalent(s): 1 Meat

The Guilt-Free "Comfort Food" Cookbook

Time: 1 hour standing time
25 minutes prep
15 minutes cooking
Yield: 8 servings

Cajun-Roasted Pork
Tenderloins

*P*ork tenderloins are the leanest cuts of pork. Our marinade keeps it moist and flavorful.

1 teaspoon plus $1/4$ teaspoon coarse (or Kosher) salt
1 clove garlic
$3/4$ cup cooked fresh (or frozen, thawed) corn kernels
2 medium tomatoes, seeded and finely diced (about $1^1/2$ cups)
3 tablespoons minced fresh cilantro

1 tablespoon freshly squeezed lime juice
1 tablespoon cider vinegar
3 tablespoons plus 1 teaspoon salt-free Cajun seasoning, divided
2 (12-ounce) pork tenderloins
vegetable cooking spray

Combine ¼ teaspoon salt and garlic in a medium bowl; crush together with back of a spoon or pestle until mixture forms a paste. Stir in corn, tomatoes, cilantro, lime juice, cider vinegar, and 1 teaspoon Cajun seasoning; cover and let stand 1 to 2 hours, stirring occasionally.

Combine remaining coarse salt and 3 tablespoons Cajun seasoning; rub tenderloins all over with mixture. Cover and let stand at room temperature 30 minutes.

Preheat oven to 400°. Coat a large nonstick skillet with cooking spray; heat over high heat. Brown tenderloins well on all sides (about 5 to 7 minutes total). Transfer to a rack in a roasting pan; roast at 400° for 12 to 15 minutes or until internal temperature reaches 160°.

Let stand 5 minutes before carving into thin slices. Serve with corn mixture.

Per Serving: 160 Calories, 4 g Fat (2 g Saturated), 65 mg Cholesterol, 385 mg Sodium, 25 g Protein, 5 g Carbohydrates
A Great Source of: Vitamin B1 (57%)
A Good Source of: Vitamin B2 (21%), Vitamin B3 (22%), Vitamin B6 (20%), Vitamin C (17%), Zinc (16%), Potassium (490 mg)
Pyramid Equivalent(s): ½ Vegetable, 1 Meat

The Guilt-Free "Comfort Food" Cookbook

Time: 8 hours marinating
30 minutes prep and cooking
Yield: 4 servings

Grilled Lamb Chops Marinated in Orange Juice, Garlic, and Rosemary

A long marinade gives even the leanest grilled or broiled lamb chops a moist and robust flavor.

*4 (5-ounce) lean lamb chops
 (1 1/2 inches thick)*
*2 cloves garlic, peeled and
 crushed*
1/2 teaspoon coarse salt
*1/2 teaspoon freshly ground
 pepper*

*1 1/2 teaspoons dried rosemary
 (or 2 tablespoons minced
 fresh rosemary)*
1/2 teaspoon curry powder
*1/2 cup frozen orange juice
 concentrate, thawed*
1 tablespoon balsamic vinegar
vegetable cooking spray

Trim fat from chops; place in a heavy-duty zip-top plastic bag. Combine garlic, salt, pepper, and rosemary in a mortar; crush with pestle, and put into a small bowl. (If you don't have a mortar and pestle, use a small food processor or mash with a wooden spoon.) Mix in orange juice and vinegar; pour over chops. Seal bag, and squeeze until chops are coated. Refrigerate 8 hours or overnight, turning bag occasionally.

Coat grill rack, or rack in a broiler pan, with cooking spray; place chops on rack, and grill over medium-hot coals or broil 6 inches from heat source 6 to 9 minutes on each side or to desired degree of doneness, basting chops frequently with marinade.

Per Serving: 300 Calories, 10 g Fat (4 g Saturated), 110 mg Cholesterol, 365 mg Sodium, 35 g Protein, 15 g Carbohydrates
A Great Source of: Vitamin B3 (40%), Vitamin B12 (48%), Zinc (32%), Potassium (690 mg)
A Good Source of: Vitamin B1 (15%), Vitamin B2 (20%), Vitamin B6 (13%), Pantothenic Acid (10%), Vitamin C (20%), Copper (12%), Iron (15%), Magnesium (12%)
Pyramid Equivalent(s): 1 Meat

The Guilt-Free "Comfort Food" Cookbook

Time: 25 minutes prep
30 minutes cooking
Yield: 4 servings

Veal Chops Stuffed with Apples, Walnuts, and Two Wheats

*C*ouscous is a tiny refined pasta; wheat berries are unrefined wheat that include the nutritious wheat bran and germ. Together they make a delicious combination; the former smooth and light, the latter chewy, moist, and nutty. We've also tried this dish with just couscous, and it's delicious—use two and a half cups cooked couscous instead of one and a half.

This is a high-protein meal, moderate to high in fat. That's what happens when you eat a six-ounce cut of veal—enough protein for an entire day, plus plenty of vitamins and minerals, fat, and calories.

Moderation doesn't mean you need to balance each meal for every nutrient, though; it's something you achieve over a day, or a few days. Nor does eating healthfully mean you have to give up a big juicy chop—once in a while. If you have a piece of veal, steak, or even chicken, for one meal, you can have low-protein meals in other meals during the day. If you have a veal chop on Tuesday, have a vegetable plate the next night. Nutritional balance doesn't have to happen over a single dish or single meal, but over several days.

$1^1/_2$ cups cooked couscous,
    cooked without salt or fat
1 cup cooked wheat berries,
    cooked without salt or fat
1 cup diced apple
$1/_2$ cup sliced green onion
$1/_4$ cup finely chopped walnuts
$1/_4$ teaspoon salt
$1/_2$ teaspoon freshly ground
    pepper

vegetable cooking spray
4 (6-ounce) lean veal loin chops
    ($3/_4$-inch thick), trimmed of
    fat
1 teaspoon dried thyme
$1/_2$ teaspoon dry mustard
1 teaspoon canola oil
$1/_4$ cup apple juice
2 ounces crumbled blue cheese

The Guilt-Free "Comfort Food" Cookbook

Combine couscous, wheat berries, apple, green onion, walnuts, and salt in a large bowl; spoon into a 9-inch square baking pan coated with cooking spray. Set aside.

Preheat oven to 350°. Rub trimmed chops all over with thyme and dry mustard. Coat a large nonstick skillet with cooking spray; add oil. Place over medium-high heat until hot. Add chops and cook until browned on each side (about 5 minutes total). Arrange chops on top of couscous mixture; drizzle with apple juice. Cover with aluminum foil, and bake for 30 minutes or until chops are done.

Transfer chops to serving plates. Stir blue cheese into hot couscous mixture; spoon on chops.

Per Serving: 620 Calories, 19 g Fat (6 g Saturated), 190 mg Cholesterol, 470 mg Sodium, 58 g Protein, 30 g Carbohydrates

A Great Source of: Fiber (4 g), Vitamin B2 (40%), Vitamin B3 (115%), Vitamin B6 (50%), Vitamin B12 (46%), Pantothenic Acid (28%), Zinc (45%), Potassium (740 mg)

A Good Source of: Vitamin B1 (16%), Folic Acid (15%), Vitamin C (10%), Vitamin E (16%), Calcium (12%), Copper (15%), Iron (17%), Magnesium (23%)

Pyramid Equivalent(s): 1¼ Breads, 2 Meats

The Guilt-Free "Comfort Food" Cookbook

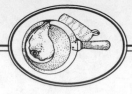

Time: 30 minutes prep and cooking
Yield: 6 servings

Peppered Lamb Stir-Fry

*I*n this quick, succulent stir-fry with red peppers, asparagus, and shallots, a pound of lamb easily serves six people. That's the kind of balance that makes comfort food guilt free. Lamb, like all red meats, gives our bodies good amounts of iron, zinc, and other minerals.

To save time, ask your butcher to trim the lamb of fat and slice thinly. That makes this quick dinner even quicker.

1 pound lean boneless leg (or shoulder) of lamb, trimmed of fat
1/2 teaspoon coarsely ground pepper
2/3 cup reduced-sodium beef broth
1 tablespoon freshly squeezed lemon juice
1 tablespoon Worcestershire sauce

2 1/2 teaspoons cornstarch
vegetable cooking spray
1 teaspoon olive oil
1/3 cup minced shallots
2 large yellow or red peppers, cored, seeded, and thinly sliced
1 pound asparagus, trimmed and cut into 1-inch lengths
3 cups cooked rice

Cut trimmed lamb into thin strips and toss with pepper. Set aside.

Combine broth, lemon juice, Worcestershire sauce, and cornstarch, stirring until smooth. Set aside.

Coat a wok or large nonstick skillet with cooking spray; add a teaspoon of olive oil. Place over medium-high heat until hot. Add lamb, and stir-fry 5 minutes. Remove from wok. Wipe drippings from wok or skillet using a paper towel.

Coat wok with cooking spray; place over medium-high heat until hot. Add shallots; stir-fry 1 minute. Add peppers and asparagus; stir-fry until crisp and tender. Return lamb and reserved broth mixture to wok; cook, stirring constantly, until mixture is thickened and hot. Serve over cooked rice.

The Guilt-Free "Comfort Food" Cookbook

Per Serving: 290 Calories, 6 g Fat (2 g Saturated), 50 mg Cholesterol, 85 mg Sodium, 22 g Protein, 37 g Carbohydrates

A Great Source of: Vitamin B3 (33%), Vitamin B12 (29%), Folic Acid (31%), Vitamin C (100%), Zinc (28%)

A Good Source of: Fiber (3 g), Vitamin A (19%), Vitamin B1 (24%), Vitamin B2 (18%), Vitamin B6 (16%), Pantothenic Acid (10%), Vitamin E (19%), Copper (17%), Iron (21%), Magnesium (12%), Potassium (560 mg)

Pyramid Equivalent(s): 1 Vegetable, 1 Meat

Note: Served over a half-cup of rice: 390 Calories; additional Pyramid Equivalent of 1 Bread.

The Guilt-Free "Comfort Food" Cookbook

CHICKEN AND TURKEY

*B*irds are rising: Sales of chicken and turkey have been steadily going up for a decade or more. One reason is cost. Another is health. Chicken and turkey are an excellent source of lowfat, high-quality protein. Half a roasted chicken breast, without the skin, which is about three and a half ounces, has only about three grams of fat. Dark chicken meat, without the skin, has a little more fat, about ten grams for a roasted three-and-a-half-ounce serving, but also more iron and other minerals.

Most of the fat in poultry is inside and outside. That is, inside the cavity and in the skin. Eat the same three-and-a-half-ounce half a chicken breast with the skin, and you'll consume not three but eight grams of fat, not counting the fat that's added in cooking. To cut fat, remove the skin either before or after cooking. Inside the cavity of a whole bird, chicken or turkey, there is another treasure trove of fat. Before cooking the bird, remove the fat with your fingers or a sharp paring knife.

Without fat, though, poultry can dry out quickly. To help, each recipe in this chapter employs a strategy for keeping chicken or turkey meat moist and succulent. A good marinade can work wonders. Country Oven-Fried Chicken (p. 163), Teriyaki-Roasted Chicken with Pine-

The Guilt-Free "Comfort Food" Cookbook

apple Salsa (p. 165), Grilled Chili-Lime Chicken with Tomato Chutney (p. 171), Herbed Mustard Chicken-and-Vegetable Skewers (p. 175), and Grilled Sweet-and-Tangy Cornish Hens (p. 180) each rely on a long marinade to infuse skinless chicken with flavor and moistness. If you can remember to marinate the bird the night before, you'll be rewarded at next night's dinner.

Another approach is to cook the poultry meat with soup stock, potatoes, vegetables, and other ingredients. That's what we do in our low-fat version of the old-fashioned American classic Cornbread Chicken Potpie (p. 176), Turkey Hash (p. 184), and Curried Chicken, Sweet Potatoes, and Rice (p. 178). Cooking cubed chicken breasts with sweet potatoes, red pepper, raisins, rice, and peanuts not only creates a unique flavor, but also creates a nicely balanced dish. Each serving provides 1 Bread, 1 Vegetable, and 1 Meat. Add a green vegetable or salad and a piece of bread and you've got a complete meal.

The Guilt-Free "Comfort Food" Cookbook

Time: 15 minutes prep
Overnight marinating
30 minutes cooking
Yield: 6 servings

Country Oven-Fried Chicken

*M*ost of the fat in chicken is in the skin. But when you take the skin off, the chicken can dry out quickly. That's why we let these skinned chicken breasts "marinate" overnight in nonfat buttermilk, then dredge them in lowfat crackers. The result is an oven-fried chicken that's crispy on the outside and temptingly moist on the inside.

1 cup nonfat buttermilk
1/2 teaspoon salt
6 (6-ounce) skinned chicken breast halves
1/2 cup finely crushed reduced-fat buttery crackers (such as Ritz)

1/4 cup self-rising cornmeal
2 tablespoons self-rising flour
1/4 cup minced fresh cilantro or parsley
1 teaspoon chili powder
1/2 teaspoon ground oregano
1/2 teaspoon red pepper

Combine buttermilk and salt in a heavy-duty, zip-top plastic bag; add chicken and seal bag. Refrigerate overnight, turning bag occasionally.

Preheat oven to 450°. Combine remaining ingredients except cooking spray in a food processor fitted with knife blade; process until blended. Pour into a shallow dish. Remove chicken from buttermilk mixture, allowing excess buttermilk to drip off; dredge in cracker mixture.

Coat a 15- x 10- x 1-inch jelly-roll pan with cooking spray; place chicken, bone sides down, in jelly-roll pan. Coat chicken with cooking spray; bake for 20 minutes. Coat again with cooking spray; bake 10 to 15 additional minutes or until juices run clear when chicken is pierced with a skewer.

Per Serving: 260 Calories, 4 g Fat (1 g Saturated), 100 mg Cholesterol, 490 mg Sodium, 42 g Protein, 12 g Carbohydrates
A Great Source of: Vitamin B3 (100%), Vitamin B6 (49%)
A Good Source of: Vitamin B1 (14%), Vitamin B2 (16%), Vitamin B12 (12%), Pantothenic Acid (15%), Calcium (11%), Iron (11%), Magnesium (15%), Zinc (11%), Potassium (530 mg)
Pyramid Equivalent(s): ½ Bread, 1½ Meats

The Guilt-Free "Comfort Food" Cookbook

Time: 45 minutes
Yield: 8 servings

Molasses-Barbecued Chicken

*M*olasses gives this dish a rich, old-time taste. It may also benefit our health: It's rich in potassium, which helps regulate blood pressure and protects against stroke. A tablespoon of molasses has almost three hundred milligrams of potassium, about 10 percent of what we need each day; blackstrap molasses has almost five hundred milligrams. White sugar, by contrast, has no potassium.

2 teaspoons olive oil
3/4 cup finely chopped onion
1/2 teaspoon garlic powder
1/4 to 1/2 teaspoon red pepper
1/2 cup molasses
1/3 cup cider vinegar
1/4 cup Dijon mustard

2 tablespoons lemon juice
1 tablespoon reduced-sodium soy sauce
8 (6-ounce) skinned chicken breast halves
salt and pepper

Light the barbecue coals. Heat oil in a heavy medium saucepan over medium heat. Add onion, garlic powder, and red pepper; saute 3 minutes. Add molasses, vinegar, mustard, lemon juice, and soy sauce; bring to a boil. Reduce heat, and simmer uncovered 10 to 15 minutes or until thickened, stirring occasionally. Cool.

Sprinkle chicken lightly with salt and pepper. Grill over medium-hot coals (350° to 400°) about 5 to 8 minutes on each side, basting often with some of the sauce, until chicken is glazed and no longer pink. Serve with remaining sauce.

Per Serving: 270 Calories, 4 g Fat (1 g Saturated), 100 mg Cholesterol, 360 mg Sodium, 40 g Protein, 17 g Carbohydrates

A Great Source of: Vitamin B3 (96%), Vitamin B6 (57%), Magnesium (26%), Potassium (785 mg)

Pyramid Equivalent(s): 1½ Meats

The Guilt-Free "Comfort Food" Cookbook

Time: 15 minutes prep
Overnight marinating
40 minutes cooking
Yield: 4 servings

Teriyaki-Roasted Chicken
with Pineapple Salsa

1 (15^1/$_2$-ounce) can
   unsweetened pineapple
   tidbits, undrained
^{1}/$_2$ cup reduced-sodium teriyaki
   sauce
^{1}/$_4$ cup white wine vinegar
^{1}/$_4$ cup firmly packed light
   brown sugar
4 cloves garlic, minced

4 (6-ounce) skinned chicken
   breast halves
vegetable cooking spray
3 kiwis, peeled and diced
^{1}/$_3$ cup minced green onion
^{1}/$_4$ cup minced fresh cilantro
2 tablespoons grated fresh
   ginger
^{1}/$_4$ teaspoon salt

Drain pineapple, reserving tidbits and juice separately. Combine juice, teriyaki sauce, vinegar, and brown sugar in a large, heavy-duty, zip-top plastic bag. Add chicken, and seal bag. Refrigerate overnight, turning bag occasionally.

Preheat oven to 450°. Coat rack of a broiler pan with cooking spray; place chicken on rack, bone sides down. Bake for 40 to 45 minutes or until chicken is no longer pink.

Meanwhile, combine reserved pineapple tidbits, kiwis, green onions, cilantro, ginger, and salt; mix well. Serve with chicken.

Per Serving: 350 Calories, 3 g Fat (1 g Saturated), 99 mg Cholesterol, 750 mg Sodium, 43 g Protein, 40 g Carbohydrates

A *Great Source of:* Vitamin B3 (100%), Vitamin B6 (55%), Vitamin C (115%), Potassium (850 mg)

A *Good Source of:* Fiber (2 g), Vitamin B1 (17%), Vitamin B2 (13%), Vitamin B12 (11%), Pantothenic Acid (17%), Vitamin E (12%), Copper (12%), Iron (12%), Magnesium (22%), Zinc (11%)

Pyramid Equivalent(s): 2 Fruits, 1½ Meats

The Guilt-Free "Comfort Food" Cookbook

Time: 10 minutes prep
1 hour to bake garlic
1$^1/_2$ hours cooking
Yield: 8 servings

Braised Chicken-Thigh Cacciatore

*T*his dish takes a little time, but the slow cooking lets the flavors of baked garlic, fennel, and tomatoes infuse the chicken with an Old World beauty. With crusty Italian bread, it's a one-dish dinner.

1 large bulb garlic
vegetable cooking spray
2 teaspoons olive oil
$^1/_4$ cup all-purpose flour
8 chicken thighs (about 1$^2/_3$ pounds), boned and skinned
2 cups sliced fresh mushrooms
1$^1/_2$ cups diced red pepper
1 cup chopped onion
1 cup thinly sliced fennel bulb

1 cup chicken broth
2 (14.5-ounce) cans unsalted whole tomatoes, drained
$^1/_4$ cup minced fresh basil or 1 tablespoon dried basil
1 bay leaf
$^1/_4$ teaspoon salt
$^1/_2$ teaspoon freshly ground pepper

Preheat oven to 400°. Remove papery skin and as much outer husk of garlic as possible without separating cloves. Wrap in heavy duty aluminum foil, and bake for 30 minutes. Unwrap foil, and slightly separate cloves of garlic so they will cook evenly; rewrap and bake 15 additional minutes or until garlic is very soft. Let cool, and peel garlic cloves; set aside. Reduce oven temperature to 325°.

Coat an ovenproof Dutch oven with cooking spray; add oil and heat over medium heat. Dredge chicken in flour; add to Dutch oven, and cook until well browned on all sides. Remove from Dutch oven, and set aside. Add mushrooms, red pepper, onion, and fennel to Dutch oven, and saute 5 minutes. Stir in chicken broth, tomatoes, basil, bay leaf, salt, and pepper; bring to a boil. Return chicken thighs to Dutch oven, and add garlic cloves. Cover tightly and bake for 1 to 1¼ hours or until chicken is very tender.

Serve over cooked white beans or rice.

The Guilt-Free "Comfort Food" Cookbook

Per Serving: 195 Calories, 6 g Fat (1 g Saturated), 78 mg Cholesterol, 350 mg Sodium, 23 g Protein, 14 g Carbohydrates

A Great Source of: Vitamin B3 (43%), Vitamin B6 (28%), Vitamin C (93%), Potassium (710 mg)

A Good Source of: Fiber (3 g), Vitamin A (20%), Vitamin B1 (13%), Vitamin B2 (20%), Pantothenic Acid (18%), Copper (18%), Iron (15%), Magnesium (12%), Zinc (16%)

Pyramid Equivalent(s): 2⅓ Vegetables, 1 Meat

The Guilt-Free "Comfort Food" Cookbook

Time: 15 minutes prep
1 hour roasting
15 minutes to freeze, reheat
drippings
Yield: 6 servings

Garlic Roast Chicken with French Herbs

*S*avvy eaters know that removing the skin from chicken cuts most of the fat and calories. But you don't have to remove the skin before roasting. Let it stay on, keeping the bird moist and succulent. Then take it off just before serving. Food scientists have actually studied this: The fat doesn't migrate into the bird, but stays in the skin. Let the skin cool, and serve some of it to your dog. It's good for the canine coat.

5 cloves garlic, finely minced
1 tablespoon minced fresh
  tarragon
1 tablespoon minced fresh
  marjoram or thyme
2 teaspoons minced fresh
  rosemary

$1/_2$ teaspoon salt
1 teaspoon freshly ground
  pepper
1 ($3^1/_2$ to 4 pounds) roasting
  chicken, trimmed
1 lemon, halved

Preheat oven to 375°. Combine garlic, tarragon, marjoram, rosemary, and salt in a bowl; mash together with a pestle, or process in a mini-food processor until finely ground.

Rinse chicken and pat dry, inside cavity and outside, with paper towels. Lift skin at tip of breast and carefully slide fingers between flesh and skin on both sides of the breast bone, loosening skin to form a pocket. Smooth herb mixture generously into pocket, spreading evenly over breast. Stuff any remaining herb mixture in cavity. Squeeze one lemon half over skin, and place both lemon halves inside chicken cavity. Tuck wings under body, and tie legs together.

Place chicken, breast side up, on a rack in a roasting pan; roast for 1 to 1¼ hours or until juices run clear when thigh is pierced and a meat thermometer inserted in the thickest part of the breast registers 180°. Transfer to a serving platter.

Pour pan drippings into a small bowl; place in freezer to solidify fat. Skim fat; reheat drippings, if desired. Before carving, remove skin; serve chicken hot or at room temperature.

The Guilt-Free "Comfort Food" Cookbook

Per Serving: 325 Calories, 8 g Fat (2 g Saturated), 185 mg Cholesterol, 385 mg Sodium, 57 g Protein, 3 g Carbohydrates

A Great Source of: Vitamin B3 (110%), Vitamin B6 (59%), Pantothenic Acid (28%), Zinc (28%), Potassium (655 mg)

A Good Source of: Vitamin B1 (14%), Vitamin B2 (23%), Vitamin B12 (16%), Vitamin C (20%), Iron (19%), Magnesium (18%)

Pyramid Equivalent(s): 2 Meats

The Guilt-Free "Comfort Food" Cookbook

Time: 15 minutes prep
20 minutes cooking
Yield: 4 servings

Honey-Mustard Chicken with Cashews

*H*ere's a quick one. For dinner, serve it with bread or over rice, with a green vegetable, such as Green Beans with Caramelized Onion and Tomato Relish (p. 257), and salad.

*4 (4-ounce) skinned and boned
   chicken breast halves
3 tablespoons all-purpose flour
1/2 teaspoon pepper
vegetable cooking spray
1/3 cup reduced-sodium chicken
   broth*

*2 tablespoons honey
2 tablespoons spicy brown
   mustard
1/4 cup chopped dry-roasted
   cashews*

Pound chicken breast halves to even thickness; cut into 2- x 1-inch strips. Toss with flour and pepper.

Coat a medium nonstick skillet with cooking spray; heat over medium-high heat. Add chicken, and saute until browned. Reduce heat to medium, and add chicken broth, honey, and mustard. Simmer, uncovered, 10 minutes. Stir in cashews; serve over rice, if desired.

Per Serving: 235 Calories, 6 g Fat (1 g Saturated), 65 mg Cholesterol, 225 mg Sodium, 29 g Protein, 17 g Carbohydrates
A Great Source of: Vitamin B3 (66%), Vitamin B6 (33%)
A Good Source of: Vitamin B1 (10%), Pantothenic Acid (11%), Copper (14%), Iron (10%), Magnesium (15%), Zinc (10%), Potassium (365 mg)
Pyramid Equivalent(s): 1 Meat

The Guilt-Free "Comfort Food" Cookbook

Time: 30 minutes to make chutney
2 hours to chill and marinate
chicken
15 to 20 minutes to barbecue
Yield: 4 servings

Grilled Chili-Lime Chicken
with Tomato Chutney

*L*ime, chili powder, and cumin make for a moist barbecue. If it's raining or cold, you can broil these in the oven four inches from the heat source.

vegetable cooking spray
1 teaspoon olive oil
1 cup chopped onion
2 tablespoons grated fresh ginger
2 cloves garlic, crushed
1 (14¹/₂-ounce) can no-salt-added stewed tomatoes, undrained
¹/₄ cup firmly packed brown sugar

3 tablespoons white wine vinegar
3 tablespoons currants or golden raisins
1¹/₂ tablespoons lime juice
1 tablespoon chili powder
1 teaspoon ground cumin
¹/₄ teaspoon salt
4 (4-ounce) skinned and boned chicken breast halves

Coat a large, heavy saucepan with cooking spray; add oil and place over medium-high heat until hot. Add onion, ginger, and garlic, and saute until onion is tender. Add tomatoes, sugar, vinegar, and raisins; bring to a boil, stirring constantly until sugar melts. Reduce heat, and simmer until mixture is reduced to 2 cups. Let cool to room temperature.

Combine lime juice, chili powder, cumin, and salt; rub on chicken breast. Place on a plate; cover and refrigerate 2 hours.

Grill chicken over medium-hot coals (350° to 400°) 7 to 8 minutes or until well browned; turn and grill an additional 6 to 10 minutes or until tender. Serve with tomato chutney.

Per Serving: 250 Calories, 3 g Fat (1 g Saturated), 66 mg Cholesterol, 450 mg Sodium, 28 g Protein, 28 g Carbohydrates

A Great Source of: Vitamin B3 (69%), Vitamin B6 (37%), Vitamin C (33%), Potassium (770 mg)

A Good Source of: Fiber (3 g), Vitamin A (13%), Vitamin B1 (11%), Vitamin B2 (10%), Pantothenic Acid (11%), Vitamin E (10%), Copper (13%), Iron (15%), Magnesium (16%)

Pyramid Equivalent(s): 1 Vegetable, 1 Meat

The Guilt-Free "Comfort Food" Cookbook

Time: 10 minutes prep
25 minutes to precook rice,
chicken, eggs
45 minutes cooking
Yield: 6 servings

Creamy Broccoli, Chicken, and Rice Casserole

ne nice way to get your vegetables is to bake them into a cheesy, low-fat casserole. Add a whole wheat roll, and fruit for dessert, and you'll have a meal that completes the Pyramid.

3 cups fresh broccoli flowerets
3 cups cooked long-grain rice
(cooked without salt or fat)
2 cups diced cooked chicken
1/2 cup sliced green onion
2 canned roasted red peppers,
rinsed, drained, and
chopped
4 hard-boiled egg whites,
chopped

1 cup nonfat ricotta cheese
1 cup evaporated skimmed
milk, divided
2 tablespoons all-purpose flour
1 clove garlic, chopped
1/2 teaspoon salt
1/2 teaspoon freshly ground
pepper
1 teaspoon lemon juice
1/4 cup grated Parmesan cheese

Preheat oven to 375°. Cook broccoli, covered, in a small amount of boiling water 10 minutes or until tender. Drain. Combine broccoli, rice, chicken, green onion, red peppers, and egg whites in a large bowl; set aside.

Process ricotta cheese, 1/4 cup evaporated skimmed milk, flour, garlic, salt, pepper, and lemon juice in a food processor or blender container until smooth. With machine running, pour remaining 3/4 cup evaporated skimmed milk through food chute. Transfer to a small saucepan; bring to a boil over medium heat, stirring constantly. Remove from heat; pour over broccoli mixture, and stir well.

Spoon into a shallow 2-quart baking dish coated with cooking spray. Sprinkle with Parmesan. Bake for 25 to 30 minutes or until hot.

The Guilt-Free "Comfort Food" Cookbook

Per Serving: 410 Calories, 10 g Fat (4 g Saturated), 75 mg Cholesterol, 460 mg Sodium, 36 g Protein, 43 g Carbohydrates

A Great Source of: Vitamin A (34%), Vitamin B2 (31%), Vitamin B3 (33%), Vitamin C (142%), Calcium (35%)

A Good Source of: Fiber (3 g), Vitamin B1 (20%), Vitamin B6 (23%), Folic Acid (15%), Pantothenic Acid (17%), Iron (18%), Magnesium (16%), Zinc (22%), Potassium (600 mg)

Pyramid Equivalent(s): 1 Bread, 1 Vegetable, 1 Meat, 1 Dairy

The Guilt-Free "Comfort Food" Cookbook

Time: 15 minutes prep (to make
dumplings)
35 minutes cooking
Yield: 8 servings

Chicken and Dumplings

*W*hen the weather cools, try this homey, lowfat dish. Southwest spices
make it especially warm.

vegetable cooking spray
1 pound skinned and boned
  chicken breast halves, cut
  into 1-inch pieces
1 cup chopped onion
1 (14½-ounce) can unsalted
  stewed tomatoes, undrained
1 cup fresh corn or frozen corn,
  thawed and drained
½ cup unsalted tomato sauce
1½ cups reduced-sodium
  chicken broth

1 tablespoon chili powder
1 teaspoon ground cumin
¼ teaspoon salt
¼ teaspoon red pepper
2 cups self-rising flour
½ teaspoon baking soda
½ cup (2 ounces) finely
  shredded reduced-fat
  Cheddar cheese
2 tablespoons stick margarine
  (or butter), softened
¾ cup nonfat buttermilk

Coat a Dutch oven or large deep skillet with cooking spray; place over
medium heat until hot. Add chicken and onion; saute until meat loses its
pink color. Stir in tomatoes, corn, tomato sauce, chicken broth, chili powder, cumin, salt, and red pepper; bring to a boil. Cover, reduce heat, and
simmer 10 minutes. Remove from heat.

Combine flour and soda; add cheese and toss. Cut in margarine with a
pastry blender until mixture is crumbly. Add buttermilk, stirring with a
fork until dry ingredients are moistened. Turn dough out onto a floured
surface, and knead lightly 4 or 5 times. Pat dough to ¼-inch thickness.
Bring chili mixture to a boil; cut off 1½-inch pieces and drop into boiling
broth. Reduce heat to medium-low; cover and cook 10 minutes or until
dumplings are cooked.

Per Serving: 280 Calories, 6 g Fat (3 g Saturated), 47 mg Cholesterol, 800 mg Sodium, 21 g Protein, 35 g Carbohydrates
A Great Source of: Vitamin B3 (46%)
A Good Source of: Fiber (3 g), Vitamin A (12%), Vitamin B1 (23%), Vitamin B2
  (16%), Vitamin B6 (20%), Vitamin C (21%), Calcium (23%), Iron (16%), Magnesium (11%), Potassium (510 mg)
Pyramid Equivalent(s): 1 Vegetable, 1 Meat

The Guilt-Free "Comfort Food" Cookbook

Time: 2 to 4 hours to chill,
marinate chicken
30 minutes to heat coals
10 minutes to make yogurt sauce
15 minutes to barbecue
Yield: 6 servings

Herbed Mustard
Chicken-and-Vegetable
Skewers

*W*hen it's barbecue season, marinate these bird breasts, and stick them in the refrigerator; you can also make the yogurt mixture in advance. Before your friends come over, thread the veggies onto skewers with the chicken, and put them back in the fridge. When your friends arrive, start the coals, and serve some cool drinks. Soon the coals will be ready....

*4 skinned and boned chicken
    breast halves, cut into
    1-inch strips
1/4 cup plus 2 tablespoons
    peppercorn-style Dijon
    mustard, divided
2 tablespoons olive oil, divided*

*1 teaspoon dried marjoram,
    divided
1 1/2 cups sliced yellow squash
12 medium mushrooms
1 1/4 cups sliced green onion
1/2 cup packed fresh basil leaves
1/2 cup 1% lowfat cottage cheese
1/2 cup plain nonfat yogurt*

Toss chicken strips with 2 tablespoons mustard, 1 tablespoon olive oil, and ½ teaspoon marjoram until well coated. Cover and refrigerate 2 to 4 hours.

Heat remaining 1 tablespoon oil in a small skillet; add green onion and saute until tender. Combine green onion, remaining mustard, olive oil, marjoram, basil, and cottage cheese in an electric blender; cover and process until smooth. Add yogurt, and blend. Set aside.

Thread chicken, squash, and mushrooms on skewers; grill over medium-hot coals (350° to 400°) 15 to 20 minutes or until cooked, turning frequently. Serve with yogurt mixture.

Per Serving: 190 Calories, 7 g Fat (1 g Saturated), 47 mg Cholesterol, 345 mg Sodium, 24 g Protein, 8 g Carbohydrates
A Great Source of: Vitamin B3 (53%), Vitamin B6 (28%)
A Good Source of: Fiber (2 g), Vitamin B2 (20%), Folic Acid (10%), Pantothenic Acid (17%), Vitamin C (18%), Vitamin E (12%), Calcium (10%), Copper (17%), Iron (11%), Magnesium (13%), Zinc (10%), Potassium (560 mg)
Pyramid Equivalent(s): 1⅔ Vegetables, 1 Meat

The Guilt-Free "Comfort Food" Cookbook

Time: 15 minutes prep
45 minutes to boil chicken
30 minutes to cool
1 hour cooking
Yield: 6 servings

Cornbread Chicken Potpie

*C*hicken potpie is a favorite at our house, and probably yours. Here's a version with a *lot* less fat. We cut the fat by skinning the chicken, letting the broth cool enough so the fat can be skimmed, using cooking spray instead of butter to saute, substituting lowfat cream of mushroom soup for the full-fat variety, and using tangy nonfat buttermilk instead of milk or cream. Instead of fat, we thicken the gravy with flour and broth. Instead of lard- or butter-based pastry, we top the potpie with down-home cornbread. Modest changes, but they add up to great flavor.

1 (3-pound) broiler-fryer, skinned
vegetable cooking spray
1 cup chopped onion
1^1/$_2$ cups cut fresh or frozen, thawed green beans (1-inch pieces)
1 cup sliced carrots
1 cup diced potatoes
^{3}/$_4$ cup fresh corn or frozen corn, thawed
^{3}/$_4$ cup plus 1 tablespoon all-purpose flour, divided

1 (10^3/$_4$-ounce) can reduced-sodium-and-fat cream of mushroom soup
1 (2-ounce) jar diced pimento, drained
1 cup lowfat baking mix (Pioneer or Bisquik)
^{1}/$_2$ cup self-rising cornmeal
^{1}/$_2$ cup nonfat buttermilk
^{1}/$_4$ cup egg substitute or 1 large egg, beaten

Cook chicken in boiling water to cover 45 minutes or until chicken is tender. Let cool to room temperature; remove chicken from broth. Skim fat from broth; measure out and reserve 1 cup broth. Reserve remaining broth for other uses, if desired. Bone and chop chicken; set aside.

Preheat oven to 400°. Coat a large nonstick skillet with cooking spray; place over medium heat until hot. Add onion, and saute until tender. Add ½ cup reserved broth, beans, carrots, potatoes, and corn; bring to a boil. Cover, reduce heat, and simmer 10 minutes or until vegetables are tender. In a small bowl, mix remaining ½ cup reserved broth and 1 tablespoon flour until smooth; stir into skillet. Stir in soup; cook over medium heat until bubbly, stirring constantly. Stir in chicken and pimento; spoon into an

The Guilt-Free "Comfort Food" Cookbook

11- x 7- x 2-inch baking dish coated with cooking spray. Cover with aluminum foil.

Combine baking mix and cornmeal in a bowl; make a well in center of mixture. Combine buttermilk and egg substitute; add to dry ingredients, stirring just until dry ingredients are moistened.

Bake casserole, covered, for 15 minutes; uncover and spoon cornmeal mixture evenly on top of casserole. Bake, uncovered, 15 minutes or until golden.

Per Serving: 585 Calories, 18 g Fat (4 g Saturated), 120 mg Cholesterol, 450 mg Sodium, 63 g Protein, 39 g Carbohydrates

A Great Source of: Vitamin A (59%), Vitamin B1 (34%), Vitamin B2 (36%), Vitamin B3 (87%), Vitamin B6 (43%), Vitamin C (28%), Potassium (745 mg)

A Good Source of: Fiber (4 g), Folic Acid (10%), Pantothenic Acid (19%), Vitamin E (13%), Calcium (13%), Copper (16%), Iron (24%), Magnesium (18%), Zinc (15%)

Pyramid Equivalent(s): 1 Vegetable, 1½ Meats

The Guilt-Free "Comfort Food" Cookbook

Time: 8 minutes prep
35 minutes cooking
Yield: 6 servings

Curried Chicken, Sweet Potatoes, and Rice

vegetable cooking spray
2 teaspoons olive oil
1 pound skinned and boned
    chicken breast halves, cut
    into cubes
3 cups reduced-sodium chicken
    broth
1 1/2 cups peeled and diced
    sweet potato
1 cup chopped red pepper
1/4 cup golden raisins

2 teaspoons curry powder
1/4 teaspoon freshly ground
    pepper
1 cup white basmati or other
    long-grain rice, uncooked
1/4 cup plus 2 tablespoons
    chopped dry roasted
    peanuts
1/4 cup plus 2 tablespoons
    minced green onions

Coat a Dutch oven with cooking spray; add oil, and place over medium-high heat until hot. Add chicken and saute until lightly browned. Stir in broth, sweet potato, red pepper, raisins, curry powder, and ground pepper; bring to a boil. Add rice; cover, reduce heat, and simmer 20 to 25 minutes or until liquid is absorbed. Serve in bowls; sprinkle each serving with 1 tablespoon peanuts and 1 tablespoon green onion.

Per Serving: 350 Calories, 8 g Fat (2 g Saturated), 44 mg Cholesterol, 375 mg Sodium, 24 g Protein, 45 g Carbohydrates

A Great Source of: Vitamin A (55%), Vitamin B3 (58%), Vitamin B6 (33%), Vitamin C (63%)

A Good Source of: Fiber (3 g), Vitamin B1 (19%), Pantothenic Acid (13%), Vitamin E (14%), Copper (13%), Iron (15%), Magnesium (15%), Zinc (10%), Potassium (445 mg)

Pyramid Equivalent(s): 1 Bread, 1 Vegetable, 1 Meat

The Guilt-Free "Comfort Food" Cookbook

Time: 10 minutes prep
25 minutes to cook
Yield: 4 servings

Quick Jambalaya Pasta

*1/2 pound skinned and boned
    chicken breast halves, cut
    into 1-inch pieces*
*2 1/2 teaspoons salt-free Creole
    seasoning, divided*
vegetable cooking spray
*4 ounces diced smoked turkey
    sausage*
1 medium onion, diced
2 cloves garlic, minced
1 medium green pepper, diced

1/2 cup thinly sliced celery
2 cups frozen cut okra, thawed
*1 (14 1/2-ounce) can Cajun-style
    stewed tomatoes, undrained*
1/2 cup unsalted tomato sauce
1 teaspoon hot sauce
*1 (9-ounce) package
    refrigerated
    cholesterol-free spaghetti
    (not egg noodles), cooked
    without salt or fat*

Toss chicken with 1 teaspoon Creole seasoning. Coat a large nonstick skillet with cooking spray; heat over medium-high heat. Add chicken, sausage, onion, garlic, green pepper, and celery; saute until chicken is opaque and vegetables are tender. Stir in okra, tomatoes, tomato sauce, hot sauce, and remaining 1½ teaspoons Creole seasoning; simmer, uncovered, 5 minutes. Pour over hot cooked spaghetti, and toss.

Per Serving: 290 Calories, 6 g Fat (2 g Saturated), 59 mg Cholesterol, 345 mg Sodium, 27 g Protein, 36 g Carbohydrates

A Great Source of: Fiber (6 g), Vitamin B3 (58%), Vitamin B6 (33%), Folic Acid (42%), Vitamin C (82%), Magnesium (26%), Potassium (950 mg)

A Good Source of: Vitamin B1 (24%), Vitamin B2 (23%), Vitamin B12 (14%), Pantothenic Acid (13%), Vitamin E (18%), Calcium (16%), Copper (20%), Iron (19%), Zinc (16%)

Pyramid Equivalent(s): 2 Breads, 3 Vegetables, 1 Meat

Time: 10 minutes prep
Overnight chilling
30 minutes to heat coals
30 minutes to barbecue
Yield: 6 servings

Grilled Sweet-and-Tangy
Cornish Hens

1/3 cup balsamic vinegar
1/3 cup honey
1 teaspoon dried thyme
3 cloves garlic, crushed
1 tablespoon prepared mustard

1/2 teaspoon freshly ground
pepper
3 (1¹/4- to 1¹/2-pound) Cornish
hens, split and skinned

Combine vinegar, honey, thyme, garlic, and mustard; mix well.

Place hens in a large shallow baking dish; brush ½ cup vinegar mixture over hens. Cover and refrigerate 8 hours or overnight, brushing marinade over hens occasionally.

Remove hens from marinade, discarding marinade. Grill over medium coals for 15 to 20 minutes on each side, basting frequently with remaining vinegar mixture.

Per Serving: 380 Calories, 7 g Fat (2 g Saturated), 90 mg Cholesterol, 740 mg Sodium, 62 g Protein, 16 g Carbohydrates

A Great Source of: Vitamin B3 (96%), Vitamin B6 (46%), Pantothenic Acid (24%), Zinc (30%)

A Good Source of: Vitamin A (11%), Vitamin B1 (10%), Vitamin B2 (23%), Vitamin B12 (11%), Vitamin E (15%), Iron (19%), Magnesium (14%), Potassium (537 mg)

Pyramid Equivalent(s): 1 Meat

The Guilt-Free "Comfort Food" Cookbook

Moist-and-Lemony Roasted Turkey Breast

3 tablespoons salt-free lemon-
  pepper seasoning
2 tablespoons garlic powder
2 teaspoons crushed dried
  rosemary
1/2 teaspoon salt

1 (6-pound) turkey breast,
  skinned
2 tablespoons olive oil
1 large (14- x 20-inch) oven-
  cooking bag
1 tablespoon all-purpose flour

Preheat oven to 325°. Combine lemon-pepper seasoning, garlic powder, rosemary, and salt in a small bowl. Rinse turkey breast and pat dry with paper towels; rub olive oil, then seasoning mixture, all over breast.

Place a large oven-cooking bag in a large baking pan. Add flour to bag; twist end and shake to coat inside. Place seasoned turkey breast in bag; close with nylon tie, and cut six ½-inch slits in top of bag. Bake for 20 minutes per pound (about 2 hours) or until meat thermometer registers 170°. Remove turkey from bag; keep warm.

If desired, pour drippings into a small bowl, and freeze to solidify fat. Remove fat, reheat drippings, and serve with turkey.

Per Serving: 230 Calories, 5 g Fat (2 g Saturated), 95 mg Cholesterol, 145 mg Sodium, 41 g Protein, 2 g Carbohydrates
A Great Source of: Vitamin B3 (47%), Vitamin B6 (46%)
A Good Source of: Vitamin B2 (11%), Pantothenic Acid (10%), Iron (13%), Magnesium (10%), Zinc (20%), Potassium (440 mg)
Pyramid Equivalent(s): 1¹/₄ Meats

The Guilt-Free "Comfort Food" Cookbook

Time: 15 minutes prep
1 hour cooking
Yield: 12 servings

Apricot-Stuffed Turkey Breast

1 (3-pound) skinned and boned
  turkey breast
3 tablespoons Dijon mustard
1 tablespoon crushed dried
  rosemary
1¹/₂ to 2 teaspoons freshly
  ground pepper

¹/₂ teaspoon garlic powder
12 dried apricots, finely chopped
1 tablespoon sugar
¹/₃ cup finely chopped pecans or
  walnuts
1 tablespoon all-purpose flour
Apricot Sauce (recipe follows)

Preheat oven to 350°. Lay turkey breast flat on wax paper, tendon sides up. Remove tendons; trim fat. From center, slice horizontally through thickest part of each side of breast almost to outer edge; flip cut piece to open up breast fillets. Pound breast to flatten and form a more even thickness.

Spread turkey breast with mustard. Combine rosemary, pepper, and garlic; sprinkle half of mixture over mustard.

Toss apricots and sugar, coating well; stir in pecans. Spoon mixture in center of width of turkey breast, leaving a 2-inch border at sides. Fold in sides of turkey breast over filling; roll up turkey breast over filling, starting from bottom. (Roll should be about 12 to 14 inches long.)

Tie turkey breast roll securely in several places with string. Place a large-size-oven cooking bag in a 13- x 9- x 2-inch baking pan. Add 1 tablespoon flour; twist end and shake to coat inside. Place turkey roll, seam side down, in bag. Close bag with nylon tie; cut six ½-inch slits in top of bag. Bake for 55 minutes to 1 hour or until meat thermometer inserted in thickest portion registers 160°. Let stand 10 minutes before slicing and serving with Apricot Sauce.

The Guilt-Free "Comfort Food" Cookbook

Apricot Sauce
Yield: 1½ cups

½ cup apricot preserves
¾ cup canned low-sodium
*   chicken broth*
1 tablespoon Dijon mustard

¼ cup apricot nectar or
*   unsweetened orange juice*
2 teaspoons cornstarch

Combine preserves, broth, and mustard in a small saucepan; cook over medium heat until hot, stirring frequently.

Combine apricot nectar and cornstarch, stirring until smooth. Add to preserves mixture; cook, stirring constantly, until thickened.

Per Serving (with two tablespoons of sauce): 265 Calories, 7 g Fat (1 g Saturated), 78 mg Cholesterol, 190 mg Sodium, 35 g Protein, 14 g Carbohydrates
A Great Source of: Vitamin B3 (38%), Vitamin B6 (33%)
A Good Source of: Vitamin B2 (10%), Iron (12%), Magnesium (11%), Zinc (18%), Potassium (445 mg)
Pyramid Equivalent(s): 1 Meat, Extras

The Guilt-Free "Comfort Food" Cookbook

Time: 5 minutes prep
30 minutes cooking
Yield: 4 servings

Turkey Hash

*O*nce, every luncheonette in America served a beef hash, sometimes with an egg or sour cream on top. Now we eat food from wrappers, and fried beef doesn't sound as wholesome as it once did. But let's not forget *all* the old ways. Our new old-fashioned turkey hash has the old-time flavor without all the saturated fat that clogs arteries.

*1 pound medium red-skinned
  potatoes
vegetable cooking spray
1 tablespoon olive oil
1 large onion
2 medium-sized sweet red or
  yellow peppers, cut into 2-x
  1/8-inch strips
1 cup shredded turkey pastrami
  (or cooked chicken)*

*1 tablespoon Worcestershire
  sauce
1/2 teaspoon hot sauce (such as
  Tabasco)
1/4 teaspoon salt
1/2 cup light or nonfat sour
  cream
2 tablespoons Dijon mustard*

Cook potatoes in boiling water 10 to 15 minutes or until tender. Cool; cut into ½-inch slices. Cut slices into ¼-inch julienne strips.

Cut onion in half vertically; place cut sides down on a cutting board, and cut into very thin slices. Coat a large heavy skillet with cooking spray; add oil. Heat over medium heat. Add onion and peppers; cook, stirring occasionally, until vegetables are very tender. Add potatoes, pastrami, Worcestershire sauce, hot sauce, and salt; cook, stirring frequently, until hot.

Combine light sour cream and mustard. Spoon hash mixture on plates; top evenly with sour cream mixture.

Per Serving: 280 Calories, 8 g Fat (2 g Saturated), 31 mg Cholesterol, 900 mg Sodium, 16 g Protein, 38 g Carbohydrates

A Great Source of: Vitamin B6 (34%), Vitamin C (151%), Copper (25%), Potassium (825 mg)

A Good Source of: Fiber (4 g), Vitamin B1 (14%), Vitamin B2 (15%), Vitamin B3 (21%), Vitamin E (11%), Iron (17%), Magnesium (13%), Zinc (12%)

Pyramid Equivalent(s): 2 Vegetables, 2 Dairy, ½ Meat

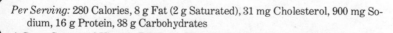

The Guilt-Free "Comfort Food" Cookbook

Turkey Piccata

1/3 cup all-purpose flour
1/2 teaspoon salt
1/2 teaspoon freshly ground
pepper
4 (4-ounce) turkey cutlets,
pounded to even thickness
and halved
vegetable cooking spray
2 teaspoons olive oil
1 clove garlic, minced

3/4 cup reduced-sodium chicken
broth
2 tablespoons lemon juice
1/2 teaspoon sugar
1 tablespoon drained capers,
rinsed
1 teaspoon grated lemon rind
2 tablespoons minced fresh
parsley

Combine flour, salt, and pepper in a shallow dish; dredge turkey cutlets in flour mixture, and shake off excess.

Coat a large nonstick skillet with cooking spray; add oil, and heat over medium-high heat. Add turkey cutlets, and cook 2 to 3 minutes on each side or until browned and meat loses its pink color. Transfer to a serving platter, and keep warm.

Saute garlic in skillet for one or two minutes, then add chicken broth, lemon juice, and sugar; bring to a boil, stirring constantly. Boil, uncovered, until mixture reduces to ½ cup. Stir in capers, lemon rind, and parsley; pour over turkey.

Per Serving: 225 Calories, 4 g Fat (1 g Saturated), 95 mg Cholesterol, 450 mg Sodium, 35 g Protein, 9 g Carbohydrates
A Great Source of: Vitamin B3 (42%), Vitamin B6 (33%)
A Good Source of: Vitamin B2 (12%), Vitamin C (11%), Iron (14%), Zinc (17%), Potassium (350 mg)
Pyramid Equivalent(s): 1 Meat

The Guilt-Free "Comfort Food" Cookbook

Time: 10 minutes prep
20 minutes cooking
Yield: 6 servings

Italian Turkey Saute

*H*ere's another quick one.

1/3 cup all-purpose flour
1/4 teaspoon salt
1/4 teaspoon pepper
4 (5-ounce) turkey cutlets
vegetable cooking spray
2 teaspoons olive oil
2 cloves garlic, minced
1 (14 1/2-ounce) can unsalted
Italian-style stewed
tomatoes, undrained

1/4 cup low-sodium chicken
broth
2 tablespoons lemon juice
1 teaspoon dried Italian
seasoning
2 tablespoons sliced ripe olives
2 tablespoons minced fresh
parsley

Combine flour, salt, and pepper in a shallow dish. Pound turkey cutlets to 1/3-inch thickness; cut in half. Dredge in flour mixture.

Coat a large heavy skillet with cooking spray; add oil, and heat over medium-high heat. Add turkey and saute 2 to 3 minutes on each side or until done. Remove from skillet; set aside.

Add garlic to skillet; saute 1 minute. Add tomatoes, broth, lemon juice, and Italian seasoning; bring to a boil. Reduce heat, and simmer uncovered 5 minutes. Add turkey cutlets, turning to coat with sauce; cover and simmer 5 minutes. Remove from heat and stir in olives and parsley.

Per Serving: 170 Calories, 3 g Fat (1 g Saturated), 65 mg Cholesterol, 360 mg Sodium, 24 g Protein, 10 g Carbohydrates
A Great Source of: Vitamin B3 (31%)
A Good Source of: Vitamin B6 (23%), Vitamin C (22%), Iron (12%), Zinc (12%), Potassium (400 mg)
Pyramid Equivalent(s): 2/3 Vegetable, 1 Meat

The Guilt-Free "Comfort Food" Cookbook

FISH AND SHELLFISH

*F*ish and shellfish are nearly perfect sources of protein. They are low in fat and very low in saturated fat. That's not surprising, if you think about the cold, watery world most fish and shellfish inhabit. Saturated fat, the kind found in butter and beef fat, is solid at room temperature. If fish contained much saturated fat, it might become solid in cold waters! Instead, fish and shellfish have a kind of "natural antifreeze" that tends to keep blood thin. These special fats are known as omega-3 fatty acids, and they have been the subject of intense scientific study. They lower blood pressure, reduce triglycerides, and reduce the tendency of blood to clot. Although the final word on the impact of fish on human health hasn't been given, some studies suggest that people who eat as little as one fish meal a week have a substantially lower risk of heart attack.

All fish contains some omega-3s. Fatty fish that swim in cold waters, such as salmon or mackerel, tend to have the highest amounts of omega-3. But lean fish such as sole also contain some of these special fats. More importantly, all kinds of fish provide excellent protein with very little saturated fat. Even shellfish, such as clams, oysters, and shrimp, contain omega-3 fats. That makes shrimp, which is also low in fat and saturated fat, a heart-healthy choice even though it does contain some cholesterol.

Fish is one of the most popular dishes ordered in restaurants. At home, however, many people shy away from cooking it. That's too bad

The Guilt-Free "Comfort Food" Cookbook

because fish, as long as it is fresh, is one of the easiest and fastest foods to cook well. A fillet of fish, wrapped in plastic with some julienned vegetables and fresh herbs, turns into dinner in two or three minutes in the microwave.

Keep in mind, though, that it's easy to ruin fish, at least nutritionally. Fish is often deep-fat fried, cooked in butter, or baked with cream. Why add saturated fat back in? Better to cook fish and shellfish in ways that utilize the unique flavors of seafood.

Embrace fish—with all your heart!

The Guilt-Free "Comfort Food" Cookbook

Time: 20 minutes prep
10 minutes cooking
Yield: 4 servings

Sole with Parmesan-Watercress Breadcrumbs

*D*on't use store-bought or stale bread for these soft breadcrumbs; use any soft bread you have in the house.

2 tablespoons lemon juice
1 teaspoon hot sauce (such as Tabasco)
1/4 teaspoon garlic powder
1/4 teaspoon salt
4 (4-ounce) sole fillets
1 cup soft breadcrumbs

1/2 cup grated Parmesan cheese
2 tablespoons reduced-fat soft margarine, melted
1/2 cup finely chopped watercress
additional watercress for garnish

Combine lemon juice, hot sauce, garlic powder, and salt in a small bowl; brush on both sides of fillets. Broil on rack of a broiler pan 6 to 8 minutes or until fish flakes with a fork.

Meanwhile, mix breadcrumbs, Parmesan cheese, and margarine; mix well and stir in watercress. Spoon breadcrumb mixture on fish; broil 2 minutes or until mixture is lightly browned. Garnish with additional watercress.

Per Serving: 215 Calories, 8 g Fat (3 g Saturated), 70 mg Cholesterol, 540 mg So-
dium, 27 g Protein, 7 g Carbohydrates
A Great Source of: Vitamin B12 (39%)
A Good Source of: Vitamin A (13%), Vitamin B2 (11%), Vitamin B3 (11%), Vitamin
B6 (13%), Vitamin C (12%), Vitamin E (13%), Calcium (20%), Magnesium
(15%), Potassium (350 mg)
Pyramid Equivalent(s): ½ Bread, ½ Dairy, 1 Meat

The Guilt-Free "Comfort Food" Cookbook

Time: 30 minutes
Yield: 6 servings

Baked Haddock with Sweet Corn Mustard Sauce

*1 (12-ounce) can evaporated
  skim milk*
3 tablespoons Dijon mustard
*2 cups fresh corn or frozen corn,
  thawed*
¹/₄ teaspoon salt

*¹/₂ teaspoon freshly ground
  pepper*
1 large onion, very thinly sliced
vegetable cooking spray
*1¹/₂ pounds haddock fillet, cut
  into 6 serving-size pieces*

Preheat oven to 350°. Combine evaporated skim milk, mustard, corn,
salt, and pepper in a small bowl. Arrange onion slices in a single layer in a
12- x 8- x 2-inch baking dish coated with cooking spray; add corn mixture.
Cover with aluminum foil, and bake for 25 minutes. Add haddock in a single layer, turning to coat with sauce; cover tightly and bake 10 minutes or
until fish flakes.

Transfer fish to a platter using a slotted spatula; cover and keep
warm.

Transfer corn and onion mixture to container of an electric blender;
process until smooth. Press through a sieve, and serve with fish.

Per Serving: 210 Calories, 2 g Fat (0 g Saturated), 70 mg Cholesterol, 345 mg So-
dium, 30 g Protein, 19 g Carbohydrates
A Great Source of: Vitamin B3 (27%), Potassium (750 mg)
A Good Source of: Fiber (2 g), Vitamin A (10%), Vitamin B1 (12%), Vitamin B2
(15%), Vitamin B6 (21%), Vitamin B12 (24%), Folic Acid (11%), Pantothenic
Acid (10%), Vitamin C (10%), Vitamin E (11%), Calcium (22%), Iron (11%),
Magnesium (22%)
Pyramid Equivalent(s): 1 Vegetable, ½ Dairy, 1 Meat

The Guilt-Free "Comfort Food" Cookbook

Poached Sea Bass with Pesto Verde

*I*f you can't find sea bass, use salmon, snapper, or grouper fillets.

2 anchovy fillets (or 1 tablespoon anchovy paste)
1 (4¹/₂-ounce) can diced green chilies
¹/₄ cup chopped shallots
¹/₄ cup chopped fresh parsley
1 tablespoon minced fresh tarragon
2 tablespoons olive oil

1 tablespoon finely chopped capers, rinsed and drained
1 tablespoon lemon juice
¹/₄ teaspoon freshly ground pepper
5 cups water
salt (optional)
¹/₂ pound sea bass (1-inch thick), cut into 6 equal fillets

Soak anchovy fillets in cold water for 15 minutes, changing water 3 or 4 times. Drain and squeeze out moisture with paper towels. Chop; place in a food processor. Add chilies, shallots, parsley, and tarragon; pulse just until mixture is minced. Transfer to a bowl; stir in oil, capers, lemon juice, and pepper. Cover and let stand, at room temperature, until serving time.

Bring water and salt (if desired) to a boil in a pot wide enough to hold sea bass in a single layer. Reduce heat to a simmer; add sea bass. Cover and poach 5 minutes or until fish is opaque. Transfer sea bass to serving plates and top with anchovy mixture.

Per Serving: 175 Calories, 7 g Fat (1 g Saturated), 50 mg Cholesterol, 390 mg Sodium, 24 g Protein, 4 g Carbohydrates
A Great Source of: Vitamin B6 (25%), Vitamin C (32%), Vitamin E (34%)
A Good Source of: Vitamin B2 (10%), Vitamin B3 (12%), Magnesium (16%), Potassium (425 mg)
Pyramid Equivalent(s): 1 Meat

The Guilt-Free "Comfort Food" Cookbook

Time: 20 minutes prep
20 minutes cooking
Yield: 6 servings

Seared Tuna with Corn Relish

vegetable cooking spray
4 cups fresh corn or frozen corn,
thawed
3/4 cup minced green pepper
1/2 cup finely chopped purple
onion
1 cup finely diced plum tomato
1 tablespoon chili powder,
divided

1/2 teaspoon ground red pepper,
divided
1/4 teaspoon garlic powder
1/4 teaspoon salt
1/4 cup nonfat sour cream
1 tablespoon canola oil
3 (11/2-inch) tuna steaks (8
ounces each)
fresh cilantro or parsley sprigs

Coat a large nonstick skillet with cooking spray; place over medium heat until hot. Add corn, green pepper, and purple onion; saute until tender. Stir in 1 teaspoon chili powder, ¼ teaspoon red pepper, garlic powder, and salt; saute 30 seconds. Remove from heat; stir in sour cream.

Coat tuna steaks on both sides with remaining 2 teaspoons chili powder and remaining ¼ teaspoon red pepper. Let stand 5 minutes. Heat oil in skillet over medium-high heat; add tuna and cook 2 to 3 minutes on each side or until desired degree of doneness. Cut tuna across grain into ½-inch slices; arrange on serving plates and top with corn mixture and cilantro.

Per Serving: 300 Calories, 9 g Fat (2 g Saturated), 45 mg Cholesterol, 170 mg Sodium, 31 g Protein, 25 g Carbohydrates

A Great Source of: Vitamin A (86%), Vitamin B1 (35%), Vitamin B3 (60%), Vitamin B6 (34%), Vitamin B12 (180%), Vitamin E (33%), Vitamin C (46%), Magnesium (26%), Potassium (725 mg)

A Good Source of: Fiber (4 g), Vitamin B2 (24%), Folic Acid (15%), Pantothenic Acid (21%), Copper (10%), Iron (12%)

Pyramid Equivalent(s): 2 Vegetables, ⅔ Dairy, 1 Meat

The Guilt-Free "Comfort Food" Cookbook

Time: 1 hour marinating
30 minutes prep and cooking
Yield: 4 servings

Steamed Greek Fish

If you don't have a fish poacher/steamer, try an oven rack or bamboo steamer over a wok, or a vegetable steamer in a deep pot. Pitted olives should be available in your grocery store's deli section; if not, buy a small jar and pit a quarter cup's worth. Carefully!

1 cup diced tomato
1/4 cup finely chopped pitted
   Nicoise or Calamata olives
1/4 cup minced green onion
1/4 cup minced fresh (or 1 1/2
   teaspoons dried) oregano

1/2 teaspoon freshly ground
   pepper
2 tablespoons lemon juice
1 tablespoon olive oil
4 (4-ounce) orange roughy, sole,
   cod, or snapper fillets
8 large spinach leaves

Combine tomato, olives, onion, oregano, and pepper in a bowl; cover and let stand at room temperature 1 hour.

Position steamer rack in fish poacher/steamer; pour water into level just below steamer rack. Bring to a boil.

Combine lemon juice and olive oil; brush on fish fillets. Place fillets on steamer rack; cover and steam 8 minutes. Remove lid and evenly divided tomato mixture on fish; cover and steam an additional 2 to 3 minutes or until fish flakes with a fork.

Line a platter or serving plates with spinach; carefully transfer fish fillets to platter using a long spatula.

Per Serving: 170 Calories, 6 g Fat (1 g Saturated), 60 mg Cholesterol, 170 mg Sodium, 25 g Protein, 5 g Carbohydrates

A Great Source of: Vitamin B12 (27%), Vitamin C (32%)

A Good Source of: Vitamin A (14%), Vitamin B3 (18%), Vitamin B6 (14%), Folic Acid (12%), Vitamin E (19%), Magnesium (14%), Potassium (600 mg)

Pyramid Equivalent(s): 1 Vegetable, 1 Meat

The Guilt-Free "Comfort Food" Cookbook

Time: 25 minutes prep and cooking
1 hour chutney standing time
Yield: 6 servings

Baja Mahi-Mahi with Fresh
Mango Chutney

*I*f it's not outdoor grilling season, or it rains, these fillets are delicious
broiled in the oven six inches from the heat.

*1¹/₂ cups seeded and finely
    diced tomatoes*
1 cup finely diced mango
*¹/₂ cup minced yellow or green
    pepper*
¹/₄ cup minced green onion

1 teaspoon curry powder
¹/₄ cup chopped mango chutney
1 tablespoon white wine vinegar
1 tablespoon honey
3 (8-ounce) mahi-mahi,

Combine tomato, mango, pepper, onion, and curry in a bowl; set
aside. Combine chutney, vinegar, and honey; mix well; reserve 3 tablespoons mixture. Stir remaining chutney mixture into mango mixture;
cover and let stand 1 hour at room temperature.

Brush reserved 3 tablespoons of chutney mixture evenly on fish fillets. Grill over medium-hot coals (350° to 400°) for 4 minutes; turn and
cook an additional 3 minutes or until fish flakes with a fork. Serve with
chutney mixture.

Per Serving: 160 Calories, 1 g Fat (0 g Saturated), 40 mg Cholesterol, 75 mg So-
    dium, 22 g Protein, 15 g Carbohydrates
A Great Source of: Vitamin C (58%), Vitamin E (25%)
A Good Source of: Fiber (2 g), Vitamin A (24%), Vitamin B6 (20%), Vitamin B12
    (10%), Magnesium (11%), Potassium (625 mg)
Pyramid Equivalent(s): 1 Vegetable, 1 Meat

The Guilt-Free "Comfort Food" Cookbook

Time: 1 to 2 hours marinating
10 minutes prep
8 minutes cooking
Yield: 4 servings

Swordfish Kabobs with Sugar Snaps

*I*f you like sugar snap peas, use a pound's worth.

*1 (8-ounce) carton plain nonfat
    yogurt
1 teaspoon toasted sesame oil
1 teaspoon salt-free
    lemon-pepper seasoning
1/4 teaspoon salt
1 pound boneless swordfish or
    halibut steaks, cut 1-inch
    thick*

*1/4 cup toasted sesame seeds
3 tablespoons cornstarch
1/2 pound large sugar snap or
    snow pea pods, ends
    trimmed
vegetable cooking spray*

Combine yogurt, sesame oil, and lemon-pepper in a shallow dish. Cut fish into 1-inch pieces; add to yogurt mixture and toss gently to coat. Cover and refrigerate 1 to 2 hours.

Pound toasted sesame seeds in a mortar with a pestle until ground; stir in cornstarch. Remove fish from marinade; coat with cornstarch mixture, and thread on skewers alternately with sugar snap peas. Place skewers on rack of a broiler pan coated with cooking spray; broil 4 inches from heat source for 8 minutes, or until fish flakes with a fork, turning once.

Per Serving: 300 Calories, 10 g Fat (2 g Saturated), 45 mg Cholesterol, 275 mg Sodium, 27 g Protein, 14 g Carbohydrates

A *Great Source of:* Vitamin B3 (53%), Vitamin B12 (34%), Vitamin C (31%), Copper (27%)

A *Good Source of:* Fiber (3 g), Vitamin B1 (12%), Vitamin B2 (16%), Vitamin B6 (24%), Vitamin E (10%), Calcium (22%), Iron (17%), Magnesium (20%), Zinc (17%), Potassium (565 mg)

Pyramid Equivalent(s): 1 Vegetable, 1 Meat

The Guilt-Free "Comfort Food" Cookbook

Time: 20 minutes prep
30 minutes marinating
8 minutes cooking
Yield: 6 servings

Tropical Grouper Stir-Fry

*1 pound (1-inch thick) grouper,
   cut into 1-inch pieces*
*¹/₄ cup plus 1 tablespoon
   reduced-sodium teriyaki
   sauce, divided*
4 teaspoons cornstarch, divided
*¹/₄ cup pineapple-orange-
   banana juice*
*1 tablespoon peanut or canola
   oil*

*1 medium-sized red pepper,
   thinly sliced*
*1 jalapeno pepper, seeded and
   minced (optional)*
*1 medium papaya, seeded and
   cubed*
*1 tablespoon minced pickled
   ginger*
3 cups hot cooked basmati rice

Combine fish, 3 tablespoons teriyaki sauce, and 2 teaspoons corn-starch; mix gently. Cover and refrigerate 30 minutes.

Combine juice, remaining 2 tablespoons teriyaki sauce, and remaining 2 teaspoons cornstarch; mix until smooth. Pour oil into wok or large non-stick skillet; heat at medium high. Add fish, and stir-fry gently 2 minutes or until opaque; remove from wok, and keep warm. Add peppers; stir-fry 1 to 2 minutes or until just tender. Add juice mixture to wok; cook, stirring constantly, until thickened. Add grouper, papaya, and ginger; cook until thoroughly heated, stirring gently. Serve with (or over) rice.

Per Serving: 270 Calories, 3 g Fat (0 g Saturated), 30 mg Cholesterol, 550 mg So-dium, 19 g Protein, 39 g Carbohydrates
A Great Source of: Vitamin C (96%)
A Good Source of: Fiber (2 g), Vitamin B1 (13%), Vitamin E (12%), Iron (11%),
   Magnesium (12%), Potassium (575 mg)
Pyramid Equivalent(s): 1 Bread, ½ Vegetable, ½ Fruit, 1 Meat

The Guilt-Free "Comfort Food" Cookbook

Time: 1 hour standing
40 minutes prep and cooking
Yield: 4 servings

Salmon with Black-Eyed Peas

*1¹/₄ cups cooked black-eyed
   peas, drained
¹/₂ cup finely chopped yellow or
   red pepper
¹/₂ cup thinly sliced celery
2 tablespoons minced fresh
   cilantro or basil
2 tablespoons olive oil
1 tablespoon white wine vinegar*

*1 tablespoon Dijon mustard
2 tablespoons lime juice
2 teaspoons cracked black
   pepper
1 pound salmon fillets or tuna
   steaks, cut 1-inch thick
vegetable cooking spray
4 cups shredded romaine lettuce*

Combine peas, peppers, celery, cilantro, oil, vinegar, and mustard in a
bowl; cover and let stand at room temperature 1 hour, stirring occasionally.

Rub lime juice and pepper on both sides of salmon fillets; refrigerate,
covered, for 15 minutes. Coat a large, heavy, nonstick skillet with cooking
spray; place over high heat until hot. Add salmon; reduce heat to medium-
high and cook 2 minutes on each side. Remove from skillet; cut lengthwise
into long, thin slices. To serve, arrange lettuce on serving plates; fan
salmon slices on plates and mound black-eyed pea mixture in center.

Per Serving: 315 Calories, 15 g Fat (2 g Saturated), 60 mg Cholesterol, 120 mg Sodium, 29 g Protein, 17 g Carbohydrates

A *Great Source of:* Fiber (6 g), Vitamin B1 (31%), Vitamin B2 (31%), Vitamin B3
   (48%), Vitamin B6 (52%), Vitamin B12 (60%), Folic Acid (48%), Potassium
   (1,000 mg)

A *Good Source of:* Vitamin A (23%), Pantothenic Acid (22%), Vitamin C (68%), Vitamin E (22%), Copper (23%), Iron (18%), Magnesium (20%), Zinc (10%)

Pyramid Equivalent(s): 1½ Vegetables, 1⅔ Meats

The Guilt-Free "Comfort Food" Cookbook

Time: 15 minutes prep
20 minutes baking
Yield: 6 servings

Sweet-Hot Pineapple Fish Rolls

*P*epper jelly comes in red and green. Use red for this recipe.

*1 (15¹/₄-ounce) can
   unsweetened pineapple
   spears, undrained
¹/₂ cup commercial pepper jelly
2 tablespoons reduced-sodium
   soy sauce*

*1 clove garlic, crushed
6 (4-ounce) skinless sole,
   flounder, or pompano fillets
6 (6-inch) green onion tops*

Preheat oven to 375°. Drain pineapple, reserving juice and spears separately. Measure out 6 spears; reserve remaining spears for other uses. Measure out ¼ cup juice; reserve remaining juice for other uses.

Combine juice, jelly, and soy sauce in a saucepan; add pineapple spears, and cook over medium heat until pineapple is hot and jelly is melted.

Place 1 pineapple spear on small end of each fillet; roll up fillets. Wrap a green onion top around each fillet roll. Place, seam sides down, in an 8-inch square baking dish. Brush half of jelly mixture over fish rolls; cover with aluminum foil, and bake for 15 to 20 minutes, or until fish flakes easily when tested with a fork.

Reheat remaining jelly mixture; serve with fish rolls.

Per Serving: 215 Calories, 1 g Fat (0 g Saturated), 60 mg Cholesterol, 300 mg Sodium, 22 g Protein, 29 g Carbohydrates
A Great Source of: Vitamin B12 (36%)
A Good Source of: Vitamin B1 (10%), Vitamin B3 (11%), Vitamin B6 (13%), Vitamin C (22%), Magnesium (16%), Potassium (425 mg)
Pyramid Equivalent(s): ⅔ Fruit, 1 Meat

The Guilt-Free "Comfort Food" Cookbook

Island-Grilled Shrimp with Peach Salsa

*I*f it's not convenient to grill outdoors, broil these four inches from the heat source in the oven, and follow the rest of the directions.

*2 pounds jumbo fresh shrimp,
    peeled and deveined*
*2 tablespoons reduced-sodium
    soy sauce*
2 tablespoons olive oil
*1 tablespoon plus 1 teaspoon
    freshly squeezed lime juice,
    divided*

1 teaspoon ground ginger
1 teaspoon curry powder
4 fresh peaches
*1 jalapeno or serrano chili
    pepper, seeded and minced*
2 teaspoons balsamic vinegar

Combine shrimp, soy sauce, olive oil, 1 tablespoon lime juice, ginger, and curry powder in a glass bowl; toss well. Cover and refrigerate 2 hours.

Combine peaches, jalapeno, and vinegar in a serving bowl; cover and let stand at room temperature until ready to serve.

Remove shrimp from marinade; discard marinade. Thread tail and neck of each shrimp on skewers so shrimp will lie flat. Grill over medium-hot coals 3 to 4 minutes on each side or until shrimp turn pink. Serve with peach mixture.

Per Serving: 230 Calories, 7 g Fat (1 g Saturated), 130 mg Cholesterol, 440 mg Sodium, 32 g Protein, 9 g Carbohydrates
A Great Source of: Vitamin B12 (29%), Vitamin E (52%)
A Good Source of: Vitamin A (11%), Vitamin B3 (22%), Vitamin C (13%), Copper (22%), Iron (22%), Magnesium (16%), Zinc (12%), Potassium (410 mg)
Pyramid Equivalent(s): ⅔ Fruit, ⅔ Meat

The Guilt-Free "Comfort Food" Cookbook

Bayou Shrimp with Grits

1/4 cup all-purpose flour
2 teaspoons canola oil
3/4 cup chopped celery
3/4 cup chopped onion
1/2 cup chopped green pepper
2 cloves garlic, minced
1 (8-ounce) can unsalted
  tomato sauce
1/2 cup water

1/2 teaspoon salt
1/2 teaspoon freshly ground
  pepper
1/4 teaspoon ground red pepper
2 pounds medium-sized shrimp,
  peeled and deveined
3 tablespoons crumbled feta
  cheese (optional)
Creamy Grits (recipe follows)

Heat a heavy, 10-inch cast-iron skillet over medium heat. Add flour; toast, stirring constantly, 7 to 10 minutes or until flour is a deep golden color. Transfer to a plate and let cool. (If flour browns too quickly, reduce heat.)

Add oil to skillet; place over medium heat. Add celery, onion, pepper, and garlic; saute until tender. Sprinkle flour over mixture; stir until vegetables are coated. Add tomato sauce, water, salt, black pepper, and red pepper; bring to a boil, stirring constantly. Reduce heat and simmer, uncovered, 10 minutes. Stir in shrimp; cook 5 to 8 minutes or until shrimp are opaque. If desired, crumble ½ tablespoon feta cheese over each serving of grits, and spoon shrimp mixture evenly on top of grits.

Creamy Grits
Yield: 3¼ cups

2 cups low-sodium chicken
  broth
1¼ cup evaporated skim milk
2/3 cup regular grits

Combine all ingredients in a small saucepan; bring to a boil, stirring constantly. Reduce heat, and simmer 10 minutes or until thickened.

The Guilt-Free "Comfort Food" Cookbook

Per Serving: 300 Calories, 4 g Fat (1 g Saturated), 130 mg Cholesterol, 780 mg Sodium, 36 g Protein, 26 g Carbohydrates

A Great Source of: Vitamin B3 (29%), Vitamin B12 (41%), Vitamin C (32%), Vitamin E (33%), Iron (34%), Potassium (625 mg)

A Good Source of: Fiber (3 g), Vitamin A (19%), Vitamin B1 (18%), Vitamin B2 (15%), Vitamin B6 (18%), Pantothenic Acid (10%), Calcium (14%), Copper (21%), Magnesium (19%), Zinc (19%)

Pyramid Equivalent(s): ½ Bread, ⅔ Vegetable, ½ Dairy, ⅔ Meat

Note: With optional feta cheese: 330 Calories, 8 g Fat (4 g Saturated), 150 mg Cholesterol, 990 mg Sodium, Calcium (23%)

The Guilt-Free "Comfort Food" Cookbook

Time: 20 minutes prep
12 minutes baking
Yield: 4 servings

Crispy Battered Shrimp

*B*aking instead of frying makes these battered shrimp crispy without much fat. Even people with elevated cholesterol levels can enjoy this low-cholesterol recipe. If you want a low-calorie, lowfat version, omit the nuts, and increase the breadcrumbs to a full cup; calories will drop to 315 and fat to nearly zero. But if you can afford a few extra calories, the pecans add a distinctive taste.

vegetable cooking spray
1/3 cup self-rising flour
1/2 cup sparkling water
1 large egg
2/3 cup cornmeal
2/3 cup fine dry breadcrumbs

1/3 cup finely minced pecans
1/4 teaspoon pepper
1 pound medium shrimp, peeled
 and deveined
lemon wedges, or Tomato
 Chutney (p. 171)

Preheat oven to 450°. Coat a rack large enough to hold shrimp in a single layer with cooking spray; place in a jelly-roll pan. Set aside.

Combine flour, water, and egg in a medium bowl; stir with a whisk until smooth. In another bowl, combine cornmeal, breadcrumbs, pecans, and pepper.

Dip shrimp in breadcrumb mixture, then egg mixture, turning to coat; dip again in breadcrumb mixture, turning with a spoon to coat evenly. Place on prepared rack, spacing evenly. Coat tops with cooking spray; bake for 10 to 12 minutes or until golden on outside and opaque in center. Serve with lemon, Sweet Onion Marmalade, or Tomato Chutney.

Per Serving: 380 Calories, 10 g Fat (2 g Saturated), 80 mg Cholesterol, 85 mg Sodium, 35 g Protein, 37 g Carbohydrates

A Great Source of: Vitamin B3 (29%), Vitamin B12 (25%), Vitamin E (50%), Copper (27%), Iron (32%)

A Good Source of: Fiber (3 g), Vitamin A (16%), Vitamin B1 (25%), Vitamin B2 (16%), Vitamin B6 (12%), Calcium (16%), Magnesium (24%), Zinc (18%), Potassium (400 mg)

Pyramid Equivalent(s): 1 Bread, 1 Meat

The Guilt-Free "Comfort Food" Cookbook

"The Works" Tuna Casserole

*5 ounces egg noodles, cooked
without salt or fat, drained*
*2 (6 1/8-ounce) cans solid white
water-packed tuna, drained
and flaked*
*1 (8-ounce) can sliced water
chestnuts, drained*
1¹/₂ cups chopped celery
³/₄ cup sliced green onion
*1 (10³/₄-ounce) can reduced-fat,
reduced-sodium cream of
mushroom soup, undiluted*

1 cup nonfat sour cream
¹/₂ cup reduced-fat mayonnaise
*³/₄ cup grated Parmesan
cheese, divided*
*¹/₂ to 1 teaspoon hot sauce
(such as Tabasco)*
vegetable cooking spray
*3 tablespoons toasted sliced
almonds*

Preheat oven to 375°. Combine noodles, tuna, water chestnuts, celery, and onion in a large bowl; set aside. Mix together soup, sour cream, mayonnaise, ½ cup cheese, and hot sauce; stir into noodle mixture. Spoon into a shallow, 2-quart casserole coated with cooking spray; cover with aluminum foil, and bake for 20 minutes. Uncover and sprinkle with remaining ¼ cup cheese and almonds; bake 5 to 10 minutes or until bubbly and lightly browned.

Per Serving: 350 Calories, 12 g Fat (3 g Saturated), 60 mg Cholesterol, 470 mg Sodium, 28 g Protein, 34 g Carbohydrates
A Great Source of: Vitamin B3 (25%), Vitamin B12 (28%), Vitamin E (31%)
A Good Source of: Fiber (3 g), Vitamin A (11%), Vitamin B1 (12%), Vitamin B2 (17%), Vitamin B6 (19%), Calcium (22%), Copper (16%), Iron (14%), Magnesium (14%), Zinc (10%), Potassium (400 mg)
Pyramid Equivalent(s): 1 Bread, 1⅓ Vegetables, 1 Dairy, ⅔ Meat

The Guilt-Free "Comfort Food" Cookbook

Time: 30 minutes
Yield: 4 servings

Linguini with Herbed Clam Sauce

𝒫art of the exquisite intensity of clams stems from their rich load of minerals from the shallow seas where they grow. Clams are very low in fat, yet rich in many B vitamins (especially B12—the percentage below is not a typo!), and minerals such as copper, manganese, and especially iron. A serving of clams (three-and-a-half ounces) provides about 75 percent of an average person's iron needs. Growing children need plenty of iron, and so do women of childbearing years. Men need somewhat less. As we cut back on meat-heavy meals, a dish such as linguini with clams makes an excellent, balanced alternative. Our version is quick, easy, cheap, filling, and delicious.

2 tablespoons olive oil
1 cup sliced green onion (4 large or small bunch)
2 cloves garlic, crushed
2 tablespoons all-purpose flour
1 cup bottled clam juice
1/3 cup vegetable or chicken broth
1 (10-ounce) can whole baby clams, undrained

1/4 cup minced fresh parsley
1 tablespoon minced fresh thyme or 1 teaspoon dried thyme
1/2 teaspoon freshly ground pepper
1/2 pound linguini
2 cups coarsely chopped arugula or spinach

Heat olive oil in a heavy deep skillet over medium heat; add green onion and garlic, and saute 2 minutes. Sprinkle flour over mixture; cook 1 minute, stirring constantly. Stir in clam juice and vegetable broth until smooth; add clams, and bring to a simmer, stirring gently. Simmer, uncovered, 5 minutes. Stir in parsley, thyme, and pepper; remove from heat and keep warm.

Meanwhile, cook linguini according to package directions, without salt or fat. Toss with arugula and clam mixture; serve immediately.

The Guilt-Free "Comfort Food" Cookbook

Per Serving: 400 Calories, 9 g Fat (2 g Saturated), 25 mg Cholesterol, 500 mg Sodium, 20 g Protein, 60 g Carbohydrates

A Great Source of: Vitamin A (31%), Vitamin B1 (27%), Vitamin B2 (25%), Vitamin B12 (945%), Vitamin C (29%), Vitamin E (27%), Copper (42%), Iron (81%)

A Good Source of: Fiber (4 g), Vitamin B3 (23%), Vitamin B6 (12%), Folic Acid (24%), Magnesium (20%), Zinc (20%), Potassium (600 mg)

Pyramid Equivalent(s): 2 Breads, 1½ Vegetables, 1 Meat

The Guilt-Free "Comfort Food" Cookbook

Capellini with Scallops and Pesto "Cream Sauce"

*C*apellini is the thinnest pasta, a.k.a. "angel hair" pasta. Dried capellini is available in supermarkets and gourmet stores. In a pinch, spaghetti would be fine. Shredded Parmesan cheese is also available in most supermarkets; it comes in big flakes. If you have a hunk of Parmesan cheese, slice off the thinnest slices you can. It makes a nice presentation.

This dish works with shrimp, too; substitute peeled, deveined shrimp for the scallops, and cook in the skillet for an extra two or three minutes. For a nice flavor alternative, substitute fresh cilantro for basil.

1 cup packed fresh basil leaves
2 cloves garlic, sliced
1/4 teaspoon salt
1/2 teaspoon freshly ground pepper
3 tablespoons reduced-sodium chicken broth
1/2 cup nonfat ricotta cheese
1/2 cup evaporated skim milk
1 tablespoon lemon juice

8 ounces capellini
2 cups packed, very thinly sliced, fresh spinach
1 teaspoon olive oil, divided
1 pound sea scallops, sliced horizontally
3 large plum tomatoes, seeded and diced
1/4 cup shredded Parmesan cheese

For pesto sauce, combine basil or cilantro, garlic, salt, pepper, chicken broth, ricotta, skim milk, and lemon juice in the container of an electric blender; process until smooth, scraping sides of blender as necessary. Transfer to a medium saucepan; cook over low heat until hot, stirring frequently. Remove from heat; cover.

Cook capellini according to package instructions, without salt or fat. Drain, place in a serving dish, and toss with spinach. Keep warm.

Coat bottom of a large nonstick skillet with ½ teaspoon oil; heat on high until hot. Add half of scallops in one layer without crowding; cook 20 to 30 seconds per side or until just opaque. Transfer to bowl of pasta; re-

The Guilt-Free "Comfort Food" Cookbook

peat with remaining olive oil and scallops. Add tomatoes and pesto cream sauce to pasta; toss gently. Sprinkle each serving with 1 tablespoon cheese.

Per Serving: 415 Calories, 5 g Fat (1 g Saturated), 50 mg Cholesterol, 570 mg Sodium, 36 g Protein, 55 g Carbohydrates

A Great Source of: Vitamin A (36%), Vitamin B1 (27%), Vitamin B2 (29%), Vitamin B12 (33%), Folic Acid (26%), Vitamin C (41%), Magnesium (36%), Potassium (885 mg)

A Good Source of: Fiber (4 g), Vitamin B3 (22%), Vitamin B6 (19%), Vitamin E (15%), Calcium (35%), Copper (17%), Iron (23%), Zinc (21%)

Pyramid Equivalent(s): 2 Breads, 1⅓ Vegetables, 1 Meat

The Guilt-Free "Comfort Food" Cookbook

Time: 25 minutes prep
40 minutes cooking
Yield: 9 cups (6 servings)

Low-Country Gumbo

*A*nother delicious, warm one-dish supper. The sodium is a little high for a single dish, but not for a meal. So serve this with a simple green salad, a loaf of bread, and fresh fruit for dessert. If you want to reduce sodium further, use one fifteen-ounce can of unsalted tomatoes plus a four-ounce can of green chilies instead of the cans of tomatoes and green chilies. Add hot sauce at table to taste.

1/4 cup all-purpose flour
1 tablespoon canola oil
1 1/4 cups chopped onion
1 1/4 cups chopped green pepper
1/2 cup diced celery
4 cloves garlic, minced
4 cups reduced-sodium chicken broth
2 (10-ounce) cans whole tomatoes and green chilies, chopped

1 1/2 cups sliced fresh okra or frozen okra, thawed
1 teaspoon Creole seasoning
1 bay leaf
1/2 cup long-grain white rice
1/2 pound medium shrimp, peeled and deveined
1 (4-ounce) skinned and boned chicken breast half, cut into 1/2-inch pieces
1/2 pint shucked oysters, drained

Heat a heavy Dutch oven over medium heat. Add flour; toast, stirring constantly, 7 to 10 minutes or until flour is a deep golden color. Transfer to a plate and let cool. (If flour browns too quickly, reduce heat.)

Heat oil in skillet over medium heat. Add onion, green pepper, celery, and garlic; saute until onion is lightly browned. Stir in flour, coating vegetables well. Gradually add chicken broth, stirring constantly; stir in tomatoes, okra, Creole seasoning, and bay leaf. Bring to a boil, stirring constantly. Cover, reduce heat, and simmer 15 minutes.

Stir in rice; cover and simmer an additional 15 minutes. Add shrimp and chicken; simmer uncovered 5 minutes or until shrimp is opaque and chicken is cooked. Stir in oysters; simmer 1 to 2 minutes or until edges begin to curl. Discard bay leaf; ladle into bowls. Serve with hot sauce.

The Guilt-Free "Comfort Food" Cookbook

Per Serving: 260 Calories, 6 g Fat (1 g Saturated), 50 mg Cholesterol, 975 mg Sodium, 18 g Protein, 32 g Carbohydrates

A Great Source of: Vitamin B3 (26%),Vitamin B12 (90%), Vitamin C (59%), Vitamin E (33%), Copper (70%), Iron (26%), Zinc (180%)

A Good Source of: Fiber (4 g), Vitamin A (13%), Vitamin B1 (19%), Vitamin B2 (11%), Vitamin B6 (21%), Folic Acid (24%), Calcium (12%), Magnesium (21%), Potassium (520 mg)

Pyramid Equivalent(s): ½ Bread, 2 Vegetables, 1 Meat

The Guilt-Free "Comfort Food" Cookbook

Time: 35 minutes prep
25 minutes cooking
Yield: 6 servings

Seafood and Artichoke Casserole

*1 (10-ounce) package frozen
    artichoke hearts
vegetable cooking spray
1/2 pound sliced fresh mushrooms
2 pounds medium shrimp,
    peeled and deveined
1/4 cup plus 1 tablespoon
    all-purpose flour
2/3 cup 2% lowfat milk*

*1 (8-ounce) can unsalted
    cream-style corn
1 (2-ounce) jar diced pimento,
    drained
2 teaspoons paprika
2 teaspoons Worcestershire sauce
1/2 teaspoon salt
2/3 cup nonfat sour cream
1/2 cup freshly grated*

Cook artichokes according to package directions without salt; drain well, and pat dry with paper towels. Cut in half.

Coat a nonstick skillet with cooking spray; add mushrooms, and saute over medium-high heat until mushrooms are tender and liquid is evaporated. Remove from skillet, and set aside. Add shrimp to skillet and saute 3 to 4 minutes or until shrimp just turn opaque. Remove from heat, and set aside.

Preheat oven to 350°. Combine flour and milk in a medium bowl, stirring until smooth with a wire whisk. Stir in corn, pimento, paprika, Worcestershire sauce, and salt; add to skillet. Bring to a boil, stirring constantly. Remove from heat, and stir in artichoke hearts, shrimp, and mushrooms. Pour into a shallow 2-quart casserole coated with cooking spray; sprinkle with Parmesan. Bake, uncovered, 20 to 25 minutes or until bubbly and lightly browned. Serve with rice, if desired.

Per Serving: 315 Calories, 6 g Fat (3 g Saturated), 110 mg Cholesterol, 635 mg Sodium, 6 g Fiber, 41 g Protein, 25 g Carbohydrates

A Great Source of: Fiber (6 g), Vitamin B2 (29%), Vitamin B3 (34%), Vitamin B12 (34%), Vitamin C (29%), Vitamin E (45%), Copper (33%), Iron (30%)

A Good Source of: Vitamin A (23%), Vitamin B1 (13%), Vitamin B6 (15%), Folic Acid (23%), Pantothenic Acid (16%), Calcium (24%), Magnesium (23%), Zinc (19%)

Pyramid Equivalent(s): 1⅓ Vegetables, 2 Dairy, ⅔ Meat

Note: When served with rice: 1 Bread.

The Guilt-Free "Comfort Food" Cookbook

VEGETABLE MAIN DISHES: RICE AND BEANS ... GRAINS AND GREENS

In this book, we've approached the twin challenges of eating right and eating well from a perspective of balance and proportion. Most of our main dishes mix animal foods with vegetables, grains, beans—even fruits. That creates satisfying dishes that help us eat the Pyramid way.

There are many ways up and down the Pyramid, though. One strategy that works for many is to balance your foods not within each main dish itself but over several meals. Perhaps you like steak. Have one—a real steak, a juicy piece. Then have another meal which contains all vegetables. All vegetables doesn't mean steamed broccoli and a salad, however. You'll still need protein. That's where beans come in.

Beans, which contain everything a newborn plant needs to survive, are rich in iron and other minerals, folic acid, and other B vitamins, trace elements, fiber, and complex carbohydrates, with almost no fat. That's why nutritionists love them. But we hope you'll love them because they are delicious when cooked correctly. Combining beans and grains balances the protein more, which is why nearly every land-based culture in the world makes a central dish from the combination.

The Guilt-Free "Comfort Food" Cookbook

Every dish in the chapter contains enough protein to qualify as a main dish. Many get their protein from beans, others from dairy foods. Each contains about fifteen to twenty grams of protein per serving. Thus, most dishes count as 1 Meat or 1 Dairy in the Pyramid. And more: Posole Bean Chili (p. 216) counts not only as 2 Meats but 2 Breads, 1 Vegetable, and 1½ Dairy. Now you're building a Pyramid! Greens and Beans over Grilled Polenta (p. 220) is not only 1 Meat, but 1½ Breads, 3 Vegetables, and ½ Dairy. And so on.

But numbers can only carry you so far. What makes these dishes hold up to the expectations of the dinner crowd is that they are filling, warm, flavorful, and real. They satisfy a hungry man, woman, or *teenager*. Fill out the plate with more vegetables from the chapters on Soups (p. 111), Salads (p. 121), and Vegetable Side Dishes (p. 227).

And leave room for Desserts (p. 259). When you incorporate a few meatless main dishes, such as these, with vegetable side dishes to produce all-vegetable meals three or four times a week, you'll be consuming less fat, much less saturated fat, and probably fewer calories. That leaves more room for occasional Extras in the form of dessert.

The Guilt-Free "Comfort Food" Cookbook

Time: 10 minutes prep
30 minutes for sauce to stand
20 minutes cooking
Yield: 4 servings

Pinto Pasta

*H*ere's a Tex-Mex main dish.

6 medium-sized plum tomatoes
1 cup drained cooked pinto
* beans*
2 tablespoons olive oil
3 cloves garlic, crushed
1/4 cup minced fresh cilantro
1/4 cup chopped green onion

1/2 teaspoon ground cumin
1/4 teaspoon red pepper
1/4 teaspoon salt
8 ounces vermicelli, uncooked
4 ounces diced reduced-fat
* Monterey Jack cheese*

Chop tomatoes over a bowl to collect juices; add tomatoes, pintos, olive oil, garlic, cilantro, green onion, cumin, red pepper, and salt, stirring well. Cover and let stand at room temperature at least 30 minutes (up to 2 hours).

Cook vermicelli according to package directions, omitting salt and fat. Drain; place in a serving bowl. Toss pasta with tomato mixture and cheese. Serve immediately.

Per Serving: 435 Calories, 14 g Fat (4 g Saturated), 20 mg Cholesterol, 240 mg Sodium, 20 g Protein, 59 g Carbohydrates

A Great Source of: Fiber (7 g), Vitamin B1 (30%), Folic Acid (26%), Vitamin C (34%)

A Good Source of: Vitamin B2 (14%), Vitamin B3 (17%), Vitamin B6 (11%), Vitamin E (17%), Copper (17%), Iron (22%), Magnesium (16%), Potassium (490 mg)

Pyramid Equivalent(s): 2 Breads, 1 Vegetable, 1 Dairy, ½ Meat

The Guilt-Free "Comfort Food" Cookbook

Time: 10 minutes prep
30 minutes for red rice
25 minutes for pineapple salsa
Yield: 6 servings

Miami Rice and Beans

*H*ere's another complete meal. It's got at least a serving from four of the five Pyramid groups. It's incredibly nutritious and delicious.

vegetable cooking spray
2 teaspoons olive oil
1 red pepper, cut into 1^1/$_2$-x
   ^{1}/$_4$-inch strips
2 cloves garlic, minced
1 teaspoon sweet paprika
^{1}/$_2$ teaspoon ground cumin
^{1}/$_4$ teaspoon ground allspice

2 (16-ounce) cans black beans,
   rinsed and drained
1^1/$_2$ tablespoons balsamic
   vinegar
1 teaspoon hot sauce (such as
   Tabasco)
Red Rice (recipe follows)
Roasted Pineapple Salsa
   (recipe follows)

Coat a large heavy skillet with cooking spray; add olive oil and place over medium heat until hot. Add pepper strips and garlic; saute until tender. Add spices; saute 1 minute. Add beans, vinegar, and hot sauce; reduce heat to low and cook, stirring gently, 3 minutes or until hot.

Spoon Red Rice evenly into bowls; spoon bean mixture evenly over rice. Top with Roasted Pineapple Salsa.

Red Rice
Yield: 3^1/$_2$ cups

1 (14^1/$_2$-ounce) can unsalted
   stewed tomatoes, undrained
1^1/$_2$ cups canned
   reduced-sodium chicken
   broth, undiluted

1 cup white basmati or long-
   grain white rice, uncooked
^{1}/$_4$ teaspoon red pepper

Bring tomatoes and chicken broth to a boil in a heavy medium saucepan; add rice and red pepper. Cover, reduce heat, and simmer 20 minutes or until rice is tender and liquid is absorbed.

The Guilt-Free "Comfort Food" Cookbook

Roasted Pineapple Salsa
Yield: 4 cups

4 cups diced fresh pineapple
2 teaspoons olive oil
2 tablespoons light brown sugar

1 tablespoon balsamic vinegar
  or lime juice
$1/4$ cup minced fresh cilantro

Preheat oven to 500°. Toss pineapple and olive oil on a large nonstick baking sheet; bake for 15 minutes or until lightly browned, stirring after 8 minutes. Transfer to a bowl; stir in brown sugar. Let cool to room temperature; stir in vinegar and cilantro.

Per Serving (rice with beans and salsa): 430 Calories, 5 g Fat (1 g Saturated), 0 mg Cholesterol, 341 mg Sodium, 17 g Protein, 83 g Carbohydrates

A Great Source of: Fiber (16 g), Vitamin B1 (46%), Folic Acid (61%), Vitamin C (84%), Copper (30%), Iron (32%), Magnesium (35%), Potassium (920 mg)

A Good Source of: Vitamin A (15%), Vitamin B2 (11%), Vitamin B3 (16%), Vitamin B6 (15%), Pantothenic Acid (10%), Vitamin E (10%), Zinc (15%)

Pyramid Equivalent(s): 1 Bread, 1½ Fruits, 1 Vegetable, 1 Meat

The Guilt-Free "Comfort Food" Cookbook

Time: 1 hour to "quick-soak"
dry beans
1$^1/_2$ hours cooking
Yield: 5 cups (5 servings)

Posole Bean Chili

*O*n a chilly winter evening, warm up with a steaming bowl of chili. It's about as American as food can get, with roots in Native American cooking of the Southwest. This version is inspired by Mexican posole made with hominy, which is corn dehulled and degermed. (Dried again and ground, hominy becomes grits.) Corn and beans combine to form a complete protein in this traditional vegetarian main dish. You won't miss the meat!

2 cups dry pinto beans
water
1 large onion, chopped
2 cloves garlic, minced
2 tablespoons chili powder
2 teaspoons ground cumin
1 teaspoon dried oregano
1 (14$^1/_2$-ounce) can Mexican-
style stewed tomatoes,
undrained
1 (16-ounce) can yellow hominy,
drained

$^1/_2$ teaspoon salt
$^1/_2$ cup minced fresh cilantro

Optional additions:
2$^1/_2$ cups cooked rice
$^3/_4$ cup plus 3 tablespoons
shredded reduced-fat cheese
$^1/_2$ cup plus 2 tablespoons
seeded and finely chopped
tomatoes
$^1/_4$ cup plus 1 tablespoon finely
chopped avocado

Rinse beans, place in a large heavy saucepan. Cover with water 2 inches above beans; bring to a boil. Boil 1 minute. Cover, remove from heat, and let stand 1 hour.

Drain and return beans to saucepan; cover with water 1 inch above beans. Add onion, garlic, chili powder, cumin, and oregano; bring to a boil. Cover, reduce heat, and simmer 1 hour, or until beans are just tender. Stir in tomatoes, hominy, and salt; simmer, uncovered, 30 minutes or until thickened. Stir in cilantro.

Serving suggestion: Spoon ½ cup cooked rice into each serving bowl, top with 1 cup chili, 2 tablespoons cheese, 2 tablespoons tomato, and 1 tablespoon avocado.

The Guilt-Free "Comfort Food" Cookbook

Per Serving (without toppings): 300 Calories, 2 g Fat (0 g Saturated), 0 mg Cholesterol, 450 mg Sodium, 14 g Protein, 59 g Carbohydrates

A Great Source of: Fiber (16 g), Folic Acid (62%), Vitamin C (31%), Copper (26%), Iron (33%), Magnesium (28%), Potassium (980 mg)

A Good Source of: Vitamin A (17%), Vitamin B1 (22%), Vitamin B2 (11%), Vitamin B6 (14%), Calcium (13%), Zinc (19%)

Pyramid Equivalent(s): 1 Bread, 1 Vegetable, 2 Meats

Per Serving (with rice, cheese, and other toppings): 575 Calories, 12 g Fat (5 g Saturated), 30 mg Cholesterol, 790 mg Sodium, 31 g Protein, 91 g Carbohydrates

A Great Source of: Fiber (17 g), Vitamin B1 (35%), Folic Acid (65%), Vitamin C (39%), Calcium (52%), Copper (31%), Iron (41%), Magnesium (33%), Potassium (1,155 mg)

A Good Source of: Vitamin A (19%), Vitamin B2 (14%), Vitamin B3 (17%), Vitamin B6 (21%), Pantothenic Acid (12%), Vitamin E (11%), Zinc (22%)

Pyramid Equivalent(s): 2 Breads, 1 Vegetable, 2 Meats, 1½ Dairy

The Guilt-Free "Comfort Food" Cookbook

Time: 15 minutes prep
1 hour to let relish stand and cook rice
12 minutes cooking
Yield: 6 servings

Black Beans and Wild Rice with Spicy Mango Salsa

*H*ere's another one-dish dinner. Make the relish first, and while it is standing, cook the rice, prep the vegetables, set the table, and then, just before you're ready to sit down, start cooking.

vegetable cooking spray
2 teaspoons olive oil
2 cloves garlic, minced
1 cup finely chopped red pepper
1/2 cup sliced green onion
3 cups cooked black beans, drained

3 cups cooked wild rice, cooked without salt or fat
2/3 cup minced fresh cilantro
Spicy Mango Relish (recipe follows)

Coat a large nonstick skillet with cooking spray; add oil, and place over medium-high heat until hot. Add garlic and red pepper; saute 5 minutes or until tender. Stir in green onion; saute 1 minute. Stir in beans, rice, and cilantro; cook 2 minutes or until hot, stirring frequently. Spoon Spicy Mango Relish over bean mixture to serve.

Spicy Mango Relish
Yield: 1 1/2 cups

1 cup finely diced mango
1/2 cup finely diced red onion
1/3 cup finely diced poblano chile peppers
1 tablespoon honey
1 tablespoon white wine vinegar

1 tablespoon olive oil
1/2 teaspoon curry powder (optional)
1/4 teaspoon salt
1/4 teaspoon red pepper

Combine all ingredients; mix well. Cover and let stand at room temperature 1 hour before serving.

The Guilt-Free "Comfort Food" Cookbook

Per Serving: 275 Calories, 5 g Fat (1 g Saturated), 0 mg Cholesterol, 95 mg Sodium, 12 g Protein, 50 g Carbohydrates

A Great Source of: Fiber (10 g), Folic Acid (42%), Vitamin C (100%)

A Good Source of: Vitamin A (22%), Vitamin B1 (20%), Vitamin B2 (10%), Vitamin B3 (10%), Vitamin B6 (15%), Vitamin E (12%), Copper (18%), Iron (15%), Magnesium (24%), Zinc (15%), Potassium (550 mg)

Pyramid Equivalent(s): 1 Bread, ¾ Vegetable, 1 Meat, ½ Fruit

The Guilt-Free "Comfort Food" Cookbook

Time: 30 minutes to make polenta
1 hour cooking
Yield: 4 servings

Greens and Beans over Grilled Polenta

ere's a complete meal. It provides servings from every Pyramid category except Fruits. That food balance is reflected in the superior nutritional profile; this dish is incredibly rich in fiber, vitamin A, vitamin C, folic acid, calcium, iron, magnesium, and potassium, yet low in fat. Tastes good too. Tastes great, actually. To save time, substitute pre-cooked polenta (if you can find it in your supermarket).

Basic Polenta (recipe follows)
vegetable cooking spray
2 slices bacon, diced
1 1/2 pounds turnip greens,
*   tough stems trimmed*
3 cloves garlic, minced
1 large onion, chopped
1 (14 1/2-ounce) can unsalted
*   Italian-style stewed*
*   tomatoes, undrained*

1 teaspoon dried thyme
1/2 teaspoon freshly ground
*   pepper*
1 (15-ounce) can cannellini
*   beans (white kidney),*
*   drained*
hot sauce

Prepare Basic Polenta; pour in 9-inch square baking pan coated with cooking spray. Cool; chill until firm.

Cook bacon in a large heavy skillet until crisp; transfer bacon with a slotted spoon to paper towels to drain; reserve 2 teaspoons drippings in skillet. Crumble bacon, and set aside.

Rinse greens and shake off excess water. Stack leaves and cut into 1-inch strips. Saute garlic and onion in drippings over medium-high heat 4 minutes. Add tomatoes, thyme, and pepper; bring to a boil. Reduce heat to medium; add greens by handfuls, stirring it down as leaves wilt. Cover and cook over medium-low heat 10 to 15 minutes or until tender, stirring occasionally.

Stir in beans; cook, stirring constantly, until hot. (Or spoon into a shallow 1½-quart casserole coated with cooking spray. Cover with aluminum

The Guilt-Free "Comfort Food" Cookbook

foil, and refrigerate until serving time; bake, covered, at 350° for 30 minutes or until hot.) Stir in hot sauce to taste.

Meanwhile, cut polenta into 8 equal triangles or rectangles. Coat a large nonstick skillet or griddle with cooking spray; heat over medium heat. Cook polenta triangles on both sides until golden. Serve with greens mixture.

Basic Polenta
Yield: 2¹/₂ cups

3 cups water
¹/₂ teaspoon salt
1 cup stone-ground yellow
    cornmeal

¹/₄ teaspoon ground red pepper
¹/₄ cup grated Parmesan cheese
vegetable cooking spray

Bring water to a boil in a heavy medium saucepan; stir in salt. Gradually pour in cornmeal, beating vigorously with a wire whisk to blend. Reduce heat and simmer, uncovered, 20 to 25 minutes or until thick, stirring frequently.

Remove from heat; stir in pepper and cheese.

Per Serving (greens and polenta): 400 Calories, 6 g Fat (2 g Saturated), 8 mg Cholesterol, 500 mg Sodium, 21 g Protein, 71 g Carbohydrates

A Great Source of: Fiber (15 g), Vitamin A (138%), Vitamin B1 (31%), Vitamin B6 (37%), Folic Acid (110%), Vitamin C (200%), Vitamin E (49%), Calcium (57%), Copper (56%), Iron (47%), Magnesium (46%), Potassium (1,530 mg)

A Good Source of: Vitamin B2 (21%), Vitamin B3 (17%), Pantothenic Acid (13%), Zinc (20%)

Pyramid Equivalent(s): 1½ Breads, 3 Vegetables, ½ Dairy, 1 Meat

The Guilt-Free "Comfort Food" Cookbook

Time: 15 minutes prep
32 minutes cooking
Yield: 6 servings

Curried Vegetable Couscous

*T*o make this into a main dish, stir in a quarter cup of toasted pumpkin or sunflower seeds and four ounces of crumbed goat or feta cheese.

vegetable cooking spray
1 tablespoon olive oil
1¹/₂ cups sliced small
   cauliflowerets
1 cup diced zucchini
1 cup diced red onion
2 cloves garlic, minced

2 teaspoons curry powder
¹/₄ teaspoon salt
¹/₄ teaspoon red pepper
1 cup canned chickpeas, drained
¹/₄ cup raisins
3 cups cooked couscous
¹/₃ cup minced fresh parsley

Preheat oven to 350°. Coat a large heavy skillet with cooking spray; add olive oil, and heat over medium-high heat. Add cauliflower, zucchini, red onion, and garlic; saute 5 minutes or until just tender. Stir in curry powder; saute 1 minute. Remove from heat.

Stir in remaining ingredients; transfer to a 1½-quart baking dish. Cover with aluminum foil, and bake for 25 to 30 minutes or until hot.

Per Serving: 210 Calories, 3 g Fat (0 g Saturated), 0 mg Cholesterol, 105 Sodium, 7 g Protein, 39 g Carbohydrates
A Great Source of: Vitamin C (29%)
A Good Source of: Fiber (4 g), Vitamin B6 (10%), Folic Acid (21%), Copper (10%), Iron (11%), Potassium (370 mg)
Pyramid Equivalent(s): 1 Bread, 1 Vegetable, ½ Meat

Note: With seeds and feta: 270 Calories, 10 g Protein, 8 g Fat (3 g Saturated), Calcium (14%); add ⅔ Dairy and ½ Meat to Pyramid Equivalents.

The Guilt-Free "Comfort Food" Cookbook

Hominy Grits, Eggplant, and Tomato Casserole

3³/₄ cups water
¹/₂ teaspoon salt
³/₄ cups hominy grits
¹/₂ cup grated Parmesan
* cheese, divided*
vegetable cooking spray

1 pound diced eggplant
1¹/₂ cups commercial fat-free
* chunky tomato sauce*
2 cups (8 ounces) reduced-fat
* shredded mozzarella cheese*

Preheat oven to 375°. Bring water and salt to a boil in a heavy medium saucepan. Gradually add grits, stirring with a wire whisk until smooth. Reduce heat and simmer, uncovered, 10 minutes or until thick and smooth, stirring frequently. Remove from heat and stir in ¼ cup Parmesan. Pour into a shallow 1½-quart casserole coated with cooking spray.

Coat a large nonstick skillet with cooking spray; place over medium-high heat. Add eggplant, and saute until golden and just tender.

Sprinkle 2 tablespoons remaining Parmesan over grits; spoon eggplant evenly on top. Pour tomato sauce over eggplant; sprinkle with remaining 2 tablespoons Parmesan and mozzarella. Bake for 30 minutes; broil 2 to 3 minutes, if desired, to brown top. Let stand 10 minutes before serving.

Per Serving: 235 Calories, 10 g Fat (6 g Saturated), 27 mg Cholesterol, 650 mg Sodium, 17 g Protein, 22 g Carbohydrates
A Great Source of: Fiber (6 g), Calcium (41%)
A Good Source of: Vitamin B2 (11%), Zinc (15%), Potassium (365 mg)
Pyramid Equivalent(s): 1 Bread, 2 Vegetables, 2 Dairy

The Guilt-Free "Comfort Food" Cookbook

Time: 10 minutes prep
10 minutes to make Alfredo sauce
7 minutes cooking
Yield: 6 servings

Fettuccine Alfredo with Spring Vegetables

vegetable cooking spray
1¹/₂ cups sugar snap or snow
* pea pods*
³/₄ cup baby carrots, trimmed
* and cut in half lengthwise*
1 cup small fresh broccoli
* flowerets*

1 cup sliced fresh mushrooms
Goat Cheese Alfredo Sauce
* (recipe follows)*
12 ounces fettuccine, cooked
* without salt or fat*

Coat a large nonstick skillet with cooking spray; place over medium heat until hot. Add sugar snap peas and carrots, and saute 2 minutes. Add broccoli and mushrooms; saute just until vegetables are crisp-tender.

Stir in Goat Cheese Alfredo Sauce; cook just until hot. Pour over hot cooked fettuccine, and toss well.

Goat Cheese Alfredo Sauce
Yield: 2 cups

1¹/₂ cups nonfat cottage cheese
4 ounces goat cheese
2 tablespoons butter-flavored
* granules*

¹/₂ cup skimmed milk
1 teaspoon dried basil leaves
¹/₂ teaspoon freshly ground
* pepper*

Combine all ingredients in container of an electric blender; process until smooth, scraping sides of blender as necessary. Pour into a small saucepan; cook over low heat, stirring constantly until hot. (Do not boil; mixture will separate. If it separates, return to blender and reprocess or press through a fine-mesh sieve.)

Per Serving (fettuccine, vegetables, and sauce): 325 Calories, 5 g Fat (3 g Saturated), 12 mg Cholesterol, 325 mg Sodium, 20 g Protein, 50 g Carbohydrates
A Great Source of: Vitamin B1 (26%), Vitamin B2 (25%), Vitamin C (63%)
A Good Source of: Fiber (4 g), Vitamin A (19%), Vitamin B3 (17%), Vitamin B6 (12%), Folic Acid (12%), Pantothenic Acid (10%), Calcium (12%), Copper (20%), Iron (21%), Magnesium (13%), Zinc (10%), Potassium (340 mg)
Pyramid Equivalent(s): 2 Breads, 1½ Vegetables, 1 Dairy

The Guilt-Free "Comfort Food" Cookbook

Time: 5 minutes prep
25 minutes to cook barley
50 minutes cooking
Yield: 6 to 8 servings

Vegetable Barley Casserole

*H*ere's another complete, meatless casserole meal. It's got servings from four of the five sections of the Pyramid. High fiber dishes such as this casserole help us feel full, which helps in weight control. For the minced herbs, use whatever you have at hand; it would be fine, for example, with just fresh basil.

1 (16-ounce) package frozen broccoli, carrots, and water chestnuts
1 cup frozen corn
1/2 cup canned diluted, reduced-sodium beef broth
3 cups cooked barley, cooked without salt or fat
1/4 cup minced fresh herbs: basil, cilantro, thyme, dill

vegetable cooking spray
1 cup egg substitute or 4 large eggs, beaten
1 (15-ounce) carton reduced-fat ricotta cheese
1/2 cup grated Parmesan cheese, divided
1/4 teaspoon salt

Preheat oven to 375°. Combine mixed vegetables, corn, and beef broth in a heavy large saucepan; bring to a boil. Cover, reduce heat, and simmer 10 minutes. Remove from heat; stir in barley and herbs. Spoon into a shallow 2-quart baking dish coated with cooking spray.

Beat egg product, ricotta cheese, ¼ cup Parmesan, and salt until smooth, using a wire whisk; spread evenly over vegetable mixture. Sprinkle with remaining Parmesan; bake for 30 to 35 minutes or until top is set and golden.

Per Serving: 325 Calories, 10 g Fat (5 g Saturated), 25 mg Cholesterol, 460 mg Sodium, 21 g Protein, 43 g Carbohydrates

A Great Source of: Fiber (10 g), Vitamin A (50%), Vitamin B2 (37%), Calcium (31%)

A Good Source of: Vitamin B1 (15%), Vitamin B3 (15%), Vitamin B6 (10%), Folic Acid (12%), Pantothenic Acid (15%), Vitamin C (13%), Vitamin E (12%), Copper (19%), Iron (15%), Magnesium (14%), Zinc (17%), Potassium (500 mg)

Pyramid Equivalent(s): 1 Bread, 1 Vegetable, 1 Dairy, ½ Meat

The Guilt-Free "Comfort Food" Cookbook

Time: 15 minutes prep
45 minutes cooking
Yield: 6 servings

Vegetable Rice Casserole

*T*ry this as a main dish for a meatless dinner one night. The dairy products provide plenty of protein, plus calcium; serve with bread and a green salad.

*1 (16-ounce) package frozen
cauliflower, broccoli, and
carrots*
*1 (15-ounce) carton reduced-fat
ricotta cheese*
*1 cup (4 ounces) shredded
reduced-fat Monterey Jack
cheese*

*$1/2$ cup reduced-fat mayonnaise
or reduced-fat sour cream*
$1/4$ teaspoon salt
$1/4$ teaspoon white pepper
$1/2$ teaspoon garlic powder
*3 cups cooked rice, cooked
without salt or fat*
*$1/2$ cup sliced green onion
vegetable cooking spray*

Preheat oven to 350°. Cook vegetables in a small amount of boiling water 5 minutes; drain well.

Combine ricotta, Monterey Jack, sour cream, salt, white pepper, and garlic powder in a large bowl; stir well. Add cooked vegetables, rice, and green onion; mix well. Spoon into a shallow 2-quart casserole coated with cooking spray. Cover with aluminum foil; bake for 20 minutes. Uncover and bake 20 to 25 minutes or until hot.

Per Serving: 385 Calories, 14 g Fat (6 g Saturated), 40 mg Cholesterol, 380 mg Sodium, 19 g Protein, 47 g Carbohydrates
A Great Source of: Fiber (5 g), Vitamin A (47%)
A Good Source of: Vitamin B1 (19%), Vitamin B2 (13%), Vitamin B3 (13%), Vitamin B6 (12%), Folic Acid (10%), Vitamin C (16%), Vitamin E (19%), Calcium (23%), Copper (11%), Iron (13%), Magnesium (11%), Zinc (12%), Potassium (315 mg)
Pyramid Equivalent(s): 1 Bread, 1 Vegetable, 2 Dairy

The Guilt-Free "Comfort Food" Cookbook

VEGETABLE SIDE DISHES

$\mathscr{E}$ating more vegetables may be the single most effective way to improve your diet. People who eat at least three servings of vegetables a day from a wide variety of sources have much lower rates of many chronic diseases.

Vegetables have dozens of protective compounds. Most are high in fiber, many are very rich in antioxidant vitamins such as beta-carotene and vitamin C, most are rich in folic acid, and many contain significant amounts of minerals such as iron. Garlic and onions have compounds that help prevent blood clots. Cabbage-family vegetables, including broccoli, cauliflower, and turnip greens, have compounds that help stimulate our livers to protect us against cancer-causing substances in the environment. Red, orange, yellow, and dark green vegetables are rich in beta-carotene and other related carotenoids, which may help protect against both cancer and heart disease.

So fill your plate with vegetables. One easy way to increase your intake is to simply have seconds. A Pyramid serving for most vegetables is quite small; for example, a half cup. So if you like a particular vegetable, and eat a cup and a half, that's 3 Vegetables right there. Our recipes make it even easier. One serving of our Five Vegetable Primavera (p. 241), counts as 3 Vegetables. Creole Okra and Tomatoes

The Guilt-Free "Comfort Food" Cookbook

(p. 250) is 2 Vegetables. So is Sweet-Sour Red Cabbage with Apples and Walnuts (p. 251). (We've also included a few grain-based side dishes in this chapter, which will help you boost your intake from the Breads group.)

Don't hesitate to make an all-vegetable lunch or dinner from this chapter alone. These dishes aren't rich enough in protein to qualify as main dishes by themselves, but put two or three or four together, and you'll easily reach the fifteen to twenty grams of protein a main dish needs. You don't need to get your protein quota at every meal. Most of us get more than we need. If you had eggs for breakfast, and a big turkey sandwich for lunch, you've gotten all you need. A vegetable-plate dinner from time to time can help you increase your fiber and vitamins while lowering your intake of fat and saturated fat.

The main purpose of this chapter, though, is to give you plenty of vegetable side dishes you can add to everyday meals. Improving the nutritional balance of a meal is often as simple as adding a second vegetable. So make room on your plate for the likes of Tex-Mex Corn Saute (p. 239), Garden Zucchini Skillet (p. 240), Sweet Potato and Pineapple Gratin (p. 244), Baked Pesto Tomatoes (p. 249), Sesame Broccoli Stir-Fry (p. 252), and Mint Peas (p. 254). It's the single most protective thing you can do for yourself and the people you love.

The Guilt-Free "Comfort Food" Cookbook

Time: 15 minutes prep
50 minutes cooking
Yield: 6 servings

Southwest Hoppin' John

*H*oppin' John, made with black-eyed peas and rice, comes from Charleston, South Carolina. It's said to be named after a lame local man named John who made his living peddling beans. We've spiced it up with some flavors more likely to be found in Albuquerque, New Mexico. If you double the serving size, this can be a main dish too.

vegetable cooking spray
1 medium onion, chopped
4 cloves garlic, minced
2 red or green bell peppers, chopped
1 jalapeno pepper, seeded and minced (optional)
1 teaspoon ground cumin
2¹/₂ cups canned reduced-sodium chicken broth, undiluted

1 (16-ounce) package frozen black-eyed peas
1 cup brown basmati rice, uncooked
¹/₄ pound diced reduced-fat, reduced-salt ham (optional)
¹/₄ teaspoon salt
2 cups seeded and finely diced tomatoes
¹/₂ cup minced cilantro

Coat a Dutch oven with cooking spray; place over medium-high heat until hot. Add onion and garlic; saute 1 minute. Add peppers and saute until vegetables are tender. Stir in cumin. Add broth, peas, rice, ham, and salt; bring to a boil. Cover, reduce heat, and simmer 45 to 50 minutes or until peas and rice are tender. Stir in tomato and cilantro; serve in bowls. Yield: 6 servings.

Per Serving (without ham): 220 Calories, 2 g Fat (0 g Saturated), 0 mg Cholesterol, 370 mg Sodium, 6 g Protein, 45 g Carbohydrates
A Great Source of: Fiber (7 g), Folic Acid (30%), Vitamin C (103%)
A Good Source of: Vitamin A (24%), Vitamin B1 (16%), Vitamin B2 (11%), Vitamin B3 (16%), Vitamin B6 (17%), Vitamin E (10%), Calcium (12%), Copper (14%), Iron (11%), Magnesium (24%), Zinc (10%), Potassium (585 mg)
Pyramid Equivalent(s): 1 Bread, 1 Vegetable, 1 Meat

The Guilt-Free "Comfort Food" Cookbook

Angel-Hair Pasta with Roasted Tomato Sauce

*W*hen you're working to slip extra vegetables into your meals, don't forget tomatoes. They're very high in vitamin C, and they contain the compound lycopene, which is distantly related to vitamin A and may help protect against cancer. When nutrition scientists study the diet of southern Italians, who have much lower rates of heart disease and cancer than we do, one thing they keep coming back to is how many more tomatoes they eat. In this recipe, roasting plum tomatoes give this sauce a depth you won't find in a jar. *Mangia!*

2 pounds large plum tomatoes (about 10)
1 tablespoon olive oil
3 cloves garlic, peeled and thinly sliced
1/4 cup sliced fresh basil leaves

1/4 teaspoon salt
1/2 teaspoon freshly ground pepper
8 ounces dried cappellini or angel-hair pasta

Preheat oven to 400°. Cut tomatoes in half crosswise and remove seeds. Toss with olive oil and garlic in a jelly-roll pan. Arrange tomatoes, skin sides up, in a single layer; bake for 23 to 25 minutes or until skins are golden brown. Transfer tomatoes and garlic to a food processor bowl; add basil, salt, and pepper. Pulse 12 to 15 times or until coarsely pureed.

Meanwhile, cook cappellini according to package directions without salt or fat. Drain and place in a serving bowl; add tomato mixture and toss well.

Note: To make this a main dish, stir in 4 ounces of feta cheese with the tomato sauce.

Per Serving: 280 Calories, 5 g Fat (1 g Saturated), 0 mg Cholesterol, 160 mg Sodium, 9 g Protein, 51 g Carbohydrates

A Great Source of: Fiber (5 g), Vitamin B1 (28%), Vitamin C (74%)

A Good Source of: Vitamin A (15%), Vitamin B2 (15%), Vitamin B3 (19%), Vitamin B6 (13%), Folic Acid (11%), Vitamin E (23%), Copper (16%), Iron (18%), Magnesium (13%), Potassium (575 mg)

Pyramid Equivalent(s): 2 Breads, 2 Vegetables

Note: With feta cheese: 355 Calories, 11 g Fat (5 g Saturated), 13 g Protein, 470 Sodium, Calcium (17%); add 1 Dairy to Pyramid Equivalents.

The Guilt-Free "Comfort Food" Cookbook

Time: 5 minutes prep
50 minutes cooking
Yield: 4 servings

Toasted Barley Pilaf with Pecans and Mushrooms

*A*re we afraid of fat? Consider pecans. Like most nuts, they are very high in fat, although they are low in saturated fat, and rich in vitamins and minerals. The key is to eat them in small amounts. In this recipe, two tablespoons helps flavor four servings. That's enough to impart a lovely flavor without much fat—comfort without guilt. Toasting barley, by the way, enhances both taste and texture.

1 tablespoon olive oil
2/3 cup medium barley
1 cup chopped green onion
1 cup thinly sliced shiitake or
*   button mushrooms*
2 cups canned reduced-sodium
*   chicken broth, undiluted*

1 tablespoon minced fresh
*   marjoram or thyme*
2 tablespoons finely chopped
*   pecans*
1/2 teaspoon freshly ground
*   pepper*

Heat oil in a heavy, medium saucepan over medium-high heat. Add barley and saute 5 to 7 minutes or until toasted. Add green onion and mushrooms; saute 3 minutes until onion is tender. Add chicken broth and marjoram; bring to a boil. Cover, reduce heat, and simmer 35 minutes or until barley is tender. Let stand, covered, 5 minutes; stir in pecans and pepper.

Per Serving: 240 Calories, 8 g Fat (1 g Saturated), 0 mg Cholesterol, 325 mg Sodium, 6 g Protein, 39 g Carbohydrates
A Great Source of: Fiber (9 g), Copper (27%)
A Good Source of: Vitamin B1 (11%), Vitamin B3 (13%), Vitamin E (13%), Iron (18%), Magnesium (10%), Potassium (295 mg)
Pyramid Equivalent(s): 1 Bread, 1½ Vegetables

The Guilt-Free "Comfort Food" Cookbook

Time: 10 minutes prep
15 minutes cooking
Yield: 4 to 6 servings

Kasha Pilaf with Dates and Walnuts

*Y*ou may know buckwheat as pancake flour. In the U.S. that's its most popular use. Kasha is buckwheat groats—the whole grain dehulled and lightly milled. It has a lovely, nutty flavor, particularly when it's toasted, as here.

1 egg white
1 cup whole grain kasha
2 cups reduced-sodium beef broth
1 cup sliced mushrooms

1/2 cup chopped onion
1/2 cup finely diced pitted dates
1/3 cup chopped toasted walnuts
2 tablespoons minced fresh parsley

Beat egg white with a fork in a medium bowl; add kasha, and toss to coat evenly with egg white.

Bring broth, mushrooms, and onion to a boil in a small saucepan. Meanwhile, toast kasha mixture in a nonstick skillet over medium-high heat 2 minutes, stirring constantly, until mixture is dry. Add to boiling broth mixture; cover, reduce heat, and simmer 7 to 10 minutes or until liquid is absorbed. Stir in dates, walnuts, and parsley.

Per Serving: 210 Calories, 5 g Fat (1 g Saturated), 0 mg Cholesterol, 600 mg Sodium, 9 g Protein, 37 g Carbohydrates

A Great Source of: Vitamin B2 (98%), Vitamin B3 (25%)

A Good Source of: Fiber (4 g), Vitamin B6 (10%), Copper (18%), Iron (10%), Magnesium (20%), Potassium (430 mg)

Pyramid Equivalent(s): 1 Bread, 1 Vegetable

The Guilt-Free "Comfort Food" Cookbook

Time: 5 minutes prep
20 minutes cooking
Yield: 6 servings

Herbed Quinoa Pilaf

*I*f you like peas, increase the peas!

2 fresh poblano chili peppers,
  seeded and coarsely
  chopped
3 cloves garlic
3 green onions, sliced
1/2 cup packed fresh cilantro
  leaves
1/4 cup packed fresh parsley
  leaves

2 tablespoons minced fresh
  oregano
2 cups reduced-sodium chicken
  broth, divided
1 cup quinoa, rinsed and
  drained
1 cup frozen petite green peas

Combine chili peppers, garlic, onions, cilantro, parsley, and oregano in an electric blender. Add ½ cup broth; cover and process until coarsely pureed.

Combine pureed mixture, remaining broth, and quinoa in a heavy medium saucepan; bring to a boil. Cover, reduce heat, and simmer 10 minutes.

Add peas; continue to cook 5 minutes or until quinoa is tender and liquid is evaporated.

Per Serving: 150 Calories, 3 g Fat (0 g Saturated), 0 mg Cholesterol, 250 mg Sodium, 6 g Protein, 26 g Carbohydrates
A Great Source of: Vitamin C (78%)
A Good Source of: Fiber (4 g), Vitamin B1 (10%), Vitamin E (17%), Copper (16%), Iron (23%), Magnesium (19%), Potassium (360 mg)
Pyramid Equivalent(s): 1 Bread, ½ Vegetable

The Guilt-Free "Comfort Food" Cookbook

Confetti Potato Patties

*C*an you imagine pan-cooked potato patties with no fat? Here they are!

1 pound baking potatoes
1 large carrot, shredded
1/2 cup minced green onions
2 egg whites
1/3 cup all-purpose flour

1 teaspoon dried thyme
1/4 teaspoon salt
1/4 teaspoon freshly ground
pepper
vegetable cooking spray

Peel and coarsely shred potatoes. In a large bowl, combine potatoes, carrots, green onions, egg whites, flour, thyme, salt, and pepper; stir well.

Coat a large skillet with cooking spray. For each patty, spoon ¼ cup potato mixture into hot skillet, pressing into 3-inch rounds with the back of a fork. Cook over medium heat 7 to 8 minutes on each side or until golden brown.

Note: To bake potato patties, spoon ¼ cup potato mixture on a non-stick baking sheet coated with cooking spray; press into 3-inch rounds with the back of a fork. Bake at 400° for 20 minutes, turning after 10 minutes.

Per Patty: 65 Calories, 0 g Fat (0 g Saturated), 0 mg Cholesterol, 70 mg Sodium,
2 g Protein, 14 g Carbohydrates
A Good Source of: Vitamin A (20%), Vitamin C (12%)
Pyramid Equivalent(s): ¾ Vegetable

The Guilt-Free "Comfort Food" Cookbook

Time: 10 minutes prep
25 minutes cooking
Yield: 6 servings

Spicy Crispy Fries

A small bag of fast-food French fries has 220 calories and twelve grams of fat (five of them saturated). A medium bag: 320 calories, seventeen grams of fat (seven saturated). A serving of our crispy spicy fries has 150 calories—and only two grams of fat!

3 large russet potatoes ($1^1/_2$ pounds)
1 large egg white
1 tablespoon olive oil

1 tablespoon lime juice
$1/_2$ teaspoon chili powder
$1/_4$ teaspoon salt
vegetable cooking spray

Scrub potatoes; cut each lengthwise into 3/8-inch ovals. Cut each oval lengthwise into 3/8-inch strips.

Preheat oven to 400°. Combine egg white and remaining ingredients in a large bowl; blend well with a wire whisk. Add potato strips; toss to coat. Spread potatoes on 2 nonstick baking sheets coated with cooking spray, leaving a little space between each. Bake for 25 to 35 minutes or until crisp, turning occasionally to brown evenly. Serve hot.

Per Serving: 150 Calories, 2 g Fat (0 g Saturated), 0 mg Cholesterol, 110 mg Sodium, 3 g Protein, 29 g Carbohydrates
A Great Source of: Vitamin C (26%)
A Good Source of: Fiber (3 g), Vitamin B6 (20%), Copper (17%), Potassium (490 mg)
Pyramid Equivalent(s): 2 Vegetables

The Guilt-Free "Comfort Food" Cookbook

Time: 15 minutes prep
25 minutes cooking
Yield: 3$\frac{1}{2}$ cups (7 servings)

Mashed Root Vegetables

1 pound russet potatoes, peeled
    and cut into 1$\frac{1}{2}$-inch pieces
$\frac{1}{2}$ pound parsnips, peeled and
    cut into 1-inch pieces
$\frac{1}{2}$ pound carrots, peeled and
    cut into 1-inch pieces
4 cloves garlic, peeled

2 tablespoons warm skim milk
2 tablespoons reduced-fat soft
    margarine
$\frac{1}{4}$ teaspoon ground ginger
$\frac{1}{2}$ teaspoon salt
$\frac{1}{4}$ teaspoon white pepper

Combine potatoes, parsnips, carrots, garlic, and water to cover in a
Dutch oven; bring to a boil. Cover, reduce heat, and simmer 15 to 20 minutes or until very tender. Drain well. Place vegetables in a large bowl,
mash with a potato masher until smooth, and cover with a plate to keep
warm.

Combine milk, margarine, ginger, salt, and pepper in a saucepan;
bring to a boil. Add to potato mixture, and beat well with a wooden spoon.
Serve immediately.

Per Serving: 115 Calories, 2 g Fat (0 g Saturated), 0 mg Cholesterol, 190 mg So-
dium, 2 g Protein, 24 g Carbohydrates
A Great Source of: Vitamin A (95%), Vitamin C (29%)
A Good Source of: Fiber (3 g), Vitamin B6 (15%), Copper (10%), Potassium (500
mg)
Pyramid Equivalent(s): 1½ Vegetables

The Guilt-Free "Comfort Food" Cookbook

Time: 20 minutes prep
30 minutes cooking
Yield: 6 servings

Chunky Vegetable Posole

vegetable cooking spray
2 teaspoons canola oil
1^1/$_2$ cups chopped onion
1^1/$_2$ cups chopped red or green
  bell pepper
3 cloves garlic, chopped
2 cups reduced-sodium chicken
  broth
2 (15^1/$_2$-ounce) cans yellow
  hominy, drained

1 (14^1/$_2$-ounce) can chopped
  whole tomatoes, undrained
1^1/$_2$ cups sliced zucchini
  (^{1}/$_2$-inch thick)
1 cup fresh or frozen corn
1 cup frozen butter beans
2 bay leaves
1 teaspoon dried oregano
1 teaspoon ground coriander
^{1}/$_2$ teaspoon crushed red pepper
3 cups cooked bulgur

Coat a Dutch oven with cooking spray; add oil, and place over medium-high heat until hot. Add onion, pepper, and garlic; saute 3 minutes. Add remaining ingredients except bulgur; bring to a boil. Cover partially, reduce heat, and simmer 20 minutes.

Spoon bulgur into serving bowls; top with vegetable mixture.

Per Serving: 245 Calories, 4 g Fat (1 g Saturated), 0 mg Cholesterol, 560 mg Sodium, 8 g Protein, 47 g Carbohydrates

A Great Source of: Fiber (9 g), Vitamin C (113%)

A Good Source of: Vitamin A (23%), Vitamin B3 (12%), Vitamin B6 (16%), Folic Acid (15%), Vitamin E (13%), Copper (15%), Iron (16%), Magnesium (21%), Zinc (13%), Potassium (560 mg)

Pyramid Equivalent(s): 2 Breads, 3 Vegetables

The Guilt-Free "Comfort Food" Cookbook

Tex-Mex Corn Saute

vegetable cooking spray
1 tablespoon olive oil
³/₄ cup chopped green pepper
³/₄ cup chopped onion
1 teaspoon ground cumin
2¹/₂ cups fresh corn
*2 large ripe tomatoes, peeled
   and chopped*

¹/₂ teaspoon sugar
¹/₄ teaspoon salt
*¹/₂ to 1 teaspoon hot sauce
   (such as Tabasco)*
*¹/₄ cup minced fresh cilantro or
   parsley*

Coat a large heavy skillet with cooking spray; add oil and place over medium-high heat until hot. Add green pepper and onion; saute until tender. Stir in cumin; add corn, and saute 3 to 5 minutes or until corn is just tender. Stir in tomatoes, sugar, salt, and hot sauce; saute 3 minutes. Remove from heat; stir in cilantro.

Per Serving: 100 Calories, 3 g Fat (0 g Saturated), 0 mg Cholesterol, 105 mg Sodium, 3 g Protein, 18 g Carbohydrates
A Great Source of: Vitamin C (45%)
A Good Source of: Fiber (3 g), Vitamin B1 (12%), Folic Acid (11%), Potassium (350 mg)
Pyramid Equivalent(s): 2 Vegetables

The Guilt-Free "Comfort Food" Cookbook

Time: 10 minutes prep
12 minutes cooking
Yield: 6 servings

Garden Zucchini Skillet

*F*or a delicious, quick dish, you can saute onions, then zucchini, and top with Parmesan shavings. This recipe adds tomatoes, fresh parsley, and fresh basil (or dill or oregano) for a memorable vegetable side dish.

vegetable cooking spray
1 cup chopped onion
1 tablespoon olive oil
4 medium zucchini (about 1³/4 pounds), sliced
1/2 pound sliced fresh mushrooms
3 medium tomatoes, seeded and chopped

1/4 cup minced fresh parsley
2 tablespoons minced fresh basil, dill, or oregano
1/2 teaspoon salt
1/2 teaspoon freshly ground pepper
2 ounces freshly shaved Parmesan cheese

Coat a nonstick Dutch oven with cooking spray; add onion, and saute over medium-high heat until tender. Add olive oil, zucchini, and mushrooms to skillet; cook 5 minutes or until crisp-tender, stirring often. Stir in tomatoes, herbs, salt, and pepper; cook 2 minutes, stirring often. Transfer to a serving dish; sprinkle with cheese. Serve immediately.

Per Serving: 110 Calories, 5 g Fat (2 g Saturated), 7 mg Cholesterol, 370 mg Sodium, 7 g Protein, 11 g Carbohydrates

A Great Source of: Vitamin C (50%), Potassium (680 mg)

A Good Source of: Fiber (3 g), Vitamin A (12%), Vitamin B1 (12%), Vitamin B2 (17%), Vitamin B3 (13%), Vitamin B6 (12%), Folic Acid (14%), Pantothenic Acid (12%), Vitamin E (12%), Calcium (17%), Copper (17%), Magnesium (12%)

Pyramid Equivalent(s): 2½ Vegetables

The Guilt-Free "Comfort Food" Cookbook

Time: 15 minutes prep
11 minutes cooking
Yield: 5 cups (4 to 6 servings)

Five Vegetable Primavera

*W*hen you look at the Pyramid, it can seem daunting to strive to eat three to five servings of vegetables every day. But if you like a vegetable, you're likely to eat more than one serving. Consider this easy, tasty dish. One of our servings has only eighty calories, yet counts for 3 Vegetables in the Pyramid. It's also incredibly rich in vitamins C and A (in the form of beta-carotene), two of the most important protective antioxidants.

1/4 cup reduced-sodium chicken broth, divided
2 teaspoons Dijon mustard
2 teaspoons white wine vinegar
vegetable cooking spray
1 tablespoon canola oil

1 1/2 cups sliced yellow squash
1 cup thinly sliced carrots
1 cup diced red pepper
3 cups broccoli flowerets
1/2 cup frozen peas, thawed
1/4 cup minced fresh parsley

Combine 2 tablespoons broth, mustard, and vinegar; mix well and set aside.

Coat a large nonstick skillet with cooking spray; add oil, and place over medium heat until hot. Add squash, carrots, and pepper; saute 5 to 6 minutes or until vegetables are just tender. Add remaining chicken broth to skillet; add broccoli and peas. Cover tightly and cook 4 to 5 minutes or until broccoli is crisp-tender. Stir in mustard mixture; saute 1 minute. Stir in parsley and serve immediately.

Per Serving: 80 Calories, 3 g Fat (0 g Saturated), 0 mg Cholesterol, 100 mg Sodium, 3 g Protein, 11 g Carbohydrates
A Great Source of: Vitamin A (110%), Vitamin C (170%)
A Good Source of: Fiber (4 g), Vitamin B6 (12%), Folic Acid (17%), Vitamin E (14%), Potassium (425 mg)
Pyramid Equivalent(s): 3 Vegetables

The Guilt-Free "Comfort Food" Cookbook

Time: 10 minutes prep
40 minutes cooking
Yield: 8 servings

Streusel Acorn Squash and Apples

*S*quash, apples, raisins, brown sugar, cinnamon, breakfast cereal, and a bit of gingersnaps turn an autumn staple into a family favorite.

2 acorn squash (1¹/₄ pounds each)
vegetable cooking spray
2 cooking apples, peeled and cut into ¹/₂-inch cubes
¹/₄ cup raisins
¹/₂ cup apple juice

¹/₄ cup Grape Nuts cereal (or whole-grain wheat nugget cereal)
¹/₄ cup crushed gingersnaps
¹/₄ cup firmly packed light brown sugar
¹/₂ teaspoon ground cinnamon

Preheat oven to 350°. Trim ends of squash; cut each squash into 4 equal-sized rings. Remove seeds and membrane. Arrange rings in a jelly-roll pan coated with cooking spray; arrange apples and raisins evenly inside squash rings. Pour apple juice evenly over apple mixtures; cover with aluminum foil and bake at 350° for 30 minutes.

Combine remaining ingredients, mixing well. Uncover squash, and sprinkle mixture evenly on squash. Bake, uncovered, 10 to 15 additional minutes or until squash is tender and topping is browned. Transfer to serving plates using a spatula.

Per Serving: 150 Calories, 1 g Fat (0 g Saturated), 0 mg Cholesterol, 54 mg Sodium, 2 g Protein, 37 g Carbohydrates

A Great Source of: Fiber (6 g), Potassium (630 mg)

A Good Source of: Vitamin A (10%), Vitamin B1 (17%), Vitamin B6 (100%), Vitamin C (23%), Iron (10%), Magnesium (14%)

Pyramid Equivalent(s): 1 Vegetable, ½ Fruit

The Guilt-Free "Comfort Food" Cookbook

Sweet Potato Souffles

**5 cups peeled and cubed sweet
potatoes**
$1/2$ cup lowfat lemon yogurt
2 tablespoons honey
2 teaspoons grated orange rind
$1/2$ teaspoon ground cinnamon

$1/4$ teaspoon ground nutmeg
4 egg whites
$1/4$ cup sugar
vegetable cooking spray
**$1/4$ cup finely crushed
gingersnaps**

Preheat oven to 325°. Cook sweet potato in boiling water to cover 15 to 20 minutes or until tender. Drain well, and mash until smooth.

In a large bowl, combine mashed sweet potato with yogurt, honey, orange rind, cinnamon, and nutmeg; mix well.

Beat egg whites in a small mixing bowl until foamy; gradually add sugar, beating until stiff peaks form. Gently fold egg whites into sweet potato mixture.

Coat 8 (¾-cup) ramekins (baking dishes) with cooking spray, and evenly spoon mixture into them. Sprinkle with gingersnaps, and place in a 13- x 9- x 2-inch baking pan. Pour hot water into pan to depth of 1 inch. Bake for 30 minutes or until set. Serve immediately.

Per Serving: 210 Calories, 1 g Fat (0 g Saturated), 1 mg Cholesterol, 77 mg Sodium, 5 g Protein, 46 g Carbohydrates

A Great Source of: Vitamin A (213%), Vitamin C (37%)

A Good Source of: Fiber (3 g), Vitamin B2 (17%), Vitamin B6 (16%), Copper (11%), Potassium (300 mg)

Pyramid Equivalent(s): 1½ Vegetables

The Guilt-Free "Comfort Food" Cookbook

Time: 5 minutes prep
1 hour and 5 minutes cooking
Yield: 6 servings

Sweet Potato and Pineapple Gratin

*Y*ou can serve these in the same casserole you bake them in (although it will be very hot when you bring it to the table). And the aromas will be so tempting, you have to remind everyone to be careful!

*1 (15¹/₄-ounce) can
    unsweetened crushed
    pineapple, undrained
2 tablespoons honey
¹/₄ teaspoon salt*

*2 medium-large sweet potatoes
    (about 1 pound), peeled and
    very thinly sliced
vegetable cooking spray
1¹/₄ cups crushed gingersnaps,
    divided*

Preheat oven to 375°. Drain pineapple, reserving pineapple and ½ cup juice separately. Add honey and salt to juice; stir well.

Arrange half of sweet potatoes in a 1½-quart casserole coated with cooking spray; spoon half of pineapple over potatoes. Top with half of gingersnap crumbs. Stir juice mixture; drizzle half over crumbs. Repeat layers of sweet potato and pineapple. Cover tightly with aluminum foil; bake for 55 minutes. Uncover, sprinkle with remaining gingersnap crumbs, and bake 10 minutes.

Per Serving: 235 Calories, 3 g Fat (0 g Saturated), 0 mg Cholesterol, 250 mg Sodium, 3 g Protein, 52 g Carbohydrates
A Great Source of: Vitamin A (130%), Vitamin C (31%)
A Good Source of: Fiber (3 g), Vitamin B1 (10%), Vitamin B2 (11%), Vitamin B6 (14%), Vitamin E (11%), Copper (13%), Iron (12%), Potassium (300 mg)
Pyramid Equivalent(s): ½ Bread, 1 Vegetable, 1 Fruit

The Guilt-Free "Comfort Food" Cookbook

Roasted Orange, Carrots, and Parsnips

*I*f parsnips aren't your favorite, try this with three-fourths a pound of medium-red potatoes—or just double the amount of carrots.

3/4 pound carrots
3/4 pound parsnips
1 1/2 tablespoons olive oil
1/4 teaspoon salt
1/4 teaspoon freshly ground
  pepper

1 tablespoon frozen orange
  juice concentrate
2 teaspoons balsamic vinegar
2 tablespoons minced fresh
  marjoram or parsley
  (optional)

Preheat oven to 450°. Peel carrots and parsnips; cut into 2 1/2- x 3/8-inch pieces. Toss with olive oil, salt, and pepper; arrange in a single layer on 2 large nonstick baking sheets. Bake for 15 minutes or until browned and tender, stirring every 5 minutes.

Transfer to a serving bowl; toss with remaining ingredients.

Per Serving: 100 Calories, 4 g Fat (1 g Saturated), 0 mg Cholesterol, 115 mg Sodium, 1 g Protein, 17 g Carbohydrates
A Great Source of: Vitamin A (160%), Vitamin C (34%), Folic Acid (52%)
A Good Source of: Fiber (4 g), Vitamin E (13%), Potassium (425 mg)
Pyramid Equivalent(s): 1⅓ Vegetables

The Guilt-Free "Comfort Food" Cookbook

Time: 15 minutes prep
1 hour cooking
Yield: 4 cups

Sweet Turnip Puree

*T*urnips are often unloved. Give them a chance! This dish sweetens turnips with pears and apple juice and then adds a tangy cheese touch at the end.

*1 tablespoon reduced-fat soft
   margarine
2 tablespoons minced shallots
2 pounds turnips, peeled and
   cut into 1-inch pieces
1/2 cup unsweetened apple juice
1/2 cup water
2 pounds pears, peeled, cored,
   and cut into 1-inch pieces*

*1/2 teaspoon salt
1/2 teaspoon white pepper
1/4 teaspoon freshly grated
   nutmeg
1/2 cup finely crumbled
   Gorgonzola cheese
vegetable cooking spray*

Melt margarine in a large heavy saucepan over medium heat; add shallots and cook until tender. Add turnips, apple juice, and water to skillet; bring to a boil. Cover, reduce heat, and simmer 10 minutes. Stir in pears; cover and continue cooking 20 to 35 minutes or until turnips and pears are very tender. Increase heat; uncover and boil, stirring frequently, until all liquid is evaporated.

Preheat oven to 350°. Transfer half of mixture to a food processor; add salt, pepper, and nutmeg, and process until smooth. Transfer to a bowl; repeat procedure using remaining turnip mixture. Stir into bowl; spoon mixture into a 1- to 1½-quart casserole coated with cooking spray; sprinkle with cheese. Bake for 10 to 15 minutes or until hot.

Per Serving: 155 Calories, 5 g Fat (2 g Saturated), 9 mg Cholesterol, 410 mg Sodium, 4 g Protein, 27 g Carbohydrates
A Great Source of: Fiber (6 g), Vitamin C (48%)
A Good Source of: Calcium (11%), Copper (12%), Potassium (400 mg)
Pyramid Equivalent(s): 2 Vegetables, 1 Fruit

The Guilt-Free "Comfort Food" Cookbook

Orange-Barbecued Limas

*O*range slices, steak sauce, and marmalade give new life to frozen limas.

vegetable cooking spray
1 tablespoon canola oil
1 large onion, chopped
¹/₃ cup spicy steak sauce (such
*   as Heinz 57)*
3 tablespoons orange
*   marmalade*
1 (10-ounce) package frozen
*   baby lima beans, cooked*
*   without salt or fat*

2 cups fresh orange sections,
*   seeded, chopped, and*
*   drained*
3 cups hot cooked long-grain
*   white or brown rice, cooked*
*   without salt or fat*

Coat a large heavy skillet with cooking spray; add oil, and heat over medium heat. Add onions; cook, stirring occasionally, 25 minutes or until very soft and lightly browned.

Stir in steak sauce and orange marmalade; add lima beans and cook 2 minutes, stirring frequently. Stir in orange sections; cook, stirring gently, until hot.

Spoon over rice to serve.

Per Serving: 280 Calories, 3 g Fat (0 g Saturated), 0 mg Cholesterol, 200 mg Sodium, 7 g Protein, 58 g Carbohydrates

A Great Source of: Fiber (5 g), Vitamin C (68%)

A Good Source of: Vitamin B1 (20%), Vitamin B3 (12%), Vitamin B6 (14%), Folic Acid (11%), Vitamin E (10%), Copper (15%), Iron (15%), Magnesium (15%), Potassium (500 mg)

Pyramid Equivalent(s): 1 Bread, 1 Vegetable, ⅔ Fruit

The Guilt-Free "Comfort Food" Cookbook

Time: 15 minutes prep
1 hour and 35 minutes cooking
Yield: 6 servings

Our Best Baked Beets

*B*eets are a wonderful source of fiber, folic acid, and vitamin C, and, perhaps surprisingly, iron. Slow cooking at low temperatures lets the beets' natural flavors develop. A brief saute in orange juice and sweet-tart balsamic vinegar with fresh chives makes them irresistible.

12 large beets (3 pounds)
2 tablespoons reduced-fat margarine
2 tablespoons frozen orange juice concentrate, thawed
1 tablespoon balsamic vinegar

1/4 teaspoon salt
1/2 teaspoon freshly ground pepper
1 tablespoon minced fresh chives

Preheat oven to 350°. Trim beets, leaving 1 inch of stem. Rinse; do not peel. Place beets in a 13- x 9- x 2-inch baking pan filled with 1/4-inch water. Cover with aluminum foil, and bake for 1 hour. Remove foil; bake 30 minutes or until tender. Let beets cool slightly; peel and slice into 1/4-inch rounds. Set aside.

Melt margarine in a medium skillet over low heat; add orange juice, vinegar, salt, pepper, chives, and beets. Cook, tossing gently, 3 to 4 minutes or until hot.

Per Serving: 115 Calories, 2 g Fat (0 g Saturated), 0 mg Cholesterol, 270 mg Sodium, 4 g Protein, 23 g Carbohydrates
A Great Source of: Fiber (6 g), Folic Acid (60%), Vitamin C (31%), Potassium (725 mg)
A Good Source of: Iron (10%), Magnesium (13%)
Pyramid Equivalent(s): 2 Vegetables

The Guilt-Free "Comfort Food" Cookbook

Baked Pesto Tomatoes

*T*ry these lovely side dishes not only for lunch or dinner, but as party food too. They're not finger food, though; you'll need plates.

1 cup packed fresh basil leaves
1 cup (4 ounces) shredded reduced-fat mozzarella cheese
1 to 2 cloves garlic, chopped
2 tablespoons reduced-sodium chicken broth (or water)
1 tablespoon olive oil

1/4 teaspoon salt
1/2 teaspoon freshly ground pepper
4 large ripe tomatoes, cut in half crosswise
3 tablespoons fine, dry breadcrumbs

Preheat oven to 400°. Process basil, mozzarella, garlic, broth, olive oil, salt, and pepper in a food processor until coarsely pureed.

Arrange tomato halves, cut sides up, in a baking dish just large enough to hold them. Spoon pesto mixture evenly on tomato halves; top evenly with breadcrumbs and Parmesan cheese. Bake at 400° for 12 to 15 minutes or until lightly browned.

Per Serving: 130 Calories, 7 g Fat (3 g Saturated), 13 mg Cholesterol, 250 mg Sodium, 8 g Protein, 9 g Carbohydrates
A Great Source of: Vitamin C (41%)
A Good Source of: Fiber (2 g), Vitamin A (14%), Vitamin E (14%), Calcium (21%), Potassium (335 mg)
Pyramid Equivalent(s): 1 Vegetable, 1 Dairy

The Guilt-Free "Comfort Food" Cookbook

Time: 5 minutes prep
30 minutes cooking
Yield: 6 servings

Creole Okra and Tomatoes

*T*his dish neatly illustrates the benefits of using small amounts of bacon for flavoring. The flavor permeates the entire dish, yet each serving has only two grams of fat, with only one gram saturated.

3 slices bacon
1 large sweet onion, chopped
4 cups sliced fresh okra or
* frozen okra, thawed*
1 (14¹/₂-ounce) can unsalted
* whole tomatoes, drained*
* and chopped*

1 bay leaf, broken
2 tablespoons minced fresh
* thyme or ¹/₂ teaspoon dried*
* thyme*
¹/₄ teaspoon salt
¹/₄ to ¹/₂ teaspoon red pepper

Cook bacon in a large heavy nonstick skillet until crisp; remove bacon, reserving 2 teaspoons drippings in skillet. Crumble bacon and set aside.

Add onion to skillet; saute over medium heat until tender. Add okra, tomatoes, bay leaf, thyme, salt, and red pepper; cover and cook 15 minutes. Uncover and cook 3 to 5 minutes or until okra is tender and liquid is mostly evaporated. Stir in bacon.

Per Serving: 80 Calories, 2 g Fat (1 g Saturated), 3 mg Cholesterol, 240 mg Sodium, 4 g Protein, 14 g Carbohydrates

A Great Source of: Vitamin C (51%)

A Good Source of: Fiber (4 g), Vitamin A (11%), Vitamin B1 (14%), Vitamin B6 (15%), Folic Acid (15%), Vitamin E (10%), Calcium (12%), Copper (10%), Iron (16%), Magnesium (19%)

Pyramid Equivalent(s): 2 Vegetables

The Guilt-Free "Comfort Food" Cookbook

Time: 10 minutes prep
30 minutes cooking
Yield: 6 cups (6 servings)

Sweet-Sour Red Cabbage
with Apples and Walnuts

*C*abbage and apples are made for each other.

**2 pounds thinly sliced red
    cabbage**
1/2 cup apple cider
*1/4 cup plus 3 tablespoons
    firmly packed light brown
    sugar*
*1/4 cup plus 3 tablespoons cider
    vinegar*
*1/4 teaspoon crushed caraway
    seeds*

1/2 teaspoon salt
*1/2 teaspoon freshly ground
    pepper*
**2 Granny Smith apples, peeled,
    cored, and cut into 8 wedges
    each**
*1/4 cup finely chopped toasted
    walnuts*

Combine cabbage and enough water to cover in a Dutch oven. Cover
and bring to a boil. Boil 5 minutes or just until tender. Drain well.

Combine cabbage, apple cider, brown sugar, vinegar, and caraway
seeds in a large saucepan. Bring to a boil, stirring constantly until sugar
melts. Cover, reduce heat, and simmer 15 to 20 minutes or until apples are
tender. Uncover and cook over high heat, stirring gently, just until liquid
evaporates. Stir in walnuts; serve hot.

Per Serving: 150 Calories, 4 g Fat (0 g Saturated), 0 mg Cholesterol, 210 mg So-
    dium, 3 g Protein, 29 g Carbohydrates
A Great Source of: Vitamin C (84%), Vitamin E (28%)
A Good Source of: Fiber (4 g), Vitamin B6 (10%), Folic Acid (17%), Magnesium
    (10%), Potassium (525 mg)
Pyramid Equivalent(s): ½ Fruit, 2 Vegetables

The Guilt-Free "Comfort Food" Cookbook

Time: 8 minutes prep
5 minutes cooking
Yield: 6 servings

Sesame Broccoli Stir-Fry

*S*tir-fries are quick and crisp. To make this into a main dish, simply add an eight-ounce block of tofu along with the broth, soy sauce, and sesame oil, and serve over half a cup or more of rice per person.

1 pound fresh broccoli
2 teaspoons peanut oil
2 cloves garlic, minced
8 ounces medium mushrooms,
*   quartered*
1 red pepper, cut into 1-inch
*   squares*

2 tablespoons reduced-sodium
*   chicken broth (or water)*
2 tablespoons reduced-sodium
*   soy sauce*
1 teaspoon sesame oil
1 tablespoon toasted sesame
*   seeds*

Trim off leaves of broccoli, and remove tough ends of lower stalks. Cut off and separate broccoli flowerets; cut stalks into ¼-inch slices. Set aside.

Pour peanut oil into wok or nonstick skillet; place over high heat until hot. Add garlic, and stir-fry 30 seconds. Add broccoli stalk slices and flowerets, mushrooms, and red pepper; stir-fry 2 minutes. Stir in broth, soy sauce, and sesame oil; stir-fry 2 minutes or until most of liquid is evaporated and vegetables are crisp-tender. Transfer to a serving bowl, and toss with sesame seeds.

Per Serving: 65 Calories, 3 g Fat (1 g Saturated), 0 mg Cholesterol, 225 mg Sodium, 4 g Protein, 8 g Carbohydrates
A Great Source of: Vitamin C (159%)
A Good Source of: Fiber (3 g), Vitamin A (19%), Vitamin B2 (16%), Vitamin B3 (11%), Vitamin B6 (11%), Folic Acid (16%), Pantothenic Acid (13%), Copper (15%), Potassium (420 mg)
Pyramid Equivalent(s): 1 Vegetable

Note: Made with tofu, and served over three cups of cooked white rice: 230 Calories, 6 g Fat (1 g Saturated), 10 g Protein, Iron (26%); Pyramid Equivalents would be 1 Bread, 1 Vegetable, and 1 Meat.

The Guilt-Free "Comfort Food" Cookbook

Neapolitan Eggplant Pizzas

ggplant slices become pizza slices!

vegetable cooking spray
2 medium eggplants (1$^1/_2$
  pounds each), unpeeled, cut
  into $^1/_4$-inch-thick slices
1 medium onion, thinly sliced
1 green or yellow pepper, thinly
  sliced
1 (15-ounce) carton refrigerated
  lowfat chunky tomato
  sauce (such as Contadina)

1 tablespoon red wine vinegar
$^1/_2$ teaspoon dried thyme
$^1/_4$ cup sliced ripe olives
1 cup (4 ounces) shredded
  reduced-fat mozzarella
  cheese
$^1/_4$ cup grated Parmesan cheese

Preheat oven to 350°. Coat a large nonstick skillet with cooking spray; heat over medium heat. Saute eggplant slices, in batches, until tender and lightly browned on both sides. Remove from skillet, and set aside. Add onion and pepper slices to skillet; saute until just tender. Set aside.

Coat a 12-inch pizza pan with cooking spray; arrange eggplant slices in an overlapping pattern to cover bottom. Combine tomato sauce, vinegar, thyme, and olives; spread evenly on eggplant to within 1 inch from edge. Arrange onion and pepper mixture on tomato sauce; bake for 30 minutes. Sprinkle with cheese; bake 5 minutes. Let cool 10 minutes; cut into wedges.

Per Serving: 105 Calories, 4 g Fat (2 g Saturated), 10 mg Cholesterol, 181 mg Sodium, 7 g Protein, 11 g Carbohydrates

A Good Source of: Fiber (3 g), Vitamin C (18%), Calcium (17%), Potassium (380 mg)

Pyramid Equivalent(s): 2 Vegetables, ½ Dairy

The Guilt-Free "Comfort Food" Cookbook

Time: 5 minutes prep
7 minutes cooking
Yield: 4 servings

Mint Peas

*F*resh chives, mint, and mint jelly give a memorable lift to peas.

2 cups frozen tiny tender peas,
  thawed
3 tablespoons chicken broth or
  water
2 tablespoons reduced-fat soft
  margarine

2 tablespoons mint jelly
1 tablespoon minced fresh
  chives
1 tablespoon minced fresh mint

Combine peas and broth in a medium saucepan; cover and bring to a simmer. Cook 3 to 5 minutes or until peas are tender. Stir in margarine, mint jelly, and chives. Cook over low heat, stirring constantly, until hot.

Note: If desired, substitute hot pepper jelly for mint jelly.

Per Serving: 110 Calories, 3 g Fat (0 g Saturated), 0 mg Cholesterol, 98 mg Sodium, 4 g Protein, 18 g Carbohydrates
A Great Source of: Fiber (5 g)
A Good Source of: Vitamin A (13%), Vitamin B1 (15%), Folic Acid (12%), Vitamin C (14%)
Pyramid Equivalent(s): 1 Vegetable

The Guilt-Free "Comfort Food" Cookbook

Asparagus with Warm Citrus Vinaigrette

*A*sparagus and orange sections combine nicely in flavors, textures, and colors. This dish helps you in the trickiest part of a quick family dinner—timing. Prep the asparagus, make the sauce, and set aside for a half-hour while you tend to the rest of dinner. Then, when everyone is already sitting down for dinner, a quick saute puts these crisply tender beauties on your plate.

*1/4 cup unsweetened orange
   juice*
*2 tablespoons white wine
   vinegar*
*1 tablespoon reduced-sodium
   soy sauce*
*1 tablespoon plus 1 teaspoon
   olive oil, divided*

1 teaspoon grated fresh ginger
1/2 teaspoon minced garlic
1/4 teaspoon ground red pepper
1 pound fresh asparagus spears
vegetable cooking spray
1 orange, peeled and sectioned

Combine orange juice, vinegar, soy sauce, olive oil, ginger, garlic, and red pepper in a jar; cover tightly and shake to blend. Let stand 30 minutes for flavors to blend.

Snap off tough ends of asparagus. Cut spears into 2-inch pieces.

Coat a large nonstick skillet with cooking spray; add 1 teaspoon oil and place over medium heat until hot. Add asparagus, and stir-fry 2 minutes. Shake orange juice mixture, and pour over asparagus; cook, stirring constantly, 2 to 4 minutes or until asparagus is crisp-tender. Stir in orange sections; transfer to a serving bowl and serve immediately.

Per Serving: 95 Calories, 5 g Fat (1 g Saturated), 0 mg Cholesterol, 150 mg Sodium, 3 g Protein, 12 g Carbohydrates
A Great Source of: Folic Acid (40%), Vitamin C (63%), Vitamin E (29%)
A Good Source of: Fiber (3 g), Vitamin B1 (13%), Vitamin B2 (10%), Copper (12%), Potassium (400 mg)
Pyramid Equivalent(s): 1 Vegetable

The Guilt-Free "Comfort Food" Cookbook

Time: 12 minutes
Yield: 5 cups (6 to 8 servings)

Creamed Peas and Onions

A quick, rich-tasting classic without the cream.

3 cups frozen petite green peas
2 cups frozen pearl onions
1/2 cup reduced-sodium chicken
  broth
1 (8-ounce) carton nonfat plain
  yogurt

1/2 cup reduced-fat sour cream
3 tablespoons all-purpose flour
1 (2-ounce) jar diced pimento,
  drained
1/4 teaspoon salt
1/4 teaspoon pepper

Combine peas, onions, and chicken broth in a medium saucepan; cover and bring to a simmer. Simmer 5 minutes or until vegetables are tender.

Meanwhile, stir together yogurt, sour cream, and flour in a small bowl until smooth; stir in pimento, salt, and pepper. Add to cooked onion mixture; cook over low heat, stirring constantly, until thickened.

Per Serving: 105 Calories, 2 g Fat (1 g Saturated), 6 mg Cholesterol, 250 mg Sodium, 6 Protein, 15 Carbohydrates

A Good Source of: Fiber (4 g), Vitamin B1 (15%), Vitamin B2 (10%), Folic Acid (11%), Vitamin C (22%)

Pyramid Equivalent(s): 1½ Vegetables, 1 Dairy

The Guilt-Free "Comfort Food" Cookbook

Time: 10 minutes prep
20 minutes cooking
Yield: 6 servings

Green Beans with Caramelized Onion and Tomato Relish

2 teaspoons reduced-fat soft
margarine
1 cup finely chopped onion
1 tablespoon sugar
1 tablespoon balsamic vinegar
4 large plum tomatoes, seeded
and chopped
1/4 teaspoon salt

1/4 teaspoon freshly ground
pepper
2 tablespoons minced fresh
basil or oregano
3/4 pound fresh green beans,
trimmed and cut into
2-inch lengths

Melt margarine in a heavy large skillet over medium heat; add onion and sugar, and saute until onion is tender and golden brown. Stir in vinegar, and saute 1 to 2 minutes or until liquid evaporates. Stir in tomatoes, salt, pepper, and basil; cook just until hot. Remove from heat and keep warm.

Cook green beans, in 2 inches of boiling water, in a medium saucepan 10 minutes or until just tender. Drain, and toss with tomato relish in a serving bowl.

Per Serving: 60 Calories, 2 g Fat (0 g Saturated), 0 mg Cholesterol, 110 mg Sodium, 2 g Protein, 12 g Carbohydrates
A Great Source of: Vitamin C (38%)
A Good Source of: Fiber (3 g), Potassium (300 mg)
Pyramid Equivalent(s): 3 Vegetables

The Guilt-Free "Comfort Food" Cookbook

Time: 20 minutes prep
1 hour letting sauce stand
22 minutes cooking
Yield: 6 servings

Kale with Spicy Relish

1 cup seeded and diced tomatoes
1/2 cup minced poblano or
    Hungarian wax pepper (or
    other mild chile pepper)
1/2 cup minced red onion

1 clove garlic, minced
2 tablespoons balsamic vinegar
1 tablespoon olive oil
1/4 teaspoon salt
1³/4 pounds kale

Combine tomato, pepper, onion, garlic, vinegar, and olive oil; cover and let stand at room temperature at least 1 hour. (Or refrigerate overnight; bring to room temperature before serving.)

Trim ¼ inch off stem ends of kale leaves; use a sharp knife to cut leaves away from stems and thick center ribs. Rinse kale and shake off excess water. Cut into bite-size pieces.

Add ½ cup water to a heavy large skillet or Dutch oven, and bring to a boil over medium-high heat. Add kale; cover, reduce heat, and cook 20 minutes or until kale is tender, stirring occasionally.

To serve, spoon tomato relish over each serving of kale.

Per Serving: 100 Calories, 3 g Fat (0 g Saturated), 0 mg Cholesterol, 315 mg Sodium, 5 g Protein, 17 g Carbohydrates
A Great Source of: Fiber (5 g), Vitamin A (121%), Vitamin C (280%), Potassium (700 mg)
A Good Source of: Vitamin B1 (12%), Vitamin B2 (11%), Folic Acid (12%), Vitamin E (21%), Calcium (19%), Copper (22%), Iron (15%), Magnesium (13%)
Pyramid Equivalent(s): 2½ Vegetables

The Guilt-Free "Comfort Food" Cookbook

ESSERTS

$\mathscr{I}$nto every healthful diet, let a little sweetness come. Embrace desserts. They won't hurt you. At least not ours. We used every skill we had, plus a few more we discovered along the way, to create recipes that are sweet, creamy, gooey, flaky, layered, chocolaty, lacy, cakey, and thoroughly satisfying. We're not talking fruit salads here. If you follow the "80/20 rule," this is the "20" part: fun foods.

We didn't strive to make these desserts as low in fat as possible, though. The first criterion, as in all recipes in this book, is taste. Often we decide we're going to do something about the way we eat, and so we cut out all our favorite foods. Then we start to crave them. A better strategy is to find versions that provide wonderful taste yet are moderately lower in fat and calories. That's what we did here.

All these desserts are lower in fat, saturated fat, and calories than most desserts you're likely to come across. Even our Banana Cream Pie (p. 271) has only eight grams of fat per serving. Chocolate Sorbet with Cinnamon and Vanilla (p. 286) has five grams; Angel Cake Pudding (p. 282) has four grams; even Marbled Chocolate-Raspberry Cheesecake (p. 269) has only nine grams of fat and 220 calories per serving.

In the Pyramid scheme of things, desserts are Extras. Some of our desserts also provide something from the Fruits, or Dairy, or even Breads group, but they also contain fat and sugar. So you probably shouldn't have a slice of our Sweetheart Peach Pie (p. 276) after breakfast, lunch, *and* dinner—even though you might want to. But it's a dessert you can serve to your family knowing that each slice is low in fat

The Guilt-Free "Comfort Food" Cookbook

(six grams) and calories (270), provides 1 Fruit and 1 Bread, and makes people happy. That's part of health too.

So as you travel the path toward a healthful diet, take a rest from time to time, and let a little sweetness in.

The Guilt-Free "Comfort Food" Cookbook

Old-Fashioned Poundcake

*P*ound of butter, pound of sugar, pound of flour. That's what a pound cake used to mean. But back then we also washed our clothes by hand, walked half a mile to the well, and plowed our fields with a mule. Now we don't even roll up the windows on our cars by hand. We change channels on TV with a click. Even farmers sit comfortably up in the air-conditioned cabs of their combines. So our pound cake has to change too.

Try this one. It's rich and moist. It's not entirely without fat, but it has about 75 percent less butter (or margarine) than truly old-fashioned pound cake. That means you can eat our Old-Fashioned Poundcake from time to time, without the pounds climbing onto your hips.

3 cups sugar
$1/_2$ cup stick margarine (or
    butter), softened
$1/_4$ cup canola oil
8 egg whites
$1^1/_2$ cups vanilla-flavored
    lowfat yogurt
1 teaspoon baking soda

2 teaspoons vanilla extract
$4^1/_2$ cups sifted cake flour
1 ($1/_2$-ounce) envelope natural
    butter-flavored granules
    (optional)
$1/_8$ teaspoon salt
vegetable cooking spray

Preheat oven to 325°. Cream sugar and margarine at medium speed on an electric mixer. Beat in oil. In a separate bowl, beat yogurt, baking soda, and vanilla until smooth; beat in egg whites until blended, and set aside. In a third bowl, stir together flour, butter-flavor granules (if using), and salt.

With mixer on low, gradually and alternately add flour mixture and yogurt mixture to sugar and margarine, beginning and ending with flour mixture. Spoon batter into a 10-inch tube pan coated with cooking spray. Bake for 60 to 65 minutes or until a wooden pick inserted in center comes out clean. Cool in pan 10 minutes; remove from pan and cool completely on a wire rack.

Per Serving: 235 Calories, 6 g Fat (1 g Saturated), 1 mg Cholesterol, 135 mg Sodium, 4 g Protein, 41 g Carbohydrates
A Good Source of: Vitamin B1 (11%), Vitamin B2 (10%), Vitamin E (11%)
Pyramid Equivalent(s): 1 Bread, Extras

The Guilt-Free "Comfort Food" Cookbook

Time: 45 minutes prep
45 minutes baking
Yield: 16 servings

Hummingbird Cake

*H*ummingbird Cake is an old Southern term for a cake made with fruits and nuts. Presumably, that makes it attractive to hummingbirds. You may find it attracts humans as well.

3¹/₄ cups sifted cake flour
1 cup sugar, divided
¹/₂ teaspoon salt
³/₄ teaspoon baking powder
¹/₂ teaspoon baking soda
1 teaspoon ground allspice
¹/₂ cup egg substitute or 1 whole
    egg and 2 whites, beaten
¹/₂ cup canola oil

¹/₄ cup nonfat plain yogurt
2 teaspoons vanilla extract
1 cup peeled and shredded apple
2 cups finely chopped banana
¹/₂ cup finely chopped pecans
3 egg whites
¹/₄ teaspoon cream of tartar
vegetable cooking spray
Vanilla Sauce (recipe follows)

Preheat oven to 350°. Combine flour, ¾ cup sugar, salt, baking powder, baking soda, and allspice in a large bowl; stir well. Make a well in center of mixture, and set aside.

Combine egg substitute, oil, yogurt, and vanilla extract; add to dry ingredients and stir just until blended. Stir in apple, banana, and pecans.

Beat egg whites and cream of tartar in a mixing bowl until foamy; gradually add remaining ¼ cup sugar, beating until stiff peaks form. Fold into batter. Pour into a 10-inch tube pan coated with cooking spray; bake for 40 to 45 minutes or until a wooden pick inserted in center comes out clean. Cool in pan 20 minutes; remove from pan and cool completely. Serve with Vanilla Sauce.

Vanilla Sauce
Yield: 1³/₄ cups

2¹/₂ cups 1% lowfat milk
1 (3-inch) piece vanilla bean,
    split lengthwise
¹/₂ cup sugar

2 teaspoons cornstarch
¹/₄ cup egg substitute or 1 large
    egg, beaten

The Guilt-Free "Comfort Food" Cookbook

Bring milk and vanilla bean to a boil in a small saucepan; remove from heat and let stand until cool. Remove vanilla bean.

Combine sugar and cornstarch, stirring until well blended. Mix sugar mixture and egg substitute into milk mixture, blending well with a wire whisk. Cook over medium heat, stirring constantly, until mixture is thick. Serve warm or at room temperature.

Per Serving (1³/₄ tablespoons of sauce): 45 Calories, 1 g Fat (1 g Saturated), 2 mg Cholesterol, 26 mg Sodium, 2 g Protein, 8 g Carbohydrates
(Not a significant source of vitamins or minerals. No Pyramid Equivalents.)
Per Serving (cake with sauce): 285 Calories, 10 g Fat (1 g Saturated), 2 mg Cholesterol, 177 mg Sodium, 6 g Protein, 43 g Carbohydrates
A Good Source of: Vitamin B1 (16%), Vitamin B2 (15%), Vitamin E (18%), Iron (11%), Potassium (245 mg)
Pyramid Equivalent(s): 1 Bread, ½ Fruit, Extras

The Guilt-Free "Comfort Food" Cookbook

Time: 35 minutes prep
45 minutes cooking
Yield: 8 servings

Carrot Cake

*W*hat a sweet way to eat carrots!

4 egg whites
1/2 cup plus 3 tablespoons
    nonfat buttermilk, divided
1/4 cup canola oil
2/3 cup firmly packed brown
    sugar
1 1/2 teaspoons plus 1 teaspoon
    vanilla extract, divided
1/2 teaspoon almond extract
2 cups cake flour, sifted
1 1/4 teaspoons baking powder

1/2 teaspoon baking soda
1/4 teaspoon salt
1 teaspoon ground cinnamon
1 1/2 cups lightly packed grated
    carrots
1 (8-ounce) can unsweetened
    crushed pineapple, well
    drained
1/2 cup raisins
vegetable cooking spray
1 1/2 cups sifted powdered sugar

Preheat oven to 350°. Whisk together egg whites, ½ cup buttermilk, oil, brown sugar, 1½ teaspoons vanilla extract, and almond extract in a large bowl. Place a wire-mesh sieve over bowl; add flour, baking powder, baking soda, salt, and cinnamon, and sift into egg mixture. Stir lightly to blend; stir in carrots, pineapple, and raisins just until blended.

Pour batter into a 9- x 5- x 3-inch baking pan coated with cooking spray. Bake for 40 to 45 minutes or until a wooden pick inserted in center comes out clean. Cool cake in pan 10 minutes; remove from pan and cool on a wire rack.

Blend powdered sugar, 3 tablespoons buttermilk, and 1 teaspoon vanilla until smooth; spread over cake, allowing mixture to coat sides of cake. Serve immediately or refrigerate.

Per Serving: 335 Calories, 7 g Fat (1 g Saturated), 1 mg Cholesterol, 265 mg Sodium, 5 g Protein, 63 g Carbohydrates
A Great Source of: Vitamin A (58%)
A Good Source of: Fiber (2 g), Vitamin B1 (19%), Vitamin B2 (14%), Vitamin B3 (10%), Vitamin C (11%), Vitamin E (18%), Iron (14%), Potassium (290 mg)
Pyramid Equivalent(s): 1 Bread, 1 Vegetable, ½ Fruit, Extras

The Guilt-Free "Comfort Food" Cookbook

Time: 30 minutes prep
4 hours chilling
10 minutes baking
Yield: 9 servings

Short-and-Sweet Strawberry Shortcakes

4 cups sliced strawberries
1/4 cup plus 1 1/2 teaspoons sugar, divided
1/2 teaspoon ground cinnamon
2 cups all-purpose flour
3 tablespoons sugar
2 teaspoons baking powder
1/2 teaspoon baking soda

1/2 teaspoon salt
1/4 cup stick margarine (or butter), cut into bits
3/4 cup nonfat buttermilk
1 egg white
vegetable cooking spray
1 1/4 cups frozen lowfat whipped topping, thawed

Combine strawberries, 1/4 cup sugar, and cinnamon in a bowl; cover and refrigerate 4 hours, stirring occasionally.

Preheat oven to 425°. Combine flour, 3 tablespoons sugar, baking powder, baking soda, and salt in a bowl; blend well. Cut in margarine until mixture forms coarse crumbs. Make a well in center of mixture, and set aside. Combine buttermilk and egg white, mixing until blended. Add buttermilk mixture to dry ingredients and stir lightly with a fork until mixture forms a ball.

Pat dough on a lightly floured surface to a 1-inch thick rectangle; cut out biscuits using a 2½-inch heart-shaped or round cutter coated with cooking spray, rerolling scraps. Place on a baking sheet coated with cooking spray; sprinkle tops of biscuits evenly with 1½ teaspoons sugar. Bake for 8 to 10 minutes or until golden.

Split warm biscuits; place bottom halves on serving plates and top evenly with strawberry mixture. Dollop each with 2 tablespoons whipped topping and replace biscuit tops.

Per Serving: 268 Calories, 11 g Fat (4 g Saturated), 20 mg Cholesterol, 365 mg Sodium, 5 g Protein, 39 g Carbohydrates
A Great Source of: Vitamin C (70%)
A Good Source of: Fiber (2 g), Vitamin A (12%), Vitamin B1 (16%), Vitamin B2 (15%), Vitamin E (12%), Calcium (13%), Iron (10%)
Pyramid Equivalent(s): 1 Bread, 1 Fruit, Extras

The Guilt-Free "Comfort Food" Cookbook

Time: 30 minutes prep
45 minutes baking
10 minutes cooling
Yield: 12 servings

Buttermilk Cornmeal Cake
with Strawberry-Mint Sauce

*B*erries (frozen or fresh, if in season) give this dessert its flair and improve its nutrition, all at once. It may not be your first thought when you put a piece of this cake in your mouth, but each serving provides a nice amount of fiber, B vitamins, vitamin C, even some calcium. Buttermilk, even though the name includes "butter," is actually low in fat or entirely nonfat.

4 large egg whites
1 cup sugar, divided
1/3 cup stick margarine (or butter), softened
2 large whole eggs (or 1/2 cup egg substitute)
2 teaspoons vanilla extract
1/2 teaspoon lemon extract
2 1/2 cups all-purpose flour
3/4 cup cornmeal
1 tablespoon baking powder
1 teaspoon baking soda

1/4 teaspoon salt
1 cup nonfat buttermilk
1/3 cup light corn syrup
vegetable cooking spray
4 cups assorted fresh berries: blueberries, sliced strawberries, raspberries (optional)
Strawberry-Mint Sauce (recipe follows)

Preheat oven to 325°. Beat egg whites in large mixing bowl until foamy; gradually add ¼ cup sugar, one tablespoon at a time, beating until stiff peaks form. Set aside.

Cream butter and remaining ¾ cup sugar; beat in eggs, one at a time, mixing well after each addition. Stir in extracts, and set aside.

Combine flour, cornmeal, baking powder, baking soda, and salt, mixing well. In a small bowl, stir together buttermilk and corn syrup, and set aside.

Add flour mixture to creamed mixture, alternately with buttermilk mixture, beginning and ending with dry ingredients. Stir ¼ beaten egg whites into batter; fold batter into remaining egg whites. Smooth into a 10-inch tube pan coated with cooking spray; bake for 42 to 45 minutes or until a wooden pick inserted in center comes out clean.

The Guilt-Free "Comfort Food" Cookbook

Cool cake in pan on a wire rack 10 minutes; remove from pan, and cool completely on rack.

To serve, arrange cake slices on serving plates; spoon ⅓ cup berries on each serving, if desired, and top with 2 tablespoons Strawberry-Mint Sauce.

Strawberry-Mint Sauce
Yield: 1½ cups

2 (10-ounce) packages frozen strawberries in light syrup, thawed

¼ cup packed chopped mint leaves

Bring ingredients to a boil in a heavy small saucepan; boil, uncovered, until reduced to 1¾ cups. Cool to room temperature; press through a fine wire-mesh sieve into a bowl, discarding solids. Chill before serving.

Per Serving (cake with sauce): 331 Calories, 7 g Fat (1 g Saturated), 36 mg Cholesterol, 365 mg Sodium, 7 g Protein, 63 g Carbohydrates
A Great Source of: Vitamin C (33%)
A Good Source of: Fiber (2 g), Vitamin B1 (17%), Vitamin B2 (18%), Vitamin B3 (10%), Vitamin E (12%), Calcium (13%), Iron (11%)
Pyramid Equivalent(s): 1 Bread, 1 Fruit, Extras

Note: With berries: 4 g Fiber, Vitamin C (54%); 1½ Fruits in Pyramid Equivalent.

The Guilt-Free "Comfort Food" Cookbook

Mocha Fudge Sundae Cake

*1/2 cup plus 2 tablespoons
   nonfat buttermilk, divided*
*1 tablespoon plus 1 teaspoon
   instant coffee powder,
   divided*
3 tablespoons canola oil
*2 teaspoons vanilla extract,
   divided*

1 cup all-purpose flour
1 1/3 cups sugar, divided
*1/2 cup unsweetened cocoa
   powder, divided*
1 1/2 teaspoons baking powder
1/2 teaspoon baking soda
1/4 teaspoon salt
1 3/4 cups boiling water

Toppings (optional):

drained crushed canned pineapple
maraschino cherries
sifted powdered sugar

Preheat oven to 350°. Heat ¼ cup buttermilk; stir in 1 tablespoon coffee powder until dissolved. Stir in remaining ¼ cup plus 2 tablespoons buttermilk, oil, and 1 teaspoon vanilla.

Place a wire-mesh sieve over a large bowl; add flour, ⅔ cup sugar, ¼ cup cocoa, baking powder, and salt to sieve. Stir and sift mixture into bowl. Add milk mixture to dry ingredients and stir just until combined.

Combine remaining ⅔ cup sugar, ¼ cup cocoa, and 1 teaspoon coffee powder in a bowl; stir in boiling water until sugar dissolves. Stir in vanilla. Pour into an 8-inch square baking dish. Spoon batter on top of sauce in large spoonfuls. Bake for 40 minutes or until top is crisp and sauce on bottom is bubbly. Let stand 10 minutes before spooning into bowls. Serve warm with toppings, if desired.

Per Serving (without toppings): 225 Calories, 5 g Fat (1 g Saturated), 1 mg Cholesterol, 210 mg Sodium, 3 g Protein, 44 g Carbohydrates
A Good Source of: Fiber (2 g), Vitamin E (11%), Copper (11%)
Pyramid Equivalent(s): 1 Bread, Extras

The Guilt-Free "Comfort Food" Cookbook

Marbled Chocolate-Raspberry Cheesecake

*M*ost cheesecakes weigh in at fifteen or twenty grams of fat and 350 calories per slice. We cut the fat to nine grams and calories to 220 per slice by combining several nonfat ingredients (cocoa, egg whites) and lowfat ones (chocolate wafer cookies, light cream cheese, lowfat cottage cheese).

vegetable cooking spray
9 chocolate wafer cookies, very finely crushed
2$^1/_4$ cups reduced-fat soft cream cheese
1$^1/_2$ cups 1% lowfat cottage cheese
1 cup sugar, divided

$^1/_2$ cup plus 2 tablespoons unsweetened cocoa powder
$^1/_4$ cup all-purpose flour
1 large egg
4 large egg whites, divided
$^1/_4$ cup seedless raspberry jam, melted and cooled

Preheat oven to 300°. Coat an 8-inch springform pan with cooking spray; sprinkle chocolate crumbs in bottom and 2 inches up side of pan. Set aside.

Process light soft cream cheese, cottage cheese, ¾ cup sugar, cocoa, and flour in a food processor just until smooth. Add egg and 1 egg white, and process just until blended.

Beat 3 egg whites in a mixing bowl until foamy; gradually add remaining ¼ cup sugar and beat until stiff but not dry. Fold into cheese batter in 3 additions.

Pour batter into prepared pan. Smooth top using a spatula. Bake for 60 to 65 minutes or until just set (center will be soft). Run a long, thin knife between cake and side of pan to release steam; let cool on a wire rack. Brush jam mixture on top of cheesecake; cover and refrigerate overnight before unmolding and serving.

Per Serving: 220 Calories, 9 g Fat (5 g Saturated), 38 mg Cholesterol, 250 mg Sodium, 10 g Protein, 28 g Carbohydrates
A Good Source of: Vitamin A (10%), Vitamin B2 (14%), Copper (10%)
Pyramid Equivalent(s): ⅔ Dairy, Extras

The Guilt-Free "Comfort Food" Cookbook

Time: 15 minutes prep
30 minutes chilling
20 minutes baking
Yield: 1 9-inch pastry

Easy Flaky Pastry

*I*t's not possible to make an attractive, flaky crust without some form of hard shortening, such as stick margarine or butter. Neither is particularly healthful—hard margarines contain cholesterol-raising trans fat while butter is rich in cholesterol-raising saturated fat. Butter contains more total cholesterol-raising fat, however, so margarine is a slightly better choice. The real trick is to use small amounts. That's what we do here. In this recipe, each serving contains only six grams of fat.

1 cup all-purpose flour
1 teaspoon sugar
1/2 teaspoon salt

1/4 cup stick margarine (or butter), melted and cooled
3 tablespoons vanilla-flavored lowfat yogurt

Preheat oven to 425°. Combine flour, sugar, and salt in a bowl; stir with a fork, and set aside. Combine margarine and yogurt, beating well with fork until blended. Immediately drizzle mixture over flour mixture; toss with fork or fingers until crumbly. Form into a ball.

Roll out pastry between two sheets of plastic wrap to a 10 ½-inch circle; fit into a 9-inch pie plate. Crimp sides and refrigerate 30 minutes. Take out of refrigerator; prick all over with a fork. Fill and bake, or bake unfilled.

Bake in lower third of oven for 10 minutes—if necessary, press pastry to pie plate with the back of a wooden spoon. (If edges begin to brown too quickly, cover lightly with a piece of foil, and continue baking.) Reduce oven temperature to 350° and continue baking 10 to 15 minutes or until pastry is golden.

Per Serving (1/8th of pie crust): 115 Calories, 6 g Fat (1 g Saturated), 0 mg Cholesterol, 200 mg Sodium, 2 g Protein, 13 g Carbohydrates
(Not a significant source of vitamins or minerals.)
Pyramid Equivalent(s): 1 Bread, Extras

The Guilt-Free "Comfort Food" Cookbook

Banana Cream Pie

$1/2$ cup plus 3 tablespoons
    sugar, divided
3 tablespoons all-purpose flour
1 (12-ounce) can evaporated
    skimmed milk
$1/3$ cup egg substitute or 1 large
    egg plus 1 egg white, beaten
$1/2$ cup reduced-fat sour cream

2 teaspoons vanilla extract
2 medium ripe bananas, sliced
$1^1/2$ cups crushed vanilla
    wafers (about 33 wafers)
3 tablespoons reduced-fat soft
    margarine, melted
3 egg whites
$1/4$ teaspoon cream of tartar

Preheat oven to 325°. Combine ½ cup sugar and flour in a heavy saucepan; mix well. Gradually stir in evaporated skim milk and egg substitute. Cook over medium heat, stirring constantly, until mixture comes to a boil. Reduce heat and simmer 1 minute, stirring constantly. Remove from heat and fold in sour cream and vanilla. Cool.

Combine wafer crumbs, 2 tablespoons sugar, and melted reduced-calorie margarine; mix well and press on bottom and up sides of a 9-inch pie plate. Spoon ⅓ of pudding mixture in pie plate; layer half of bananas on top. Repeat layers, ending with pudding mixture. Set aside.

Beat egg whites, cream of tartar, and remaining 1 tablespoon sugar in small bowl of an electric mixer until stiff peaks form. Spread meringue over pudding, sealing to edges. Bake for 15 minutes or until meringue is browned. Cool to room temperature or chill before serving.

Per Serving: 315 Calories, 8 g Fat (2 g Saturated), 2 mg Cholesterol, 200 mg Sodium, 9 g Protein, 53 g Carbohydrates

A Good Source of: Vitamin A (15%), Vitamin B1 (11%), Vitamin B2 (21%), Vitamin B6 (10%), Vitamin E (13%), Calcium (14%), Potassium (360 mg)

Pyramid Equivalent(s): ½ Fruit, 1 Dairy, ½ Meat, Extras

The Guilt-Free "Comfort Food" Cookbook

Apple Crumb Pie

*H*ere's a delicious, lowfat, low-saturated fat version of a classic. It's lower in calories than most versions as well, although it's not a low-calorie dessert. So save it for a once-a-week occasion, not every night.

8 large, crisp cooking apples, peeled, cored, and thinly sliced
1/4 cup nonfat buttermilk
2/3 cup firmly packed light brown sugar
3 tablespoons all-purpose flour

1 teaspoon ground cinnamon
1/4 teaspoon apple pie spice
1 Easy Flaky Pastry (p. 270), baked for only 8 minutes at 425°
Streusel Crumbs (recipe follows)

Place apples in a large mixing bowl. In a small saucepan, combine buttermilk, brown sugar, and flour; mix until smooth. Cook over medium heat, stirring constantly until sugar melts and mixture thickens. Pour over apples in bowl; gently toss.

Arrange apples snugly in pastry shell, mounding into a firm shape. Cover pie plate with aluminum foil, and bake at 425° for 15 minutes. Uncover pie, and sprinkle with Streusel Crumbs. Reduce oven temperature to 350°, and continue baking 30 minutes or until fruit is tender. Let cool; serve warm or at room temperature.

Streusel Crumbs

Yield: topping for 8- or 9-inch pie

These sweet, nutty, crunchy crumbs make a nice topping for many kinds of pies and fruit crisps.

1/3 cup regular oats, uncooked
1/2 cup all-purpose flour
1/4 cup Grape-Nuts cereal
1/3 cup firmly packed light brown sugar

1 teaspoon ground cinnamon
2 tablespoons stick margarine (or butter), melted

Spread oats in a single layer on a nonstick baking sheet; bake at 350° for 15 to 20 minutes or until toasted.

The Guilt-Free "Comfort Food" Cookbook

Combine all ingredients except margarine; mix well. Mix in margarine until crumbly.

Per Serving (topping only): 102 Calories, 3 g Fat (1 g Saturated), 0 mg Cholesterol, 2 g Protein, 17 g Carbohydrates, 1 g Fiber, 55 mg Potassium, 60 mg Sodium
(Not a good source of vitamins or minerals. No Pyramid Equivalents.)

Per Serving (one slice with topping): 400 Calories, 10 g Fat (2 g Saturated), 1 mg Cholesterol, 275 mg Sodium, 5 g Protein, 77 g Carbohydrates
A Great Source of: Fiber (6 g), Vitamin E (28%)
A Good Source of: Vitamin A (16%), Vitamin B1 (21%), Vitamin B2 (14%), Vitamin B3 (12%), Vitamin B6 (10%), Vitamin C (21%), Copper (10%), Iron (14%), Potassium (390 mg)
Pyramid Equivalent(s): 1 Bread, 1 Fruit, Extras

The Guilt-Free "Comfort Food" Cookbook

Time: 5 minutes prep
65 minutes for pastry
45 minutes baking
Yield: 8 servings

Pumpkin Spice Pie

*T*his pie has half the fat of a regular pumpkin pie. And pumpkin itself is a nutritional plus—like most members of the squash family, it's loaded with vitamin A (as beta-carotene).

1 cup 1% lowfat cottage cheese
1¹/₄ cups canned solid-pack
   pumpkin
²/₃ cup egg substitute or 1 large
   whole egg plus 4 large egg
   whites
¹/₃ cup light or dark corn syrup

¹/₄ cup sugar
1 tablespoon all-purpose flour
1 tablespoon pumpkin pie spice
1¹/₂ teaspoons vanilla extract
1 baked Easy Flaky Pastry
   (p. 270)
lowfat frozen yogurt (optional)

Preheat oven to 400°. Process cottage cheese, pumpkin, egg substitute, corn syrup, sugar, flour, pumpkin pie spice, and vanilla extract in an electric blender until smooth. Pour into pastry shell; bake for 20 minutes. Reduce oven temperature to 325° and continue baking 25 to 30 minutes or until pie is just set. Let cool on a wire rack; serve at room temperature or chilled with frozen yogurt, if desired.

Per Serving: 235 Calories, 7 g Fat (1 g Saturated), 2 mg Cholesterol, 380 mg Sodium, 9 g Protein, 35 g Carbohydrates
A Great Source of: Vitamin A (97%)
A Good Source of: Fiber (2 g), Vitamin B1 (12%), Vitamin B2 (13%), Vitamin E (15%), Iron (11%)
Pyramid Equivalent(s): 1 Bread, 1 Vegetable, Extras

Note: Served with a half cup of lowfat frozen yogurt: 337 Calories, 9 g Fat (3 g Saturated), 13 g Protein, Calcium (21%); additional ½ Dairy.

The Guilt-Free "Comfort Food" Cookbook

Time: 20 minutes prep
40 minutes baking
Yield: 8 servings

Peach-Blueberry Cobbler

**4 cups fresh peach slices or
  frozen peach slices, thawed
1¹/₂ cups fresh blueberries or
  frozen blueberries, thawed
¹/₄ cup sugar, divided**

**1 tablespoon lemon juice
¹/₄ teaspoon allspice
¹/₄ teaspoon ground cardamom
Biscuit Topping (recipe follows)**

Preheat oven to 375°. Combine fruit, 2 tablespoons sugar, lemon juice, and spices in a 10-inch tart pan or quiche dish. Mix well, and spread in an even layer. Spoon biscuit topping evenly over fruit; sprinkle with remaining 2 tablespoons sugar. Bake for 30 to 40 minutes or until biscuits are cooked. (If necessary, cover lightly with aluminum foil after 20 minutes to prevent overbrowning.) Serve warm.

Biscuit Topping
Yield: topping for 10-inch cobbler

**1¹/₂ cups cake flour
¹/₄ cup sugar
1 teaspoon baking powder
¹/₂ teaspoon baking soda
¹/₄ teaspoon salt**

**³/₄ cup plain nonfat yogurt
2 tablespoons stick margarine
  (or butter), melted
¹/₄ cup egg substitute or 1 large
  egg, beaten**

Combine dry ingredients and sift into a large bowl; set aside. Whisk together yogurt, margarine, and egg substitute; stir into dry ingredients all at once just until blended.

Per Serving (with topping): 210 Calories, 4 g Fat (1 g Saturated), 0 mg Cholesterol, 260 mg Sodium, 5 g Protein, 42 g Carbohydrates
A Good Source of: Fiber (3 g), Vitamin A (10%), Vitamin B1 (14%), Vitamin B2 (12%), Vitamin B3 (11%), Vitamin C (17%), Vitamin E (14%), Calcium (10%), Iron (10%), Potassium (300 mg)
Pyramid Equivalent(s): 1 Bread, 1 Fruit, Extras

The Guilt-Free "Comfort Food" Cookbook

Time: 45 minutes prep
40 minutes baking
Yield: 1 9-inch pie (8 servings)

Sweetheart Peach Pie

When peaches are in season, make this one for *your* sweetheart.

**Processor Pastry (recipe
    follows)**
3 pounds fresh peaches
1 tablespoon lemon juice
$1/3$ cup sugar
$1/4$ cup cornstarch

**1 tablespoon quick-cooking
    tapioca**
$1/4$ teaspoon ground allspice
$1/8$ teaspoon ground nutmeg
$1/8$ teaspoon ground ginger

Transfer ⅔ of pastry mixture to a large sheet of heavy-duty plastic wrap; press gently into a disc, and cover with another sheet of plastic wrap. Roll dough, covered with plastic, into a 12-inch circle. Place dough in freezer for at least 15 minutes; meanwhile, prepare peach mixture.

Peel peaches, remove pits, and cut into 1-inch slices. Toss with lemon juice in a large bowl. Combine sugar and remaining ingredients in a small bowl; mix well and toss with peaches until well coated.

Remove pastry from freezer; fit into a 9-inch pie plate dusted lightly with flour. Spoon peach mixture into pastry; refrigerate.

Preheat oven to 400°. Transfer remaining one-third pastry to a large sheet of heavy-duty plastic wrap; press gently into a disc, and cover with another sheet of plastic wrap. Roll dough, covered with plastic, into a 10-inch circle; place on a baking sheet and freeze 5 minutes. Remove top sheet of plastic wrap; invert pastry over peaches, and remove remaining sheet of plastic wrap. Trim edges of pastry and flute, moistening edges of pastry with water to adhere. Using tip of a sharp knife, cut 6 (2-inch) slits in top of pastry. Bake for 35 to 40 minutes; cover loosely with foil after 20 minutes to prevent overbrowning. Let cool on a wire rack before serving.

Processor Pastry

1 cup all-purpose flour
$1/2$ cup whole wheat flour
2 tablespoons sugar
$1/4$ teaspoon salt

**$1/4$ cup stick margarine (or
    butter), chilled and cut into
    4 pieces**
**$3 1/2$ to 4 tablespoons ice-cold
    water**

The Guilt-Free "Comfort Food" Cookbook

Combine flour, sugar, and salt in a food processor fitted with knife blade; pulse just until combined. Evenly distribute margarine over flour mixture; pulse just until mixture resembles coarse meal, about 10 to 12 times. With processor running, gradually add ice water through food chute, processing just until combined. (Do not form a ball.)

Per Serving (one slice): 270 Calories, 6 g Fat (1 g Saturated), 0 mg Cholesterol, 135 mg Sodium, 4 g Protein, 53 g Carbohydrates
A Great Source of: Fiber (5 g)
A Good Source of: Vitamin A (16%), Vitamin B1 (12%), Vitamin B2 (10%), Vitamin B3 (15%), Vitamin C (20%), Vitamin E (22%), Potassium (390 mg)
Pyramid Equivalent(s): 1 Bread, 1 Fruit, Extras

The Guilt-Free "Comfort Food" Cookbook

Time: 35 minutes prep
45 minutes baking
Yield: 10 to 12 servings

Meringue Fruit Tart

*M*eringue isn't the tart topping. It's the shell!

1 (8-ounce) carton lowfat
    vanilla yogurt
1/2 cup nonfat ricotta cheese
1/4 cup sifted powdered sugar
1 teaspoon vanilla extract
1 cup frozen reduced-fat
    whipped topping, thawed
vegetable cooking spray
1 teaspoon cornstarch
4 large egg whites

1 tablespoon cornstarch
1/4 teaspoon cream of tartar
1 cup sugar
1 teaspoon vanilla extract
1/2 teaspoon almond extract
4 cups assorted fresh fruit:
    blueberries, strawberry
    halves, sliced kiwifruit,
    peaches, or plums

Spread yogurt ½-inch thick on several layers of paper towels; place 2 layers paper towels on top of yogurt. Let stand 15 minutes. (The paper towels quickly absorb the water from the yogurt and improve consistecy.) Scrape yogurt into a food processor bowl fitted with knife blade; add ricotta cheese, sugar, and vanilla. Process until smooth. Transfer to a bowl; fold in whipped topping and refrigerate until well chilled.

Mark a 13- x 8-inch rectangle on wax paper; place on a baking sheet. Coat rectangle with cooking spray; dust with 1 teaspoon cornstarch. Set aside.

Preheat oven to 275°. Beat egg whites, 1 tablespoon cornstarch, and cream of tartar at high speed of an electric mixer until foamy. Gradually add sugar, ¼ cup at a time, beating until stiff peaks form and sugar dissolves. Beat in 1 teaspoon vanilla and almond extract. Spread meringue into the 13- x 8-inch rectangle on prepared wax paper. With a spatula or back of a spoon, shape edge into a 1½-inch-high rim. Bake for 35 to 45 minutes or until crisp and dry.

Turn off oven, and leave in oven 10 minutes to dry. Transfer to a wire rack, and cool completely. Carefully remove wax paper; place meringue on a serving platter. (Meringue may be prepared up to 24 hours ahead; store, loosely covered, in a dry area.)

The Guilt-Free "Comfort Food" Cookbook

Just before serving, spread topping mixture on meringue shell; arrange fruit on top of filling.

Per Serving: 145 Calories, 1 g Fat (0 g Saturated), 4 mg Cholesterol, 46 mg Sodium, 4 g Protein, 31 g Carbohydrates
A Great Source of: Vitamin C (39%)
Pyramid Equivalent(s): ¾ Fruit, Extras

The Guilt-Free "Comfort Food" Cookbook

Magnolia Buttermilk Pie

6 egg whites
$1^1/_2$ cups sugar
1 cup nonfat buttermilk
2 tablespoons stick margarine
(or butter)

$^1/_4$ cup all-purpose flour
$1^1/_2$ teaspoons vanilla extract
$^1/_2$ teaspoon almond extract
1 baked Easy Flaky Pastry
(p. 270) or prebaked shell

Preheat oven to 350°. Process all ingredients except pastry in a food processor until smooth. Pour into pastry shell; bake for 50 minutes or until a knife inserted in center comes out clean and top is golden. Cool before cutting.

Per Serving: 325 Calories, 9 g Fat (2 g Saturated), 1 mg Cholesterol, 310 mg Sodium, 6 g Protein, 56 g Carbohydrates

A Good Source of: Vitamin A (11%), Vitamin B1 (11%), Vitamin B2 (16%), Vitamin E (15%)

Pyramid Equivalent(s): 1 Bread, Extras

The Guilt-Free "Comfort Food" Cookbook

Mango-Lime Sorbet with Grilled Fruit

$\mathcal{W}$e grill meats, poultry, fish, vegetables; why not fruit? Mangoes are so rich in antioxidant vitamins that a single serving provides nearly half your daily needs for vitamin C and more than half for vitamin A (in the form of beta-carotene).

$^1/_2$ cup plus 1 tablespoon sugar, divided
$^3/_4$ teaspoons ground ginger, divided
$^3/_4$ cup water

$^1/_4$ cup plus 1 tablespoon fresh lime juice, divided
2 cups pureed mango
2 small bananas
3 peaches

Combine ½ cup sugar, ¼ teaspoon ground ginger, and water in a small saucepan; bring to a boil over medium heat, stirring constantly until sugar dissolves. Remove from heat; let cool. Stir in ¼ cup lime juice and mango puree. Freeze in an ice cream maker according to manufacturer's directions (or in plastic ice cube trays; see directions under introduction to Chocolate Sorbet with Cinnamon and Vanilla [p. 286]); transfer to freezer containers and freeze until solid.

Refrigerate six dessert plates. About 30 minutes before serving, cut bananas into 1-inch slices. Peel peaches and cut each into 6 wedges. Mix 1 tablespoon lime juice, 1 tablespoon sugar, and ½ teaspoon ginger; add to fruit and toss well. Let stand 15 to 30 minutes, stirring occasionally.

Thread fruit on skewers; grill over medium-hot coals until fruit is lightly browned, turning frequently.

To serve, scoop ½ cup sorbet onto each 6 chilled dessert plates; arrange fruit around sorbet.

Per Serving: 200 Calories, 1 g Fat (0 g Saturated), 0 mg Cholesterol, 415 mg Potassium, 4 mg Sodium, 1 g Protein, 51 g Carbohydrates
A Great Source of: Fiber (5 g), Vitamin A (43%), Vitamin C (65%)
A Good Source of: Vitamin B6 (19%), Vitamin E (16%), Copper (10%)
Pyramid Equivalent(s): 2 Fruits, Extras

The Guilt-Free "Comfort Food" Cookbook

Time: 2$^1/_2$ hours
Yield: 8 servings

Angel Cake Pudding

*M*ake everyday angel food cake into a brand new dessert that's destined to become a family favorite.

5 cups packed commercial angel food cake (packaged, or from cake mix), cut into 1-inch cubes
3$^1/_2$ cups skim milk
$^2/_3$ cup sugar
$^3/_4$ cup egg substitute (or 6 egg whites)
$^1/_2$ cup dried cranberries or dried cherries
1 tablespoon vanilla extract
$^1/_2$ teaspoon butter extract (optional)
1 teaspoon ground cinnamon

2 tablespoons slivered almonds, toasted
1$^1/_2$ cups cranberry-raspberry juice, cranberry-strawberry juice, or cranberry juice cocktail
3 tablespoons sugar
3 tablespoons reduced-fat soft margarine
$^1/_4$ teaspoon ground cinnamon
$^1/_2$ cup water
1 tablespoon plus 1 teaspoon cornstarch

Preheat oven to 250°. Arrange cake cubes in a single layer in a jelly-roll pan; bake for 30 minutes or until dry. Turn off oven.

Combine milk, sugar, egg substitute, cranberries, vanilla extract, butter extract (if using), cinnamon, and almonds in a large bowl; mix well, as with a pudding. Add cake cubes, and toss gently. Let stand 1 hour, stirring gently occasionally.

Preheat oven to 350°. Spoon mixture into a 9- x 5- x 3-inch loaf pan coated with cooking spray; bake for 1 to 1¼ hours or until set. Meanwhile, combine juice, sugar, margarine, and cinnamon in a small saucepan. Cook over medium heat, stirring frequently until sugar dissolves. Combine cold water and cornstarch; stir well, and add to juice mixture. Bring to a boil; cook, stirring constantly, until clear and thickened.

To serve, spoon warm pudding in serving dishes; spoon warm sauce around pudding.

The Guilt-Free "Comfort Food" Cookbook

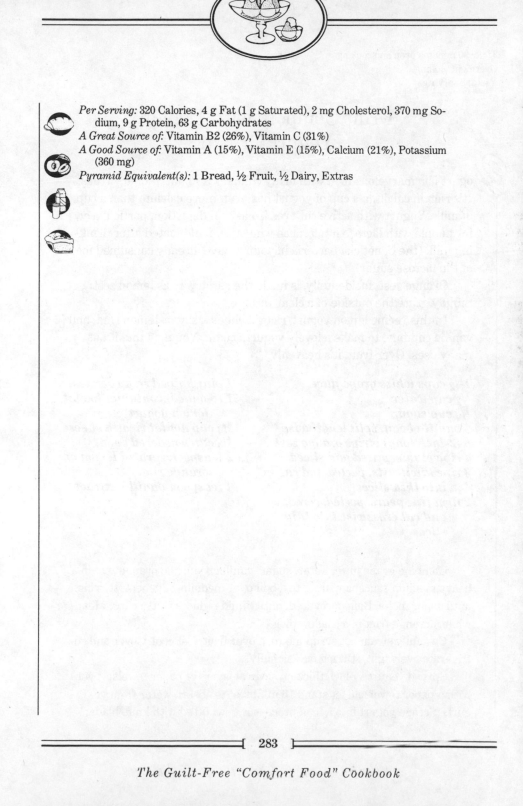

Per Serving: 320 Calories, 4 g Fat (1 g Saturated), 2 mg Cholesterol, 370 mg Sodium, 9 g Protein, 63 g Carbohydrates

A Great Source of: Vitamin B2 (26%), Vitamin C (31%)

A Good Source of: Vitamin A (15%), Vitamin E (15%), Calcium (21%), Potassium (360 mg)

Pyramid Equivalent(s): 1 Bread, ½ Fruit, ½ Dairy, Extras

The Guilt-Free "Comfort Food" Cookbook

Time: 30 minutes prep and cooking
Overnight chilling
Yield: 8 servings

Fruit Compote with Lemon Yogurt Cream

*Y*ogurt is a marvelous food with many culinary and nutritional virtues. It's rich in calcium; a cup of yogurt has even more calcium than a cup of milk. Yogurt with active cultures is easy on digestion, particularly for people with lactose intolerance who often feel bloated after drinking milk (the beneficial bacteria in yogurt have already consumed most of the lactose sugar).

Orange zest, incidentally, is made the same way as lemon zest: Simply grate the outside of a clean orange.

In this recipe lemon yogurt, ricotta cheese, sugar, lemon rind, and vanilla combine to make a lovely yogurt cream. You may find it has many uses. Over fruit, it's heavenly.

1½ cups white grape juice
½ cup water
¼ cup sugar
1 vanilla bean, split lengthwise
6 (2-inch long) strips orange zest
4 ripe plums, pitted and sliced
3 ripe kiwifruits, peeled and cut into thin slices
2 firm ripe pears, peeled, cored, and cut crosswise into thin slices

1 pint halved strawberries
1 (8-ounce) container lowfat lemon yogurt
³/₄ cup nonfat ricotta cheese
¼ cup powdered sugar
2 teaspoons grated lemon or orange rind
1 teaspoon vanilla extract

Combine grape juice, water, sugar, vanilla bean, and orange zest in a heavy medium saucepan; bring to a boil over medium-high heat, stirring until sugar melts. Boil, uncovered, until liquid reduces to 1⅓ cups. Meanwhile, arrange fruit in a shallow dish.

Carefully strain hot syrup mixture over fruit. Let cool. Cover and refrigerate overnight, stirring occasionally.

Spread yogurt ½-inch thick on several layers of paper towels; cover with a paper towel and let stand 15 minutes (to absorb water from yogurt). Scrape yogurt into a food processor bowl fitted with knife blade;

The Guilt-Free "Comfort Food" Cookbook

add ricotta cheese, powdered sugar, vanilla, and lemon rind. Process until smooth.

To serve, spoon fruit into serving dishes; spoon syrup evenly over fruit. Top evenly with yogurt cream.

Per Serving: 195 Calories, 3 g Fat (1 g Saturated), 8 mg Cholesterol, 50 mg Sodium, 5 g Protein, 40 g Carbohydrates
A Great Source of: Vitamin C (90%)
A Good Source of: Fiber (3 g), Vitamin B2 (12%), Calcium (14%), Potassium (420 mg)
Pyramid Equivalent(s): 2 Fruits, Extras

The Guilt-Free "Comfort Food" Cookbook

Time: 1 hour
Yield: 3$^1/_4$ cups (6 servings)

Chocolate Sorbet with Cinnamon and Vanilla

A lowfat frozen dessert that's richly chocolate? Of course. This one is delicately accented with cinnamon and vanilla. Cocoa powder not only gives flavor without fat, but nutrition; it's rich in magnesium and copper, both of which tend to be in low supply in the American food supply. It's almost a virtuous dessert!

We made it in an ice cream maker (Donvier makes a nice one), but you can make it without: Instead of the last step, just pour liquid into plastic ice cube trays. Freeze until hard, about three hours, then let stand at room temperature a few minutes. Process in the bowl of a food processor a few minutes, until it reaches the desired consistency.

2 cups water
1/2 cup evaporated skim milk
1/3 cup light corn syrup
1/3 cup sugar
pinch of salt
2 (3-inch) sticks cinnamon

1/3 cup unsweetened cocoa powder
2 ounces finely chopped unsweetened chocolate
2 teaspoons vanilla extract

Combine water, skim milk, corn syrup, sugar, salt, and cinnamon in a saucepan; bring to a boil over medium heat, stirring occasionally. Remove from heat and cool completely. Remove cinnamon sticks.

Whisk in cocoa and chocolate; cook over low heat, stirring constantly until smooth. Let cool completely. Stir in vanilla.

Freeze sorbet in an ice cream maker.

Per Serving (1/2 cup): 160 Calories, 5 g Fat (3 g Saturated), 1 mg Cholesterol, 85 mg Sodium, 3 g Protein, 30 g Carbohydrates
A Good Source of: Fiber (3 g), Copper (18%), Magnesium (14%)
Pyramid Equivalent(s): Extras

The Guilt-Free "Comfort Food" Cookbook

Time: 10 minutes
1 hour freezing
Yield: 5 cups

Lemon Sherbet

It's easy to make no-fat frozen sherbet at home. For a nice presentation, serve in frozen lemon "cups." Instead of squeezing the lemons for juice in the normal manner, cut off the top third of each lemon, and then scoop out the insides with a sharp knife and a spoon; juice the pulp. Freeze the hollowed-out lemons. Then, when the sherbet is partly frozen, scoop it inside the lemons, and continue to freeze. You'll serve lemon-sherbet-in-a-lemon. As an alternative, you can also serve this sherbet, or any commercial sherbet or sorbet, inside melon halves. It's an easy way to sneak more fruit into your family's meals!

2 cups nonfat buttermilk
1 (12-ounce) can evaporated
*   skim milk*

1 (6-ounce) can frozen
*   lemonade concentrate,*
*   thawed*
1/2 cup fresh lemon juice

Combine all ingredients, stirring until sugar dissolves. Freeze in an ice cream maker. (Or freeze in plastic ice tray; see instructions in introduction of Chocolate Sorbet with Cinnamon and Vanilla [p. 286].)

Note: If desired, add 1½ cups sliced strawberries, blueberries, or chopped peaches during last 30 minutes of freezing.

Per Serving: 135 Calories, 3 g Fat (2 g Saturated), 12 mg Cholesterol, 90 g Sodium, 4 g Protein, 25 g Carbohydrates
A Good Source of: Vitamin B2 (12%), Vitamin C (16%), Calcium (15%)
Pyramid Equivalent(s): ½ Fruit, ½ Dairy, Extras

The Guilt-Free "Comfort Food" Cookbook

Time: 30 minutes prep
15 minutes cooking
Yield: 2 dozen

Old-Fashioned
Oatmeal-Raisin Cookies

*A*pple butter, which has no fat, helps keep these cookies moist. Because they are low in fat, they don't store well; they taste best the same day they are baked. But you can freeze the *batter* in a freezer zip-top bag for up to a month (or refrigerate it up to a week). Just defrost in the refrigerator, scoop out the batter, and bake as directed. If you divide the batter into halves (enough for twelve cookies) or quarters, then freeze or refrigerate, you can even have freshly baked, portion-controlled cookies at a moment's notice!

2 cups regular oats, uncooked
1/3 cup stick margarine (or
    butter), softened
1/2 cup sugar
1/2 cup firmly packed light
    brown sugar
1/2 cup egg substitute or 1 egg
    and 2 whites, beaten
3 tablespoons apple butter

1 teaspoon vanilla extract
1 1/2 cups all-purpose flour
1 teaspoon baking powder
3/4 teaspoon baking soda
1/2 teaspoon salt
1 cup lightly crushed oat bran
    flake cereal (such as
    Quaker Toasted Oats)
1/2 cup raisins

Preheat oven to 350°. Spread oats in a single layer in a jelly-roll pan; bake for 15 minutes or until toasted, stirring occasionally.

Cream margarine; gradually add sugars, beating at medium speed of an electric mixer until light and fluffy. Add egg substitute, apple butter, and vanilla; beat well.

Stir together flour, baking powder, baking soda, and salt. Add flour mixture to creamed mixture, and mix well. Stir in oats, cereal, and raisins.

Drop level tablespoonful of dough 2 inches apart onto baking sheets coated with cooking spray. Bake for 12 to 14 minutes. Remove from baking sheets, and let cool completely on wire racks.

The Guilt-Free "Comfort Food" Cookbook

Note: For larger cookies, drop 2 level tablespoonsful of dough 2 inches apart onto baking sheets coated with cooking spray. Bake for 12 to 15 minutes.

Per Cookie: 130 Calories, 3 g Fat (0 g Saturated), 0 mg Cholesterol, 160 mg Sodium, 3 g Protein, 23 g Carbohydrates
A Good Source of: Vitamin B1 (10%)
Pyramid Equivalent(s): 1 Bread, Extras

Time: 10 minutes prep
20 minutes baking
Yield: 16 brownies

Rich-and-Fudgy Brownies

*C*ocoa powder is a health-conscious dessert lover's best friend. It's fat-free, cholesterol-free, and low in calories (unlike chocolate, which is made with cocoa butter, whole milk, and sugar). The trick is to use co-coa powder to impart true chocolate taste, keeping other ingredients low in fat and making sure the final product is moist and chewy. Which we did. The result is a brownie that's as delicious as brownies with twice the calories and fat.

2/3 cup unsweetened cocoa
*   powder*
1/3 cup all-purpose flour
1/2 teaspoon baking powder
1/3 cup canola oil
1/2 cup firmly packed light
*   brown sugar*

1/2 cup sugar
4 large egg whites
2 teaspoons vanilla extract
vegetable cooking spray
1/4 cup raspberry jam, melted
*   (optional)*
3 tablespoons powdered sugar

Preheat oven to 350°. Blend cocoa powder, flour, and baking powder in a small bowl until well combined; set aside. Combine oil, sugar, egg whites, and vanilla in a large bowl; mix with a wire whisk until smooth. Stir in flour mixture.

Spread batter in an 8-inch square baking pan that has been coated with cooking spray. Bake for 20 to 22 minutes or until edges just begin to brown and pull away from sides of pan. Do not overcook.

For a nice added touch, brush warm jam on top of warm brownies; cool completely in pan on a wire rack. Sift powdered sugar on top of brownies. Cut into squares. (To cut cleaner pieces, chill before cutting.)

Per Brownie: 110 Calories, 5 g Fat (1 g Saturated), 0 mg Cholesterol, 28 mg So-dium, 2 g Protein, 16 g Carbohydrates
A Good Source of: Vitamin E (10%)
Pyramid Equivalent(s): Extras

The Guilt-Free "Comfort Food" Cookbook

INDEX

The Guilt-Free "Comfort Food" Cookbook

The Guilt-Free "Comfort Food" Cookbook

The Guilt-Free "Comfort Food" Cookbook

The Guilt-Free "Comfort Food" Cookbook

The Guilt-Free "Comfort Food" Cookbook

The Guilt-Free "Comfort Food" Cookbook

The Guilt-Free "Comfort Food" Cookbook

warm citrus, asparagus with, 255
vision, 10
vitamins, 10-12
    in fruits, 19
    in meats, 21
    in vegetables, 17-19

W

walnut(s)
    and apples, sweet-sour red cabbage
      with, 251
    and apples and two wheats, veal
      chops stuffed with, 156-57
    bread, whole wheat, 87
    and dates, kasha pilaf with, 233
weight loss, 2
wheat
    and apples and walnuts, veal chops
      stuffed with, 156-57
    bread, toasted oat and, 90-91
    crispbreads, sesame, 101
    lavash, whole, 95
    and oat muesli, 76
    walnut bread, whole, 87

Y

yogurt
    -basil dressing, cool broccoli salad
      with, 123
    lemon cream, fruit compote with,
      284-85

Z

zinc, 13
zucchini
    -corn salsa, crispy potato skins with,
      50-51

The Guilt-Free "Comfort Food" Cookbook

$\mathscr{A}$BOUT THE AUTHORS

Georgia G. Kostas, M.P.H., R.D., has been director of nutrition at The Cooper Clinic, the medical division of The Cooper Aerobics Center in Dallas, Texas, since 1979. She is the author of *The Balancing Act: Nutrition and Weight Guide,* and the nutrition chapters in several of Dr. Kenneth Cooper's books, including *The Aerobics Program for Total Well-Being, Controlling Cholesterol,* and *Overcoming Hypertension.* She is a frequent contributor to magazines, including *Reader's Digest, Self, Runner's World, Family Circle, Shape, Living Fit, Woman's Day, Good Housekeeping, Ladies' Home Journal, American Health,* and *Working Woman.* She received her B.A. in biology from Rice University, her M.P.H. in Nutrition from Tulane University, and completed her residency at Oschner Hospital in New Orleans. She lives in Dallas, Texas.

Robert A. Barnett is a journalist who specializes in food and nutrition. He is the editor of *The American Health Food Book* (Dutton, 1991) and a contributor to many magazines, including *Food & Wine, Travel & Leisure, US News & World Report, Mirabella, Money, Men's Journal, Hippocrates, Rx Remedy, Family Circle,* and *Working Woman.* He is the former senior editor for Food and Nutrition for *Anerican Health* magazine. He received his B.A. in philosophy from Haverford College. He lives in New York City with his wife, Chris, and their dog, Jackie.

The Guilt-Free "Comfort Food" Cookbook